THE COPPER SPIKE

THE COPPER SPIKE

LONE E. JANSON

ALASKA NORTHWEST PUBLISHING COMPANY
Anchorage, Alaska

Published 1975
Fifth Printing 1984

Library of Congress cataloging in publication data:
Janson, Lone E.
  The copper spike.
  Bibliography: pp. 65, 105, 133 and 165.
  1. Copper River and Northwestern Railway.
2. Valdez, Alaska — History. 3. Cordova, Alaska — History.
4. Katalla, Alaska — History. I Title.
HE2791.C9155J35   385'.09798'3   75-16446
ISBN 0-88240-045-2
ISBN 0-88240-066-5 (pbk.)

Edited by Robert N. De Armond
Design by Susan Hyde
CartoGraphics by Jon.Hersh
Cover design by Roselyn Pape
Cover photo by E.A. Hegg

Alaska Northwest Publishing Company
Box 4-EEE, Anchorage, Alaska 99509

Printed in U.S.A.

CONTENTS

FOREWORD

Lone Janson is one who knows and loves Alaska. Out of experience, out of observation and memory, out of research in old newspapers and diaries and books of reminiscences, out of conversations with Alaska old-timers, she has dug a slab of valid Alaska life of the turn of the century. This is the tale of the building of the Copper River & Northwestern Railway, built to bring copper out of the tremendous Bonanza Mine in the Wrangell Mountains.

It is an eventful tale, full of the vagaries of Alaska weather, the crags and glaciers of Alaska mountains, the daring and resourcefulness of Alaska pioneers. In the background are the legal and political battles reaching all the way to Washington, D.C., the financial struggles and schemes involving the giants of Wall Street, and all the colorful scenes of America in the years when the Gay Nineties closed in a whirl of boom or bust philosophy, and the new century began with a surge of excitement and high endeavor.

Lone Janson's book is full of vivid and memorable pictures of the adventures and escapades of the pioneer railroad builders. Those were the days when people literally stumbled upon wealth, sometimes in the most unexpected ways and places; a startling instance was the time when some bear hunters, in Katalla, almost fell into a pool of oil, and one of them lighted a match and started a fire which burned gloriously for a week. Gold was never Alaska's only mineral wealth, though for a time it outshone all else in the popular imagination. Copper, like that in the Bonanza Mine, could be quite as lucrative to those who understood its potentialities. This was a whole mountain of high-grade copper ore, "the richest copper mine ever discovered."

The story is replete with narratives like Jack McCord's story of what he called the "Battle of B.S. Hill," a tale of the meeting of rival railroads, of shooting, dynamiting, cable-cutting and bluffing, and with briefer episodes and enlightening comments from the memories of other old-timers.

In *The Copper Spike* we have a piece of the life of the old Alaska, of the seekers and builders of Alaska's wealth, of flaring success and fizzling failure, of tremendous effort against terrific obstacles, and of the effortless triumphs of fortune's favorites. I hope that many will read and enjoy the stories packed in this book, and I am sure the historians of the future will make use of the unique information here gathered together about one of the greatest enterprises of the Alaska of pioneer days.

E. L. Bartlett
(Written in February 1961 by the late Senator E. L. "Bob" Bartlett.)

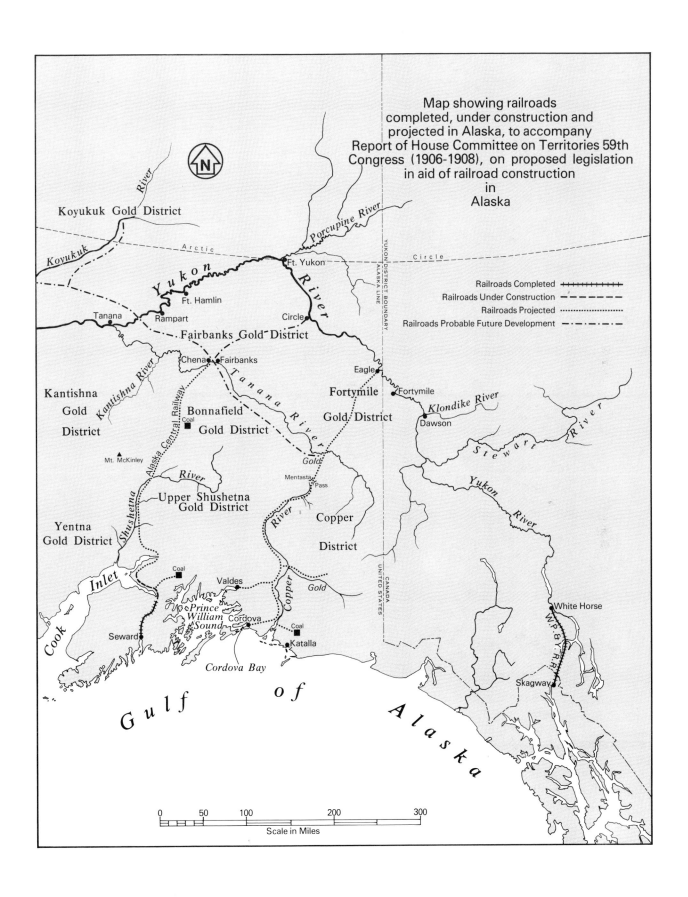

Map showing railroads completed, under construction and projected in Alaska, to accompany Report of House Committee on Territories 59th Congress (1906-1908), on proposed legislation in aid of railroad construction in Alaska

Koyukuk Gold District

Koyukuk River

Arctic

Circle

Porcupine River

Yukon River

Ft. Yukon

Ft. Hamlin

Tanana

Rampart

Circle

Fairbanks Gold District

Chena Fairbanks

Eagle

Fortymile Gold District

Fortymile

Kantishna River

Kantishna Gold District

Bonnafield Gold District

Coal

Klondike River

Dawson

Mt. McKinley

Alaska Central Railway

Tanana River

Gold

Mentasta Pass

Stewart River

Yukon River

Upper Shushetna Gold District

Shushetna River

River

River

Copper District

Yentna Gold District

Cook Inlet

Coal

Valdes

Copper River

Gold

White Horse

Prince William Sound

Cordova

Seward

Coal

Katalla

W.P.&Y.R.R.

Cordova Bay

Skagway

Gulf of Alaska

Railroads Completed ++++++++++
Railroads Under Construction – – – – – –
Railroads Projected ················
Railroads Probable Future Development –·–·–·–·–

YUKON DISTRICT BOUNDARY
ALASKA LINE
CANADA
UNITED STATES

0   50   100   200   300
Scale in Miles

PART ONE
A TALE OF THREE CITIES

PART ONE
A TALE OF THREE CITIES
Valdez,
Cordova
and Katalla

1 PROLOGUE

Just when the United States was adjusting to the new northward focus of the Alaskan gold rush, copper was discovered. And then coal to process that copper was found. And then oil. Alaska and the country were reeling with the excitement of discovery. But these rich finds were worthless without transportation and since rail provided the most economical way of moving these goods the iron horse race was on!

The copper mines of the region (Kennecott-Bonanza-Nicolai) were so rich that no less than 50 railroad concerns made some attempt to open a line in the region.

By the early 1900's railroad developers had lost the blanket protection and encouragement of the federal government. Subsidies and land grants to railroad builders were no long available. Railroads were given four years to complete a designated route, and at the end of the four years they were taxed $100 per operating mile per year. Many people thought that was an impossible burden to carry, and felt great anger about it. One Congressman of the time described the feeling when he said, "We have forbidden railroad building in Alaska." But even though expenses soared, five separate railroad lines were actually begun. Of the five railroad lines begun, however, the Copper River & Northwestern Railway was the only one that succeeded.

The Copper River & Northwestern Railway had the extensive financial backing needed to build a railroad through the Alaska wilderness, and, more importantly, it had the incentive of private ownership. The Copper River & Northwestern Railway was owned and operated by the Guggenheim and Morgan Alaska Syndicate. The Syndicate had vast holdings in gold mines, fish canneries and copper. But for all of its organization and related holdings the Syndicate grew at an unpopular time for big business. Accusations of monopoly and "trying to control all of Alaska" were hurled against them. As their unpopularity mounted and as Congress grew more uneasy about the monopoly charges levied against the Syndicate, the Copper River & Northwestern Railway was forced to overcome yet other problems raised by bureaucracy and mother nature. Nearby coal mines held by the Syndicate were "temporarily" withdrawn by the federal government—this forced the Guggenheims to import an inferior high-cost Canadian coal rather than mine their own. The problems of labor shortages, hard winters, movement of equipment and men haunted them.

The Copper River & Northwestern Railway story is typically American in its inception and typically Alaskan in its frustration.

Opposite—**Copper River Indians, whose chief commanded the river canyon and its water traffic.**

MOSS COLLECTION. ALASKA HISTORICAL LIBRARY   ALASKA HISTORICAL LIBRARY

LEWIS A. LEVENSALER PHOTO. RALPH E. MACKAY COLLECTION

Top—The village of Nuchek on Port Etches, Hinchinbrook Island, at the entrance to Prince William Sound, about 1904.
Above—A Tlingit of the Katalla area in ceremonial costume.
Middle right—Breaking in packhorses in front of the Amy & Woods barn in Valdez.
Right—A Tlingit canoe builder in the Katalla area. Canoes were hewed from a single log.

MOSS COLLECTION. ALASKA HISTORICAL LIBRARY

2 BEFORE COPPER—GOLD!

The Copper River & Northwestern Railway began before the first spike was driven and the first plans laid. It began with the dream of an All-American railroad in the gold fields of the Klondike ten years before Cordova existed.

Transportation to the gold fields was primitive at best—usually by foot—until Michael J. Heney, a determined young engineer, built the White Pass & Yukon and opened the Alaska-Yukon country to the Klondike's "Ton of Gold." The building of the railroad introduced Heney to the peculiarities of Northland construction and gave him the confidence to say "Give me enough snoose [snuff] and dynamite and I'll build you a road to Hell!"

In the years to come Heney would draw on his Klondike experience to build a road to the copper fields. But at this time copper wasn't what was on everyone's mind—nor was coal or oil. Gold!

But the White Pass & Yukon was limited. It was a semi-Canadian route with only 22 miles of rail in Alaska. The prospectors clamored for a railroad that would range into the Interior to the Yukon River, the major Alaskan travel artery.

The U.S. Army responded in 1898 by sending Lt. W. R. Abercrombie to Alaska's Southcentral coastal town of Port Valdez. He established Fort Liscum as a base and leaving a small contingent of troops there to winter he went "Outside" to gather men and material for the next year's activities.

During his absence the bitter Alaskan winter clamped down on the unprepared prospectors of '98 forcing an exodus of frightened and desperate men from the gold camps of the Interior to the coast and Valdez.

Out of the North they came, broken, destitute, scurvy-ridden; as sad a company as was ever seen poured out of the Copper River country that winter of 1898-1899. They were unfit for the Northland hardships and the country broke them.

Those who stayed in the Copper River valley were often just too proud to turn back, and as the winter progressed they became more and more uneasy. In a rising panic they could think of nothing but to get away. Somehow. Anywhere. So a number of them, knowing they were dead men if they stayed, made a desperate gamble for life by attempting the passage down Valdez Glacier in midwinter. They were told it was madness and certain death, but still the exodus began. Two-thirds died.

The panic was complete.

In Valdez wild tales of battles with glacier demons were told and everyone who had made the trip firmly believed the truthfulness of these stories. Abercrombie said that those who had survived the trip walked with a characteristic limp, and were called "glacier striders." Almost all of them were demoralized and "more or less mentally deranged, faces hidden by beards, and eyes with a wild light in them."

Quartermaster Brown, who had spent the terrible winter in Valdez watching the exodus, declared, "My God, Captain, it has been clear Hell! I tell you the early days of Montana were not a marker to what I have been through this winter! It was awful!" He waved his arm toward the little graveyard that had sprung up over the winter.

Abercrombie's party immediately set about relief activities. They built a hospital, dispensed medicine and sent out relief details to the Interior to see what could be done for others still there. Transportation home was arranged for the destitute through the Pacific Steam Whaling Company and various religious groups.

Once this task was attended to they began exploration of the country to find feasible routes for a military road and for a future All-American railroad. The Valdez Glacier was abandoned as a possible route. They then focused attention on Keystone Canyon, a previously impassable gorge. This narrow, steep-sided canyon was three miles long and wildly beautiful with rushing glacier streams, silvery waterfalls and precipitous rock walls plunging to the torrent below. And it was the only way through, a fact which was to make Keystone Canyon very important to the future of railroad building in Alaska.

Railroad engineer Edward Gillette wasted no time in drawing up contour maps and making a preliminary report on a highly feasible railway route through Keystone Canyon.

From Valdez the route led out through a level country of cottonwood and scrub spruce until it reached the canyon at Mile 14. Here the road had to be chiseled out of Keystone's three miles of solid rock.

North of the canyon there were two alternative routes. One ran directly north over Thompson Pass and on to the Yukon River. The other turned eastward to the Copper and Chitina rivers by way of Marshall Pass. If current rumors of new copper strikes in that area were true, this would be an important spur.

Gillette stressed the importance of Valdez in any railroad considerations as it possessed a deep-water, ice-free port at the lower end of a pass to the Interior. "The southern coast of Alaska affords very few good harbors," he wrote. "This appears to be greatly due to the fact that all streams emptying into the ocean carry vast amounts of silt . . . which forms numerous deltas and fills up the neighboring coast line to such an extent that sufficient depth of water for ordinary vessels, especially at low water, is seldom obtained.

From the shore back into the interior the coast range presents few practicable routes. Nearly all the canyons and drainages along these mountains are filled with ice and where the natural routes to the interior, as a rule, would be found, an absolutely prohibitory condition for travel exists. The stupendous masses of mountains and ice-filled canyons and valleys back of the green wooded islands along the seacoast, while forming probably the grandest scenery on this continent, give(s) [*sic*] no encouragement to the explorer or engineer in search of a practicable route for a railroad into the interior of the country, combined with that of starting from a good harbor."

Valdez was a natural gateway to the Interior offering light grades and easy curves. These encouraging factors were compared with the White Pass & Yukon's grades and curvatures in the report:

Maximum grade on WP&Y: 206 ft. per mile
on both sides of pass.
Maximum grade on Valdez route: 150 ft.
going north and 125 ft. south.
Maximum curvature on WP&Y Ry: 16 degrees.
Maximum curvature on Valdez route:
10 degrees.
Elevation of summit WP&Y Ry: 2,880 feet.
Elevation of summit Valdez route: 2,550 feet,
or 1,700 via Marshall Pass.

Gillette found many advantages to this new route and proceeded to outline them: ". . . it is understood that the White Pass & Yukon Railroad is handicapped greatly in its operation by snowslides. On the Valdez route this serious impediment to travel has been practically eliminated by the peculiar formation of the country and the careful placing of the line. The very important condition is also obtained for this country in having a route completely in United States territory and thus avoiding all the complications resulting from endeavoring to develop a vast territory full of mineral wealth across 400 miles of foreign soil."

It was recommended that the railroad be built to a gauge of three feet, significantly under the standard gauge of four feet, eight and one-half inches, though it was pointed out that should the need arise to change the gauge it could be done without any relocation of the line because of the relatively light grades and curvatures involved.

It was a very promising report, and was the basis for the railroading fever that broke out in the next few years in Valdez. But there was one thing missing: economic feasibility. What would the railroad carry? Destitute miners? True, there was gold up around Fairbanks, and some promising new placer properties up on the Chistochina and other places, but scarcely enough to warrant a railroad.

But then, there were the rumors.

Rumor was the "staff of life" in early Alaska. It floated on the surface of daily life like foam on beer. It filtered down into the dregs of living like the grounds in the miners' boiled coffee. It planted gold at the grass roots. It found copper mines worth a fortune. It brought faith and hope to the new prospector, and sometimes despair to the winter-bound miner. This was an age of faith, and each new whisper was greeted with a fresh wave of belief. Skepticism was reserved for a future generation. Now there were only the golden and copper-tinted rumors, and just often enough, they proved to be true.

The rumors were strengthened by such men as H. G. Allis. Allis and a ragged, wild-eyed little party had straggled out to Valdez in the general exodus of the winter before with a harrowing tale of winter cold and scurvy, both of which had overtaken them near the Bremner River. Some had died. One man, Peterson, being too weak to travel had been taken in by Chief Nicolai's people at Taral on the Copper River. The men who got out left their supplies cached on the Bremner and brought out specimens of bright green and blue copper nuggets—enough to arouse the interest of grubstakers back in Minnesota.

Now, as tales of copper filled the air, people remembered the stories of the copper mine owned by Chief Nicolai of the Copper River Indians, a mine reported by Lt. Henry T. Allen 13 years earlier in 1885.

3 HI-YU CHIEF

Chief Nicolai's house is supposed to be in the heart of the mineral region, and by him we were shown the locality of a vein of copper which was at that season of the year, April, above the snowline.

—Lieutenant Allen
Reconnaissance in Alaska, 1885, p. 158

Chief Nicolai of Taral was known to the Copper River Indians as "Hi-Yu Chief," Big Chief. There were other chief Nicolais around, called "Sanford Nicolai" or "Nicolai No. 2," but it was Taral Nicolai who was considered the Big Tyone (Superior Chief) of the Copper River country.

Taral Nicolai, despite his 18 summers, enforced his position by a dictatorial command of the narrow gorge of the Copper River which his main village, Taral, commanded. Since the village was located at the head of the narrow, steep-walled Woods Canyon, no one could pass up or down without his consent or without paying a toll. During his lifetime he forbade any active commerce between the upriver Indians and the whites, often firing on Native boats to ensure obedience. It was this command of the river traffic which made him Hi-Yu Chief.

In 1885 Abercrombie sent Allen to explore the Copper River and meet Nicolai.

Hunger marched with Allen's men as they finally neared Nicolai's hunting camp on the Chittystone River. On the trail the explorers had celebrated Allen's birthday "with a little rotten moose meat." But now such a luxury was absent as the men were weak from a diet of "snowballs and rabbit tracks."

Outside Nicolai's camp, Allen and his men paid tribute to the Copper River Indians' chief with a volley of rifle fire. The number of volleys fired indicated the rank of a chief, and as it was considered the poorest of taste not to answer every volley, Allen and his men were compelled to use up precious ammunition paying diplomatic homage. Nicolai's men fired bullets of copper-silver alloy from their own mines.

Later, inside the lodge, with the warm glow that comes from a full stomach, Allen and his men had a chance to inspect the young chief. Sitting with the firelight ruddy on his broad face, he was a handsome, even-featured young man, with strength of character showing in the cut of his jaw and the pride of his bearing.

With Nicolai as a guide, Allen made the first effective exploration of the Copper and Chitina rivers. The autocrat of the Copper River showed Allen many signs of mineral wealth of the region: copper utensils, bullets made of copper-silver alloy, huge nuggets of pure native copper and Nicolai's own vein of copper, which Allen reported in his narrative of the trip.

In 1898 the U.S. Army again visited Nicolai. Once again volleys of rifle fire were discharged and answered as long as courtesy and the pride of Nicolai demanded.

The Tyone waited aloof and composed while his squaws ran out to meet Abercrombie's emissary, J. J. Rafferty. With great dignity Chief Nicolai received the gifts of the "Waston men," and pretended to understand nothing. Rafferty tried various ways to thaw out the still young chief, but met with little success. Nicolai didn't seem to understand. At last he showed Nicolai the picture which Allen had made of the Tyone and his wives and children. A look of surprise spread over Nicolai's face. Immensely pleased, he momentarily forgot his aloof stance. Clutching the picture he stared at it, sighing with admiration. It was the first time he had ever seen a picture of himself. His comprehension of the Chinook trading tongue miraculously restored, he settled back to entertain his guests with tea served in china cups and saucers, and dried salmon from china dishes.

At the conclusion of the meal, Rafferty launched into a formal speech, saying that the expedition had come from the same chief who had sent Allen—a chief who ruled over people as numerous as the trees on the mountain opposite. This great chief, Rafferty said, had sent him to see how the "Stick Siwash" fared.

Nicolai declared that he liked the "Waston men"—as he pronounced the Chinook term "Boston men," or white men—and told of Allen's visit. Nicolai was unquestionably a man of intelligence and force, but with an engaging innocence; such a personality as would sell a multimillion-dollar copper mine for a cache of food.

4 COPPER DISCOVERIES

From 1899 to 1901 four of the most important copper discoveries were made. Without them there would have been no Copper River railroad story to tell. They were the Billum, Nicolai and Bonanza—all tied together by a chain of circumstance and by common names. These claims were joined a little later by the Hubbard-Elliott group, located and developed by Harry Bratnober and others.

The copper country was big. It eventually comprised some 200 groups totaling about 4,000 claims, both copper and gold, spread over a large area of the Copper and Chitina rivers. But these four groups were the springboard. They formed the economic basis for railroad building in the copper section of Alaska.

The chain of circumstances began in 1899 with the formation by the H. G. Allis party of a prospecting company called the Chittyna (original spelling of Chitina) Company. The company consisted of 11 prospectors grubstaked by about 25 others, mostly people in Minnesota. They had a plan for beginning a systematic search for copper in the spring of 1899. They would start with the Nicolai and the Billum.

The Billum

The Allis company had learned of the Billum from two prospectors, known as Downey and Young, who had straggled out during that terrible winter of 1898-1899 with a strange story of a copper find which they called the Billum after a medicine man who lived near the Kotsina River. The story involved claim jumping, pulling stakes and the burning of tents. However, three prospectors, Hoffman, Wilson and another, also claimed to have found the Billum.

The story was confused and it was one group's word against the other.

Now, as spring approached, the Chittyna Company prepared to race with Downey and Young to the site of the Billum mine. Members of the contending parties traveled together—necessarily—in the first packtrain taken by Abercrombie's men across the Valdez Glacier in the spring of 1899. At Chitina they split up and the race was on.

In a 1901 newspaper article, B. F. Millard of the Chittyna Company related:

"For a few days we traveled all the horses could stand. On the Chitina we divided into several parties. Warner and I started for the known Billum; McClellan and McCarthy for the lower Chitina (Nicolai's mine) [to negotiate with Nicolai for the Nicolai mine] and Gates and McNeer to prospect across from Taral.

"We [Warner and Millard] raced on foot up the Kotsina for the Billum. Downey and Young, now joined by Scotty, were after us with horses.

"They passed us in the night of July 4 and got to the Billum ahead of us. Siwash Jack informed us it would take half a day to reach the mine or we would have gone up that night. It was only two miles away; we reached it in an hour next morning and found the others in possession. The vein was staked; the notice was a slab of wood against the face of a rock."

The Nicolai

Disappointed, Warner and Millard headed for Taral to meet McClellan and McCarthy. McClellan and McCarthy were to try to persuade Chief Nicolai to reveal his copper site.

They found the Copper River Indians in the grip of one of their interminable bouts of famine. Each winter, despite weeks spent drying and smoking salmon, hunger returned to the people and that winter the Chief himself had been ill. Nicolai had promised Peterson, the sick prospector who was left at Taral by the Allis party, that during the following fall he would show him where the Nicolai copper vein was.

Now Warner, Millard, McCarthy and others of the Chittyna Company joined forces in trying to persuade Nicolai to reveal the mine even sooner. A powwow was held with the Chief and after hours of talking around the problem, Indian-style, a bargain was finally struck. The company would give Nicolai all the supplies that Allis had cached on the Bremner the previous year, if Nicolai would send someone to show them the copper.

Nicolai agreed and thus sold a multimillion-dollar copper mine for a cache of food. Taral Jack would be their guide. The Chief told the group confidently that it would take eight days for the trip, two at the site, and then two days for the return by raft. Provisioned for 12 days they started out.

It took them 13 days to reach the mine, and by then they were themselves experiencing "ha-lo muck-a-muck." The trail was over high country, and was 120 miles long. To eke out their food supply, they managed to kill a mountain goat and also found a small sack of cornmeal cached by travelers along the White River passes.

The lode they found was rich. Some of it was bornite ore containing 85 percent copper. It was located on the upper right-hand limits of the Nizina River, a tributary of the upper Chitina.

Immediately they staked out three claims for the company and the following day they started down the swollen Chitina River by raft. They had to pack around several canyons and build new rafts on the other side. Once McCarthy fell overboard and Gates saved him by grabbing his hair and pulling him back onto the bucking raft.

Meanwhile, at Taral, their comrades watched the expected day of return come and go. With mounting worry they waited as the days went by. At last, 19 days after the departure, Millard and other members of the party heard gunshots from upriver.

Millard describes the homecoming: "We were lying in our tents when we heard three shots. We ran out and saw a dark object moving on the water. The current was a good ten miles per hour. We soon saw four men coming, motioning for help. We threw a line and they were soon ashore.

"Not a word was spoken, but Ed Gates stood up holding a large piece of bornite ore in his hand at arm's length above his head. This spoke volumes to us on shore.

"They were hungry, Indian and all. Everyone talked and ate at once. It was August 22, 1899. We closed out the combination, signing a contract defining each man's interest."

The Bonanza

In the fall of 1899 members of the Chittyna Company met in Valdez to settle their affairs and make plans. The membership of the group, which was constantly changing, once more underwent a shift with new members coming in and old ones dropping out. Captain Abercrombie seems to have held a share in the company at this time.

During the winter the Chittyna Exploration Company was incorporated in San Francisco under California laws. Its purpose was to do assessment and

LEWIS A. LEVENSALER

LEWIS A. LEVENSALER

Left, from top—A train of pack-horses about to ford the Kusku-lana River. Indian houses along the Copper River. A Copper River Indian child.
Right, from top—The Indian chief Dr. Billum, second from right, with his family and a freighter. A Copper River Indian.

ALL PHOTOS FROM THE RALPH E. MACKAY COLLECTION

development work on the Nicolai claims. R. F. McClellan was hired to supervise the work.

So, in the spring of 1900, McClellan, several other members of the original Chittyna Company and additional prospectors went into the Copper River country for a season's work. McClellan and his group went directly to the Nicolai claims and began their work there.

In the meantime he was one of the grubstakers for a company of prospectors which became known as the McClellan party. McClellan himself did not take part in their prospecting activities.

The McClellan party split up into pairs and drew lots for prospecting several sections of the country. The upper Chitina was drawn by Clarence Warner and Jack Smith. Smith was an old Arizona prospector known as the "Arizona Centipede" or "Tarantula Jack."

Warner and Smith prospected their area rather extensively, and came to the area encompassed by Kennicott Glacier on one side of the ridge and McCarthy Creek on the other. They had gone only a few miles when Warner sprained an ankle. The two men sat down to rest and eat and while they were eating Smith saw an unusual green patch high up on

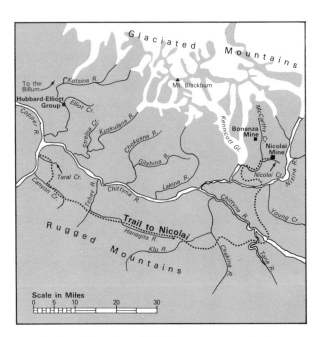

Taral Jack guided members of the Chittyna party over the Hanagita Trail to the Nicolai copper deposits. "There is a trail running up Chittyna from the mouth, and another, known as the Hanagita trail, which runs from Taral, up Hanagita valley, across Tebay, Klu and Charina rivers, to the Tana, which it strikes a short distance from the junction with the Chittyna; from here it runs northerly to the Nicolai mine. This route is comparatively open, with good forage for horses."—*Valdez Prospector,* March 27, 1902.

the mountainside. He thought it should be investigated.

Warner, nursing his sore ankle, told Smith that he could go tramping up the mountain to look at a mountain goat pasture if he wanted to, but he could go alone. Then the two men noticed a silvery chip of rock in the creek, a bit of ore that prospectors call "float." They examined it; it appeared to be silver, or at least some sort of mineral. So, forgetting his sore ankle, Warner joined Smith and they worked their way on up the creek, picking up more bits of float as they went. The farther they went, the more numerous the silvery chips, and they seemed to lead to the patch of "mountain goat grass." To their surprise, when Warner and Smith climbed the mountain they found that it was not grass at all but an outcropping of green mineral, a copper ore of immensely high grade.

The discovery was on the very peak of a sawtooth ridge, overlooking the Kennicott Glacier, 5,000 feet below. The ore was found in rich masses on the very pinnacle of sharp upthrusting rocks. From the face of this sheer ridge, the copper ore had been weathered away and had fallen on both sides of the mountain in slide areas that were themselves rich, nature-mined ore dumps.

The discovery was only 18 or 20 miles from the Nicolai mines. During the month of July and part of August the discoverers staked out a dozen claims in the names of members of the McClellan party.

5 VALDEZ: RAILROAD FEVER

"$1,100,000 Sale of 45 Copper Claims from Original Locators to Alaska Copper Company," announced the *Valdez Prospector* on March 6, 1902. Options taken by mining engineer Stephen Birch from the locators of the Bonanza were to be purchased by a firm of eastern capitalists with H. O. Havemeyer as president. Outlining the transaction the *Valdez News* stated that: "A transaction involving the proposed construction and equipage of a railway from Valdez to the interior of the Copper River country and the transfer of rich copper properties in the latter district, is reported affected in Chicago. . . . The capitalization of this company is placed at $9,000,000. The price paid for the mining properties was $1,125,000, upon the terms of $55,000 down and the remainder when experts for the company return a favorable judgment of the value of the claims."

Implicit in this agreement was the building of a railroad, and with this Valdez felt itself vindicated. For over a year the lusty little glacier town had been in the grip of "railroad fever," which had been set off by the Gillette surveys of 1899. The excitement had reached its greatest pitch in June 1901 with the arrival of the biggest name in Alaskan railroading: Michael J. Heney.

"M. J. Heney Now in City," exulted the *Valdez News*. Heney, fresh from his triumph in building the White Pass & Yukon Railroad, was looking over the All-American route, and Valdez was exuberant. "Heney's reputation is to 'work first and talk afterward,'" report the *News* happily. He had just arrived on the steamer *Bertha* with his engineer Sam Murchison and a third man identified as H. Harper. The party had six horses, camping gear, and would travel overland from Valdez to Eagle, visiting copper and placer deposits en route.

Two months later Heney emerged from his expedition by way of Skagway. Rumor had it that he had floated bonds on the London market to build the All-American railroad. Heney would be quoted on just one thing; that he was "not given to excursions in wild country for pleasure."

Valdez was excited. This little town had grown a great deal since the days when the Valdez Glacier had been in use. Valdez had become the metropolis of Southcentral Alaska—as metropolitan standards went in early Alaska. Now, with the great All-American railroad just around the corner, Valdez would naturally be its terminus. Great days were ahead.

Then M. J. Heney dropped a "bomb."

The *Seattle Post-Intelligencer* carried an interview with the frontier railroad builder in which Heney reported adversely on the possibilities:

"WILL NOT BUILD THE ROAD," read the headline, and the descending headers said: "M. J. Heney Reports Adversely on Valdez-Yukon Route"— "Grain Raising is Possible"—"Not Enough Business in the Copper River Valley to Warrant the Construction of a Railroad from Valdez to Eagle City—Wonderful Agricultural Possibilities—Rich Deposits of Virgin Copper."

The article reported that Heney said:

"'So far as I can see, there is absolutely no excuse for promoters or capitalists interesting themselves in the construction of a railroad through that part of the country, or in other words, from Valdez to Eagle City. If the conditions were such as to warrant the construction of a railroad it would have been done long ago, but it will be many years before a locomotive is seen in the Copper River Valley.

"'. . . I should say that it would cost, at the very lowest estimate, $12,000,000 to construct a railroad between the two points mentioned. I expected, when I went into the country, to find that there was at least some chance for local business, but it is of such an inferior nature that it is not worth considering. No

survey was made, but only a general reconnaissance of the country.'"

In the interview Heney noted that:

"'From my own observations I would say that the future of that part of Alaska depends much more upon the development of its agricultural resources than upon its mineral wealth. I am convinced that it is possible to raise all the hardier grains in that country, and they would thrive there as well as in Norway or Sweden. Alaska would furnish a market for all of the grain raised, and then it is probable that a railroad would be constructed. The Department of Agriculture should take the matter in hand and the proper experiments be made at once.

"'Without a railroad this section of Alaska will never be developed, and until it is developed it will be difficult to get capital to invest in such an enterprise. If it was the Canadian government, they would probably render assistance of such a nature that the road could be built.'"

Mr. Heney exhibited several bullets made from the native copper by the Tanana Indians. However, Heney also said that the copper was valueless without transportation.

It was a stunning blow. Heney was "Mr. Railroad" in Alaska, and his words carried great prestige. His estimate of things caused a general raising of hackles in Valdez. Sniffed the *Valdez News* rather stiffly: "There are other railroad builders in the country, and more than one has his eye on the All-American route."

Indeed there were other builders interested in the Valdez route. Over the next couple of years the Valdez papers reported on a constant stream of railroad builders and financiers.

August 3, 1901: "More Railroad Men Coming—To Inspect the All-American Route." Roswell Miller of the Chicago, Milwaukee & St. Paul was on his way to Eagle, with a side trip to the copper district. However, it was the opinion of the paper that he did not represent the Chicago, Milwaukee & St. Paul, but rather a group of stockholders of the Burlington & Missouri Railroad.

This same article reported, "A rather peculiar state of affairs exists in regard to M. J. Heney and his trip through the country, if the information at hand is true. It is said that there is a clash between the English and American capital in the White Pass & Yukon over something about the extension of the road on down the river. In fact, the trouble is so serious that one side will, or already has, withdrawn from the company and will build a road of their own to the Yukon from Valdez, and according to rumor, M. J. Heney is now completing the final arrangements for the consummation of that scheme."

COURTESY J. S. MACKINNON SR.

E. A. HEGG PHOTO

When it came to Heney, or to Close Brothers of London, who financed him, or to E. C. Hawkins, who had been Heney's chief engineer on the White Pass & Yukon Railroad, rumor indeed died hard. On September 28, 1901, the *Valdez News* had "More Talk of Railroads—Close Brothers said to be Promoters—E. C. Hawkins reigns. Several weeks ago the *News* published a rumor that some of the capitalists of the White Pass & Yukon Railroad would draw out of that company and construct a railroad over the All-American route to the Yukon. If the *Alaska-Yukon Mining Journal* is well informed in this matter, as it claims to be, the rumor had more foundation that it was first thought. The *Journal* says: '. . . At the present time all indications point to the Close Brothers of London, who were the promoters and builders of the White Pass & Yukon Railway, will be promoters of the Valdez railroad scheme. . . .'"

On June 19, 1902, a year after Heney's trip through the country, they went so far as to report: "Contract is Let—M. J. Heney has Received the Contract—" This was to build "to the Big Bonanza." The contract was spoken of as "almost a certainty."

In August, the *Valdez Prospector* threw in a new railroad connection to one already in progress: "Word was received by the last mail that the Valdez, Copper River & Yukon Railroad had secured control of the Hawkins road, or as it is better known, the Dawson & Indian River road. This road is to start from Dawson and will run to the Indian River country, a distance of 80 miles toward American territory. . . .

"In the meantime, the surveyors of the [Valdez, Copper River & Yukon] road are actively running lines, and are now nearly to Keystone Canyon. They have run a number of different lines and the most suitable will be decided upon when Mr. Gillette arrives. . . ."

The rumors were too persistent and reported by too many sources not to have some basis. It is likely that the London, Loan Mortgage & Trust Company, or Close Brothers, or both, were involved in the promotion and financing of the Valdez, Copper River & Yukon Railroad for reasons of their own, very likely having to do with the reported falling out between English and American capital in the White Pass & Yukon Railroad. Nevertheless M. J. Heney apparently did not have any contract to build the railroad, as was rumored.

The Burlington & Missouri people were very active as indicated by an October 26, 1901, story:

"Right-of-Way Has Been Granted to Burlington Company." A right-of-way for a railroad from Valdez into the Interior for a distance of 20 miles had been granted to the Burlington company. How the right-of-way came to be granted for only 20 miles could not be determined by the *Valdez News* staff, but "it appears on the face of it that the object in getting the 20-mile right-of-way is to possess the key to the situation in Keystone Canyon."

That was just the beginning. The files of the *Valdez News* and *Valdez Prospector* are studded with headlines of copper and railroads. They form a staccato medley of rumor and fact:

"PRELIMINARY SURVEY BEGUN,
Alaska, Copper River & Yukon Railroad."
(February 13, 1902)

"RAILROADS TO BEGIN. Iles & Bannister have incorporated a new company capitalized at $25 million." (March 13, 1902)

"ALASKA COPPER COMPANY WILL BUILD TO THEIR [copper] PROPERTIES ON CHITINA, CALLED THE ALASKA, YUKON & GULF RAILWAY."
(April 10, 1902)

"STILL ANOTHER RAILROAD."
(May 22, 1902)

"MORE COPPER, MORE RAILROAD EXPERTS," again and again, all through 1901 and 1902.

The promoters in many cases remained the same, but their interest shifted from one scheme to another.

There were at least nine distinguishably different railroad schemes reported in the Valdez papers—and schemes such as the Valdez, Marshall Pass & Northern, Alaska Midlands Railway (from Cordova Bay), Valdez-Yukon Railroad and the Alaska Railroad Company, were not reported on.

Railroad activity was not confined to the Valdez scene.

In Washington, D.C., an active lobby was being established and efforts were being made to liberalize the restrictive laws regarding railroad building in Alaska. A land grant bill was introduced in Congress on behalf of the Alaska, Yukon & Gulf Railway Company. It didn't pass. None of the many similar bills passed, but the promoters kept trying.

Promoters and financiers were urged on by the continuation of Alaska's gold rush and the promise of success. The White Pass & Yukon Railroad had established the importance and economic feasibility of a railroad. And new strikes were being made at Nome, around Fairbanks and other places. Encouragement also came from the promise of huge copper profits. And rather than concentrate on gold many entrepreneurs bent their efforts on reaching the copper district first in the expectation that the first railroad on the ground would be a real money-maker. Indeed, without a railroad the copper of the Interior was worthless, regardless of the richness of the ore or its extent, both of which still remained to be proved.

The Burlington Railroad promoters, who had the surveyed route through Keystone Canyon, had by now acquired terminal facilities. The promoter for their terminal tract townsite was a vigorous Valdezan, George Cheever Hazelet. His townsite had been taken out as early as May 1901 and was located on the northern shore of Valdez Bay, opposite the townsite where Valdez was growing. Some 63 years later following the 1964 earthquake it became the site of New Valdez. Describing the area the *Valdez News* reported that "The latest to appear in the arena of townsites on Valdez Bay, and one which bids fair to outstrip all its rivals, is what is now known as 'Hazelet's Hay Ranch.' . . . Hazelet and associates have surveyed and scripted 720 acres. . . . The tract surveyed and located includes one of the best wharf sites on the whole bay, being sheltered from strong winds, free from ice and 36 feet of water at a distance of 200 feet from the line of high tide. . . . It is generally believed that the Burlington and Missouri railroad people are backing Mr. Hazelet . . . and that this tract is intended for railroad terminals, and it is known beyond all question of doubt that G. W. Holdridge, general manager of the Burlington & Missouri Railroad is interested with Mr. Hazelet in this townsite matter in the amount of several thousand dollars. . . ."

By mid-1902, active construction was ready to start. "Surveys Commenced—Valdez, Copper River & Yukon Railroad Has Commenced Active Operations." Fifteen engineers had arrived on the steamer *Santa Ana* and had begun their surveys. Edward Gillette, chief engineer, was expected in about three weeks with a party of 20. Mr. Gillette, noted the article, now held a responsible position with the Burlington Railroad in Montana; but he was "careful to say that it is not a Burlington project, though some of the men financially interested in the latter corporation may be behind the new venture. . . ." A vessel was reported on its way around the Horn with enough rails for 70 miles of road. Great promise was in the air. Active construction was really under way.

Then another blow fell. The Bonanza copper mines, around which most of this prosperity revolved, were involved in a dispute that was to stop all progress for nearly three years. The Chittyna Exploration Company (now called the Copper River Mining Company) was suing R. F. McClellan and the original locators of the Bonanza for possession of the Bonanza group of claims.

6 BATTLE FOR THE BONANZA

Big Suit over Mining Properties," reported the *Valdez News*. "Notice has been filed in the commissioner's office that suit will be brought by the Chittyna Exploration Company against R. F. McClellan and others who are interested in the Bonanza group of claims. This suit has been brought by the exploration company on the grounds that the locators of said claims were in the employ of the company at the time the locations were made.

"All the parties concerned who are now here, are very reticent about the matter, and refuse to be interviewed on the subject. . . ." The suit was filed on August 11, 1902.

There were some surprisingly prominent names among the attorneys, especially for the Chittyna company. Senator Heyburn of Idaho was one; Congressman Cushman of Washington another; and Andrew F. Burleigh, who was one of the receivers of the Northern Pacific Railroad. The Northern Pacific, at this time, held almost half of the stock of the Burlington & Missouri Railroad, which in turn was cited as interested or affiliated with the Valdez, Copper River & Yukon Railroad, which had already begun building to the copper properties now in dispute. It is not surprising, in view of these facts, that all railroad work came to an abrupt halt on the filing of this suit.

Attorneys for the original locators were Frank D. Arthur of New York, John A. Carson of Oregon, Fred M. Brown of Valdez and others.

To add to the difficulty and confusion, two years had passed since the discovery, and many of those involved had moved on, some as far away as the Philippine Islands. Therefore, it was agreed that much of the testimony could be presented by deposition. The taking of this written testimony from many parts of the world, in an age when mail often traveled by sailing ships, was a slow process and required most of a year to complete. The collected testimony comprised a volume of over 2,000 pages. All was in readiness for the court's arrival in Valdez.

So it was that in October of 1903 a man who would be closely connected with the railroad story first became acquainted with the famous Bonanza copper claims. He was Judge James Wickersham, who was already renowned in the Northland as the "Dog Team Judge," the man who had traveled to the far districts of Alaska, in many cases by dog team. Wickersham had been sent to Eagle in 1900 as the first judge for Alaska's Third Judicial District.

U.S. District Judge James Wickersham.

The court which convened in Valdez that fall was the first term of court ever held there and was known as the "floating court" because it traveled between many coastwise communities by revenue cutter. Members of the judicial entourage had left Rampart (on the Yukon) on August 12, 1903, and stopped at ports in Bristol Bay and the Aleutian Islands en route. They held court in Nushagak, Unalaska, Belkofsky, Unga, Karluk, Sand Point, Kodiak, Seldovia and Nuchek before arriving in Valdez on September 17. They had taken the United States court to nine isolated communities and had traveled 3,000 miles in 37 days.

At Valdez, the lusty new metropolis of Southcentral Alaska, they proposed to build a courthouse, and Judge Wickersham obtained a piece of ground and requested money for this purpose. Meanwhile he rented space in the Hemple Building for hearing the cases before him. Since there was no jail in Valdez he rented a log cabin.

The Bonanza case came up in November.

The dispute revolved around the oral agreements made at the time R. F. McClellan was hired to do the development work on the Nicolai claims. At the time of incorporation all the Nicolai claims went into the

hands of the corporation for the purpose of development. The principals accepted stock in return. McClellan was made supervisor in charge of this work.

The fact of McClellan's employment was conceded. The debate was about the verbal agreements concerning his duties to the company.

The Chittyna Company claimed that as a part of the agreement McClellan was to do additional prospecting "to locate and have located all other mines in the vicinity for the company..." along with the development work on the Nicolai claims. Therefore, anything discovered while in their employ belonged by rights to the company. The original locators, they contended, held title in trust for the company.

McClellan, on his part, claimed he had grubstaked the men on his own, a practice common at that time. Matters were further complicated by the fact that he had used some company horses and food in the prospecting activities, and that several of the McClellan party had been hired for periods of time as packers and in other jobs connected with the Nicolai development work.

Judge Wickersham took three weeks to render his decision. He considered the 2,000-page volume of testimony and ruled in favor of the McClellan party, the original locators of the Bonanza claims.

"The burden of proof," asserted the judge, "is upon the one who seeks to establish a trust in a mining claim against both the record and the quiet possession of the locator...." Under such circumstances, it was up to the Chittyna Company to prove their claim by "full, clear and satisfactory evidence."

The McClellan party had been in peaceful possession of the Bonanza claims for two years before any attempt was made by the Chittyna Company to press action. "The Bonanza group of copper claims," said Wickersham in his decision, "... was discovered, marked and located, and every act necessary to a full, valid, and legal mining location thereof was made and done, by John H. Smith and Clarence Warner, without the physical aid of any person whatever," at various dates between July 4 and August 26, 1900.

Countervailing proofs cited by Wickersham included several official documents of the company prior to 1902 which made no mention of any interest or share in the Bonanza group, and the failure of the company to do any assessment work in 1901.

It had been recounted by McClellan, and apparently unrefuted, that several agents of the Chittyna Company visited him at the Nicolai camp late in July 1900 and were told of the Bonanza discoveries. McClellan showed them a sample of the ore, and sent for Warner to give them a tour of the Bonanza claims. McClellan informed these men at this time that the

Bonanza had not been taken up for the Chittyna Company, but in the individual names of the locators.

Wickersham rendered his decision on November 28, 1903. The case was immediately appealed to the U.S. Circuit Court of Appeals, which upheld Wickersham's decision. An application to the Supreme Court was denied.

It was a most stubbornly fought case, and some of the attorneys for the plaintiff, Senator Heyburn, Congressman Cushman and Andrew F. Burleigh, would use their influence to oppose Wickersham's reappointment to the federal judgeship in Alaska.

By the time the title to the Bonanza was cleared of this litigation it was late 1904.

While the court battle was going on, another less dramatic "battle" for the Bonanza was being waged, the fight to show the value of the claims. When the Alaska Copper Company had taken options to purchase the property, it was with the stipulation that the balance of the purchase price was to be paid when the experts returned a favorable judgment of the worth of the mines. But preliminary examination by the company's experts had cast some doubt upon them. It appeared that the outcroppings were very similar to those found in the Lake Superior region. These mining men urged caution, pointing out that such showings were often mere surface indications with no substance underneath; they would play out quickly.

As the engineer who had negotiated the options and the sale, it was up to Stephen Birch to prove them.

The name of Stephen Birch first appeared on the Alaskan scene in the orders to Captain Abercrombie for the expedition of 1899. He was hired as a guide with that expedition. Birch was a young mining graduate fresh out of Columbia University at that time. His special interest was copper. He had heard of the indications of copper in the Copper River country and had looked on the expedition as a means to get to that area.

When he had finished his work with Abercrombie that year, young Steve Birch took horses and Indian guides and traveled north to the Yukon River looking the country over as he went. He then returned by way of Skagway. He was in Valdez in 1900 when news of the Bonanza discovery reached there. Never one to let things come to him, he went in to find out for himself and to purchase a share.

It was Birch who interested the Havemeyer company in the Bonanza claims and negotiated the purchase agreement. So it was he who had to prove them. With undiminished faith in the find, he set about development work. He dug a 200-foot tunnel and drifts, plus test bores in the large slide area on the face of the mountain.

No one questioned his ability, but still Stephen Birch was not popular with his men. One old-timer who worked with him tells how he loved his tea boiled up extra strong, Canadian-style, and would raise a terrific stir if it wasn't strong enough to suit him.

He was fussy about little things.

"I recall one time I was rolling myself a smoke of Bull Durham," another pioneer prospector said. "I was just minding my own business, constructing me a cigarette, when up comes Birch and jumps me about me smelly smokes. 'Just how much of this country do you own?' I asked him, 'If it's not too far, I'll walk off of it and smoke in peace!' "

Prospectors on the upper Copper River were inclined to be plain-spoken men, as further illustrated by one who informed Birch that he was the "meanest S.O.B. I ever worked for!" The man hesitated, thought for a moment and added, "No, I take that back. I worked for your brother once."

Contemporary histories refer to Birch as reserved and taciturn, somewhat aloof in his relations with all but his companions of the trail and close associates in business.

But of his abilities there is unanimous agreement. He knew his business thoroughly. The result of his development work was the uncovering of about $20 million worth of copper ore, enough to convince even the most skeptical of the experts and more importantly enough to finance transportation and smelters.

Alaska Monthly magazine issue of May 1907 describes the Bonanza discovery area this way: "On the ledge are pinnacles of ore 65 feet high, 32 by 9 feet at the base standing up like a steeple, that average 50 percent copper and $20 per ton in gold and silver. . . .

"[Below this ledge] there is a slide 2,000 feet long, 3,000 feet wide at the bottom and 15 feet deep; 3,500 test holes have been put in this mass of copper ore mined by nature, and the average value is 28 percent. . . . "

Meanwhile, another large group of prospects was brought in by Harry Bratnober, the Hubbard-Elliott group. Bratnober did his work in a most resourceful manner. He brought a river steamer of very shallow draft to the head of the Tanana River, from where a short portage put his heavy mining machinery on the grounds. This steamboat idea was to bear rich fruit later.

In the year 1905 the properties of the Nicolai, Bonanza and certain of the Hubbard-Elliott (Bratnober's) groups of claims, and possibly others, were all bought and consolidated into a single large Syndicate. The Syndicate was organized by Birch, Bratnober, the Guggenheim brothers, J. Pierpont Morgan and others. Financiers for this venture were

GUY F. CAMERON PHOTO

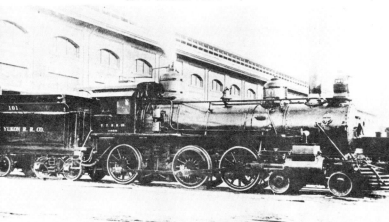

ALASKA HISTORICAL LIBRARY

Top—Joseph A. Spenard, who operated a transfer business, used both dogs and horses at Valdez. He later moved to Anchorage where a lake and a townsite were named for him.

Middle—This Rogers locomotive was built in 1881 for the Southern Pacific. Around 1906 the Southern Pacific sold it to the Valdez-Yukon Railroad, which numbered it 101 but never actually used it. They sold it to the Copper River & Northwestern, where it became No. 50, and was one of the workhorses in the early years of the railroad.

Bottom left—McKinley Street in Valdez at an early date.

Bottom right—Judge James Wickersham applied for funds to build a courthouse at Valdez.

ALASKA HISTORICAL LIBRARY

GUY F. CAMERON PHOTO

four eastern banking houses: the Havemeyer firm, the House of Morgan, the Guggenheims and Kuhn, Loeb & Company. The Guggenheims were a mining concern, so they became the operating partner in the Syndicate.

It was called the Alaska Syndicate. Steven Birch was elected president of this newly founded organization. The Syndicate then formed several subsidiary companies acquiring a large existing concern which had a steamship line, commercial enterprises, gold mines, fish canneries and one railroad company, the Northern Railway Company. The Syndicate acquired about 47 percent of most of these companies and all of the stock for the Northern Railway Company. The railroad company became the Copper River & Northwestern Railway Company. John Rosene became president. Rosene's chief engineer was M. K. Rogers, a very highly rated professional.

7 VALDEZ: HOME OF THE GUGGENHEIM-MORGAN SYNDICATE, 1905-1906

Valdez was booming; the *Valdez Prospector* reported: "Now the copper magnates from the interior are beginning to appear, and one can hear talk of bornite, glance, 600-foot ledges and millions on every corner. One prospector says that there is so much copper where he was this summer that even the water in the swamps carries a green stain and the grass was also tinged with green."

The glacier town had taken on all the appearance of a substantial business community with wide orderly streets, mercantile houses, a dock, and was "practically the seat of the United States District for the Third Division in Alaska."

So promising was Valdez's future that the *Seattle Mail & Herald* devoted an entire issue to it, the "Valdez Edition" of March 17, 1903. There were pages of articles on copper, gold, fur farming, Prince William Sound, the coal and oil of nearby Katalla, and on the town of Valdez itself. It reported:

"Valdez has continued to grow and improve during the past two years beyond the fondest hopes of the most sanguine. From the little village of log cabins of three years ago it has grown into a modern little city with large buildings and stores, nice and commodious hotels, pretty and comfortable homes, school, elegant church, city hall, lodges, clubs and all the conveniences of a modern city. The town is lighted by electricity, has a good telephone system, telegraph communication with the outside world and is connected with Seattle by several elegant and commodious steamers.

"There is no doubt that Valdez will in the near future, if it is not now, be the most important city in Alaska. . . .

"The only route to the great interior country of Alaska that is open the entire year, is through Valdez. Valdez is the commercial center of Southern and Western Alaska and is the distributing point for a large country. The only feasible route for an All-American railroad to the Yukon is from Valdez, and there is no doubt whatever that a railroad will be built from this place to the Yukon, and when this road is built it will open the greatest and richest mining, agricultural and grazing country in Alaska."

Descriptions of Valdez's business enterprises were impressive, especially for a town not yet five years old: six large general merchandise houses, one large dry goods store, a wholesale house carrying groceries and general produce, three drugstores, two hardware stores, four candy and cigar stands, two jewelry stores, three blacksmiths, two sawmills, four transfer lines, three hotels and so on.

More and more distinguished and important dignitaries were making a point of visiting Valdez.

In 1902 Governor John Green Brady visited the booming Valdez accompanied by General Adolphus W. Greely. It was a strange prelude for the tragic adventure that was to follow for Governor Brady a few years later.

That same year another group of important visitors was given a grand tour of Prince William Sound

GUY F. CAMERON PHOTO

In the early years of Valdez, the skin *bidarka* was still in common use by the Natives of Prince William Sound.

copper properties and the Bonanza copper claims of the Interior. They were representatives of financial houses back east, and their guide was Stephen Birch. "So well did he conduct the tour," said the *Valdez News,* "that it seemed like a picnic."

Valdez was becoming politically active, and its politics were marked by their excitement and rhetoric. "Home Rule" for Alaska was the big theme. Alaska was campaigning for an elective legislature, and Valdez residents decided to dramatize their demands in a way that could not be ignored. The Yukon Territory of Canada was just at that time gaining an elective Territorial Council. Hawaii and the Philippines, both American districts, had each been given a Delegate to Congress. Alaska had no representation at all. The people of Valdez decided to do something about the situation, so on President Theodore Roosevelt's inauguration day, March 4, 1905, the following telegram was sent:

On behalf of 60,000 American citizens in Alaska, who are denied the right of representation in any form, we demand, in mass meeting assembled, that Alaska be annexed to Canada!

The telegram created a gratifying stir for Valdez citizens on the editorial pages of the nation. In 1906 the first delegate elections were held, though it is doubtful if the "Annex Alaska to Canada" telegram had much to do with it.

Valdez was the headquarters for the new Alaska Syndicate, often called the Guggenheim-Morgan Syndicate, or the Guggenheims, or more popularly— the "Googies."

It would have seemed incredible in 1905, but the "Googies" were destined to become the "eye of the hurricane" in a major political storm. The Guggenheims were just what was needed. They represented capital, and it was known that it takes millions of dollars to develop copper mines.

They were welcome in Alaska, and the press was very favorable. An interview in the *New York Times* with Daniel Guggenheim, mining engineer and patriarch of the Guggenheim family, quoted in the *Alaska Monthly* showed that:

"The Guggenheim capitalist interests, which during three generations in the industry, have grown to be among the largest in the country, contemplate the development on a scale larger than anything that has been done in the states. . . .

"Such is the statement of Daniel Guggenheim, head of the firm. . . . 'We want to go into the Territory,' he said, 'And build railroads and smelters and mining towns and bring men there and populate the country and do for it what the earlier figures of American railroad building did for sections of the great West.'

" 'The American Smelting and Refining Company,' said Mr. Guggenheim, 'Will not only build a railroad but will build smelting works at Valdez for the reduction of the ores.' Speaking of the matter of fuels

he says that the engineers have reported . . . valuable coal deposits which need only development. . . . 'If they fall short of expectations,' he went on, 'California fuel oil will be used in the reduction works.' "

This was one of the first references to a matter which was to become the key to the railroad situation in Alaska, the discovery of high-grade coal on the southern coast of Alaska, some 100 miles from Valdez, near a place called Katalla.

The first important item of business for the new Alaska Syndicate was to reach the copper at Bonanza. This would give the railroad tonnage and insure its success. To that end, the Copper River & Northwestern Railway Company was formed. Thus, when this company first appeared on the scene, its plan was to build from Valdez. Exactly what it planned is shown by a map of the proposed route, which appeared in the *Alaska Monthly* of April 1906. This showed that the Copper River & Northwestern contemplated two northern terminals, one at Fairbanks and the other at Eagle. It also planned a copper spur over Marshall Pass to the Chitina River country and the Bonanza mines.

At about this same time, the coal and oil discoveries at Katalla were attracting attention. Since the combination of coal, copper and railroads is an obvious one, the Syndicate sent George Cheever Hazelet and some railway engineers to survey the route from Katalla up the Copper River, as well as the Valdez routes, and to recommend the best one.

Due to the difficulty of bridging the Copper River between Miles and Childs glaciers, the Copper River & Northwestern Railway Company's engineers advised against trying to build up the Copper River from Katalla.

Acting on the advice of these prominent engineers, Mr. Hazelet submitted a report recommending construction from Valdez. The Copper River & Northwestern Railway Company therefore proceeded to file on two Valdez routes, one by way of Thompson Pass and the other by way of Marshall Pass. The Copper River survey was inadvertently forgotten. Neglecting to file on this survey was to be a quarter-of-a-million-dollar mistake.

However, the company had other problems. It was notified that both of its surveys were in conflict with two previous ones in Keystone Canyon. The applications were denied. Consequently the Copper River & Northwestern Railway Company began negotiations with the owners of the other two surveys (Valdez, Copper River & Yukon Railroad and the Burlington & Missouri) and obtained relinquishments from both companies in 1906. On January 25, 1906, the Secretary of the Interior received a letter from the Commissioner of the General Land Office stating that

the relinquishments were on file, and on January 27, the applications for the Keystone Canyon surveys of the Copper River & Northwestern Railway were approved.

Work on clearing and grading for the Copper River & Northwestern had been in progress, and the grade was clear for several miles out from Valdez. Rock work was also under way in the canyon. A rock grade was completed for about 2,000 feet from the entrance to the canyon. The grade ended in a sheer rock face. In the rock face two working tunnels were started, one about 40 feet and the other about 45 feet in length. These tunnels, more commonly known as "coyote holes," were to be loaded with dynamite to blast off the rock wall. About $85,000 had been spent on the rock work up to this time.

O. A. Nelson of Chitina described the coyote hole as a "tunnel driven into the solid rock as small as can be worked in, about three feet wide and three or four feet high. Some of them were over a hundred feet long. Sometimes it took a few days to load a long coyote hole with up to twenty-five kegs of black powder and say, a hundred cases of dynamite. When it went off, it shook up the scenery for miles around."

The competition was on! At about the same time construction on the Valdez & Yukon Railroad under Col. A. W. Swanitz was begun. This project was reported in the April 1906 *Alaska Monthly* "Railroad Rumblings": "Col. A. W. Swanitz, of the Valdez & Yukon Railroad, says the construction of the road is absolutely assured, and that work on a large scale will be resumed as soon as the weather will permit. Grading was carried on as late as Dec. 19. When completed the road will pierce the heart of the Copper River country and will then run on to Eagle."

Two or three miles of the Valdez-Yukon Railroad had been graded by the slow and laborious process of working with wheelbarrows. They had some flatcars, pulled by horses. Neither company ever had a locomotive in Valdez, though a later company brought one in.

It gave Valdez a comfortable feeling to have two railroads actually building their All-American route, and more in the talking stages.

In 1906, a number of things happened, and events were now conspiring to take the railroads away from Valdez. One of these events concerned a "paper railroad" which, if approved, would have stopped all other railroad building on the southern coast of Alaska. It was the Alaska Railroad Company and its terminus was to be at a townsite called Nelson.

Opposite—**Valdez was the southern terminus of the Valdez Trail. This team had come over the trail from Fairbanks in the record time of seven days, eight hours.**

8 THE NELSON TOWNSITE AND THE JARVIS MEMORIAL

Washington, D.C., was the real capital of Alaska. For this reason much of the Alaska railroad drama took place in the nation's capital where there was an extremely active railroad lobby at work.

The railroad lobby was a confusing array of persons interested in the various Alaska railroad building schemes. Bills were constantly being introduced to give this railroad or that relief from taxation, extensions of time, land grants, subsidies and bond guarantees.

But now the railroad lobby in Washington was in an uproar. The reason all these gentlemen, with their divergent interests, were now united in common opposition was the introduction, in February of 1906, of Senate Bill S.191, asking that Congress itself incorporate and give special inducements to a railroad to the Yukon River. Not just any railroad, but the one backed by Andrew F. Burleigh and Donald A. McKenzie, along with some New York and Pennsylvania capitalists.

It was to be called the Alaska Railroad Company, sometimes referred to as the Pacific & Yukon. (Not the same railroad as the Valdez-Yukon, backed by Col. A. W. Swanitz from Valdez.)

Andrew F. Burleigh, it may be remembered, was one of the attorneys for the Chittyna Exploration Company in its efforts to wrest the Bonanza claims from the original locators. He was a man of considerable political weight; associates of his in that trial were members of Congress and led the fight to oppose confirmation of Judge Wickersham to the federal bench again and again.

The Alaska Railroad Company enterprise had chosen as its terminus a townsite which it named Nelson, in honor of Senator Knute Nelson of Minnesota, known in Congress for his interest in Alaskan legislation.

The Nelson townsite was later billed as the "San Francisco of the North" by its promoters, who had grandiose plans for their future metropolis. The Nelson townsite was located at the head of Orca Bay (often called Cordova Bay), about ten miles from the present town of Cordova. It is a setting strikingly similar to Valdez and Skagway with a broad level expanse of land at the head of a fjord, with one or two canyons leading back through the mountains.

While on the ground this site looks like a promising one, a glance at any modern map shows that there is absolutely no pass through the mountains, either toward Valdez on the northwest or to the Copper River on the east. Every possible pass and canyon leading through is blocked by glaciers and ice fields. The only possible way to build from Nelson is south, along the almost perpendicular flank of the mountains to Cordova and thence across to the Copper River.

However, this presented no problem to the promoters, because they had never had a surveyor on the ground, nor were there any modern maps to disillusion the legislators as to the merits of Nelson as a terminus. S.191 was introduced in Congress, and represented as the salvation of Alaska, the quickest and most effective way to get an All-American railroad without letting any of the wicked corporations do it. This was the era of Teddy Roosevelt and the "trust-busting" psychology. But the special privileges and other inducements called for in S.191 were so liberal as to, in effect, eliminate every other railroad enterprise already at work in Alaska.

All Alaskan railroads were subject to the rather severe provisions of the Act of 1898, which among other things, limited the amount of terminal land a railroad could own, provided that no pass or canyon could be dominated by any one railroad and required a surveyed route to be completed within four years or be subject to forfeiture, as well as imposing other restrictions designed to prevent a monopoly. This new venture would be subject to none of these provisions, because it would be incorporated by Congress itself. In addition, if S.191 passed, it would be given special rights and grants available to no other line.

The Jarvis Memorial was a protest against this unfair favoritism.

David H. Jarvis was a very well-known Alaskan at this time, almost a folk hero. He had become famous in his dash to Barrow with reindeer to feed ice-bound whalers in the winter of 1897-98. He had been a member of the Revenue Service at that time (the Revenue Service later became the Coast Guard). After that he became collector of customs and served outstandingly in that post. He was with Wickersham when the famous "floating court" made its rounds. He had even been offered the governorship of Alaska by Teddy Roosevelt, but had turned it down. On Roosevelt's recommendation, he had been offered a position, and accepted it, with the new Alaska Syndicate.

It was in his capacity as representative for the Alaska Syndicate that he presented the Jarvis Memorial, an eloquent protest against the blatant favoritism of S.191. It read in part:

"Honorable the Senate of the United States, Washington, D.C.:

"As one long interested in the development of the District of Alaska, and now extensively engaged in commercial, transportation, and other business in the district, I desire to protest against the passage of the bill [S.191] entitled 'A bill to aid in the construction of a railroad and telegraph and telephone line in the district of Alaska,' for the following reasons:

"First, this bill proposes that Congress incorporate the Alaska Railroad Company and grant it a blanket right-of-way from the Gulf of Alaska, at or near the head of Cordova Bay, to a point on the Yukon River within two miles of Eagle. In addition to this proposed railroad company, there are now four others, in one of which, the Copper River & Northwestern Railroad Company, I am interested, building or proposing to build the same field. These four companies have completed more or less of the laying out and grading of the line or route by which they are to build, and at least one of them has definitely, with the approval of the Land Office and the Secretary of Interior, located a considerable part of its permanent right-of-way. *This proposed Alaska Railroad Company is the only company desiring to enter that particular field, asking of Congress special incorporation and special privileges in the shape of a right-of-way not taken under existing law. . . .*"

The injustices of S.191 were pointed out clearly and devastatingly by Jarvis.

He pointed out that the bill would confer a right-of-way from Cordova Bay to the Yukon River by the most eligible route that shall be determined by the company. "No one else dare move," Jarvis said, "until this company determines what it wants. It is a blanket right-of-way covering all the region."

The matter of land grants was exceedingly generous, giving the Alaska Railroad Company 100 acres *more* than any other railroad entitlement for terminal tracts, plus the mud flats or tide lands in front of the terminal tract. Also, not granted to any other line were the 2,560 acres of public lands and 640 acres of coal lands. This 640 acres was four times what was allowed any other locator in Alaska by law, and further than that, there was no provision that the area be rectangular. ". . . Since a section need not be taken in a rectangular form, the limit to the amount of coal lands which may be taken under such a grant can hardly be estimated," declared Jarvis.

There were several irregularities in the granting of the right-of-way under the proposed act; the mere filing of a preliminary plat would automatically pass the right-of-way to the company. ". . . That right-of-way passes absolutely to the company on the mere filing of a paper, which can be prepared in the company's office without a survey or without a single official ever having been on the ground." There were several paragraphs discussing other similar irregularities, including the fact that no performance bond was required and that even the provisions requiring fair and indiscriminate use by all shippers had been omitted.

Eight years, instead of four, were allowed this favored company for completion of its route. Further, it would have provided, "That if said Alaska Railroad Company shall not complete and put into operation at least 20 miles of its said railroad within three years from the passage of this act, all the lands granted by this act shall revert to the United States." "That is to say," wrote Jarvis, "if the proposed corporation builds 20 miles of railroad in three years, its title to all the lands, coal, terminal, and otherwise, herein mentioned, vests absolutely in the corporation. . . . This is a request for favoritism."

Jarvis' arguments were well-stated and cogent: "The preamble setting forth the object of the bill states that it is to aid in the construction of a railroad in the district of Alaska. It is a mistake to say that such an act would encourage or aid railroad building in the district. On the contrary, it would in a measure kill all of the enterprises heretofore started. This proposed corporation should take its chances under that act [of 1898] as all the rest of us have done."

He concluded his presentation of the railroad situation in Alaska that early spring of 1906 by summarizing: "The Copper River & Northwestern Railroad starts at Valdez and goes over the Marshall Pass to the Copper River where it meets the right-of-way which the proposed bill would give to the Alaska Railroad Company. It has already completed and cleared all obstructions from a definite survey to this point of meeting and for some distance up the river. It has filed in the General Land Office a preliminary survey for that distance and a permanent survey for half the distance, the latter having been approved by the land office and the Secretary of the Interior.

"It has built at Port Valdez docks and other improvements, and has graded its right-of-way from that point to Keystone Canyon, 12 miles; it has about completed a very difficult piece of rock work through this canyon, a distance of four miles, and is continuing this work along its right-of-way as fast as the inclement winter season will permit. The financial arrangement for the building of this—the Copper River & Northwestern Railroad—has been fully made, and its completion is assured.

"I am informed that the Copper River Railroad Company [Heney's road] and the Alaska Pacific & Terminal Railroad Company have on file in the General Land Office preliminary surveys covering 130 miles of their proposed routes, which would also be covered by the right-of-way asked for in this bill, and are fully prepared, financially and otherwise, to build their roads. The Alaska Central Railroad Company [from Seward] has already built and in operation 45 miles of railroad under the general law and has asked for no special act of incorporation.

"There is no evidence on file in the Land Office to show that the proposed company, asking for these special favors, has ever been over its route with instruments; it has made no survey or measurements, as shown by the testimony of its chief engineer before the Committee on Territories, House of Representatives, February 1, 1906, p. 60, Hearings on Railroads in Alaska.

"In conclusion, I wish to reiterate that this bill should not pass unless Congress desires to put a cloud upon the titles of all these companies already at work in the region, which will be a menace for eight years to all railroad building in the country.

—Respectfully, D. H. Jarvis."

The bill did not pass.

The Alaska Railroad Company never got off the ground, but the Jarvis Memorial was to become a lasting legacy to Alaskan railroading.

Despite the fact that the Jarvis Memorial was addressed as a protest against a single piece of legislation, it would be used in later years as one more red herring to confuse and incite the public against the Alaska Syndicate. Foes of the Guggenheim-Morgans would twist its meaning in an effort to prove that the Syndicate opposed all railroad building but their own.

It may well be that the Guggenheims did not favor government aid to other railroads, but to cite the Jarvis Memorial is grossly unfair. To have granted what was asked to the Alaska Railroad Company would have been to grant special privileges with no guarantee that the desired transportation would ever be built. The granting of these privileges would have killed every other railroad enterprise in Alaska. What was needed was general legislation for all railroads, not special privilege for one.

The net effect of the Jarvis Memorial was to strengthen in the minds of the U.S. Congress the aversion to aiding railroads by land grants and subsidies as had been done in the 1800's. It was clear that from now on, there would be no special favors forthcoming to railroad builders in Alaska beyond the few extensions of time and occasional tax relief.

However, there were some new developments in these years from 1900 to 1906 which made it clear that at least some of the lines could be economically viable. If they had a product for tonnage, such as copper from the Bonanza-Kennecott region, combined with cheap fuel, such as a good coal from a local source, they had every chance of success. Good coal had been found at Bering River near Katalla (on the coast,

U.S. ARMY PHOTO, ALASKA HISTORICAL LIBRARY

Left, from top—Aerial view of the Katalla townsite on September 12, 1954, looking toward the south or southeast. John Krey and his family outside their home at Katalla in 1907.
Right, from top—A survey party of four on the line out of Katalla, 1907. An oil rig near Katalla. Katalla Natives working on the railroad right-of-way.

ALL PHOTOS EXCEPT TOP LEFT ARE FROM THE MOSS COLLECTION, ALASKA HISTORICAL LIBRARY

about 100 miles from Valdez), and new fields were being explored in the Matanuska area.

Coal was not the only rich resource discovered in the Katalla area. From 1901 on exciting explorations in oil also were taking place there.

9 KATALLA: BLACK GOLD AND ANTHRACITE

Oil!

The gusher that sprang from the bowels of the earth in September of 1902 rose 85 feet in the air, and flowed at an estimated rate of 1,600 barrels per day. Katalla's first oil well had been brought in by the "English company," a syndicate which had contracted with the Alaska Development Company to drill the promising new oil prospects at the mouth of the Bering and Copper rivers.

The "oil rush" was on. Within a few years, four legitimate companies were actively drilling, and many were staking lands. With them came the shady curbstone dealers selling phony stock. Journalist Preston H. Wilson in an article for the March 17, 1903, edition of the *Seattle Mail & Herald* wrote that, "The winter at Katalla has been one of unusual severity, and the snow lies about eight-feet-deep, but this has not prevented quite a rush to 'stake' lands. The whole country way out on the mountains and glaciers has been staked on the snow, and recorded, and in many instances several times over, and it is such cases as this in which the grafter and curb broker are now offering at any price on the street, and the myriad of fly-by-night fakes are being organized, and this statement is printed in order that intending investors may take notice. Many good companies will be in the field, but watchfulness and care must be exercised to avoid irresponsible ones. There can be no question of the genuineness of the discovery nor of the excellence of the product, and wealth beyond the dreams of avarice will undoubtedly be realized there in the near future. . . . "

The Katalla region had been the site of the farthest west Tlingit Indian settlement in Alaska; the earliest settlement was the trading post and village on Kayak Island.

On April Fool's Day of 1903 the Juneau papers noted the northbound passage of the steamer *Portland* with men and drilling tools for the Alaska Petroleum and Coal Company. The ship was headed for the new townsite of Katalla (translated, Katalla means "oil") which had just been laid out by that company and platted. It was a vigorous new town, and grew rapidly. Most of the residents on Kayak moved to the mainland shore with the opening of the new town. At the mouth of Katalla Slough there had for years been a fine deep anchorage where schooners and barkentines were said to lay. Safe anchorages were rare along that shallow coast. But an earthquake of great intensity occurred in 1899, and there is evidence that the Katalla region was uplifted (as it was again in 1964) by that temblor. Just as the new town was being built, that anchorage suddenly filled, leaving the landing at Katalla an open roadstead. It did not diminish the fervor of the oil rush in the slightest.

The oil strikes at Katalla were not news to old-timers such as Tom White, who is credited with the first discovery of oil there in 1894.

Tom was a great talker in an age when the lack of radio and television made virtuosos of interesting storytellers. He loved to tell of his hilarious misadventures in this oily region when in 1896 he discovered oil by literally falling into it. He was on a bear hunt but since his gun was fouled by the black stuff, he returned home to clean it so the hunt could continue. He took samples of the oil home and used it to start his morning fires. On an impulse he returned to the pool, lit a match and threw it in "to see what would happen." The pool burst into flame and continued burning, a flaming orange pyre pouring thick black smoke into the air for over a week.

Tom and his two buddies, George T. Barrett and Michael Davoll, bent every effort to getting capital interested in the oil, and thus became known to coastwise skippers as "The Three Greases."

In 1897 "The Greases" interested R. C. Johnston in the oil. He took samples to Seattle for analysis. Chauvenant Brothers of St. Louis submitted a report on this surface seepage, pool oil, which showed it to be of a remarkably high-grade paraffin base; with 48.50 percent illuminating oil, 36.92 percent lubricating oil and 14.54 percent residuum or tar with only .05 percent light or naptha. Other sources say Katalla oil was so high in products such as gasoline and kerosene that it did not even come into competition with lower grade California fuel oils which were used extensively in crude and stove oil forms.

Oil flowed from seepages all over the Katalla region. And then there was coal. Both oil and coal were attracting attention to this area, but the unworkable coal laws prevented any exploitation until 1904.

The coal land law of 1904 marks a turning point in this history. From the time that Bering River coal began to be mined, or was expected to be, Valdez was doomed to lose her railroads. Coal, copper and railroads made too obvious a combination—coal to run the railroads, coal to smelt the copper to sell to a ready market.

The coal country was big and the more it was prospected, the better it looked.

Many people were interested in the Bering River coal and had staked claims. One of the claims in the Bering River field was held by M. J. Heney, another by his brother P. A. Heney. Michael Heney, somewhat at loose ends after his White Pass & Yukon success, was dabbling in various ventures, using money he had earned in the building of that railroad. Mostly unknown to everyone in the vicinity, Michael Heney held an executive post with the English company, which, also not generally known, was financed in part by the Close Brothers of London. The English company held a block of claims in the coal fields and was naturally interested in seeing a railroad built to take the coal to tidewater.

By 1905 there were two railroads working on that project. One was the Alaska Pacific & Terminal Railroad Company (the Bruner Line) and the other was the Catalla & Carbon Mountain Railroad (Clark Davis Road). The Bruner Line planned to build from a terminus on one of the Martin Islands near Katalla, up the Katalla River and across Bering Lake by means of a long trestle and then on up to the coal fields.

The Clark Davis Road was to run down the Bering River flats to a terminus on Okalee Channel in Controller Bay.

At the time both of these Katalla projects were merely coal tonnage roads. They were projected only to tap the Bering River coal fields and to bring that product to tidewater on Controller Bay.

No one in 1904 dreamt that it was possible to build up the Copper River. Even if it could be done they felt that the route would prove financially unfeasible, but it was an obvious route as it followed a river course. Anyone who could overcome the difficulties of spanning the two glaciers that contained the river would be able to tie the coal and copper together with steel rails. Success would mean that copper could be smelted in Alaska and that local coal would be available for tonnage and operation of the railroad.

That was the state of things in 1904 during the formation of the Guggenheim-Morgan Syndicate and its subsidiary company, the Copper River & Northwestern Railway Company. News of the coal and oil of the Katalla region prompted the Syndicate to send out its engineers under George Cheever Hazelet to look at the Copper River route and report on its feasibility. Rejection of the route came only after at least two competent railway engineers reported adversely on the possibility of bridging the Copper River between Miles and Childs glaciers. Instead of following normal procedure and filing this survey, it was forgotten—a mistake which was to cost the Syndicate dearly.

At about the same time that the Guggenheims showed an interest in the Copper River route the Bruner Line was in the process of organization and became interested in the possibilities of building up the Copper River. Accordingly, they also surveyed the route, but they were a year too late, for by this time other events had intervened.

10 REENTER M. J. HENEY

Late in 1904, Michael J. Heney visited London and paid a call on his old friends and associates at the Close Brothers offices.

During the conversation there, he became aware of their intense interest in the various railroad projects on the coast of Alaska. But the Close Brothers were not happy with Katalla as a port for their coal and oil. They felt that harbor was too unprotected, too given to sudden violent storms, especially in the fall. Heney felt that the location of the cannery at the Indian village of Eyak would offer a better harbor. He was also well aware of the pass through the mountains from Copper River flats to Eyak Lake commonly used by the fishermen of the region.

He was aware, too, that the Guggenheim capitalists had looked over the Copper River as a means of bringing the coal and copper together, but had rejected it, and were even now preparing to start their construction from Valdez.

The Copper River was a natural gateway to the Interior, as Heney was aware. When he found out about the interest of Close Brothers in the route, he immediately did two things. He bought the U.S. War Department's *Narratives of Exploration,* containing Lieutenant Allen's account of his travels up the Copper River, and he sent a telegram to Siegley, his secretary and confidential advisor, telling him to contact all of "his boys," those who had worked with him on the White Pass & Yukon, and to put them on the payroll immediately.

After initiating his entry into the new railroad, he set sail for Seattle. During the ten-day journey he read carefully the War Department accounts dealing with the Copper River. By the time he landed in Seattle he had a fair idea that there were two keys to the Copper River route and if they could be surmounted, a railroad could be built. The primary key involved the bridging of the Copper River between the Miles and Childs glaciers. Abercrombie Canyon was the second key. Heney felt that if he could chisel out a rail line along its rocky face and get through, he could build a railroad up the Copper River.

To determine the feasibility of the line he planned to travel up the Copper River with Sam Murchison and Jack Dalton and look for himself. But fate took a hand. Heney came down with a very bad cold on his trip across the Atlantic and his physician, Dr. Fenton B. Whiting, forbade him to make the trip. In his place, Heney sent J. L. McPherson, a very competent surveyor. McPherson, Murchison and Dalton were to look over the route and pay stringent attention to the two "key" positions.

When the three men completed their survey they were to wire Heney and use an agreed-upon code. If the route was feasible, they were to say, "Meet me in Juneau," and give a date. If not, they should wire simply, "Will be home on the first boat."

At last the telegram came—the trio would meet him in Juneau in four days. Heney found a steamer leaving immediately from Seattle for Juneau. He arrived there ahead of his crew. At the land office, he asked if there were any surveys filed for the Copper River and found that there were none. He was the first, and made a verbal preliminary filing on the spot. When the three Copper River voyagers arrived, they made out a map of a preliminary route and filed it with the General Land Office.

That was the birth of the Copper River Railway. The year 1905 was spent in preliminary work, buying the abandoned cannery at Eyak for a headquarters and other such arrangements.

The cannery complex at what is now known as Old Cordova became the headquarters for the railroad.

When they felt the time was ripe, Samuel Graves, representative of Close Brothers, presented himself to the financial powers behind the Copper River & Northwestern Railway and attempted to secure a sale or merger. He tried to convince them that building up

the Copper River by way of the new survey would be a far superior route, but was peremptorily dismissed. The Guggenheims had already surveyed that route and decided against it. They saw no reason to change their minds. The *Alaska Monthly* in May of 1906 reported that ". . . the negotiations, if such they can be called, were a failure."

Michael Heney and Close Brothers determined to go ahead with their route. Now there were two copper railroads competing from Valdez (the Valdez-Yukon Railroad and the Copper River & Northwestern Railway), and two coal lines from Katalla (Alaska Pacific & Terminal Railway Company and the Catalla & Carbon Mountain Railroad). The Copper River Railway intended to tap both coal and copper from Eyak.

11 CORDOVA: APRIL FOOL!

On April Fool's Day 1906, Michael J. Heney engaged the big gamble. On that day the first shipload of men and equipment was landed at Eyak on Orca Bay. Eyak was a small canning community, which had been the site of the Alaska Packers Association salmon cannery, located on a neck of land between Odiak Slough and Eyak Lake.

The village made its living by catching salmon, which were found in great abundance both in the Copper River and in Prince William Sound. More importantly, Eyak had a deep-water anchorage which made it the scene of such feverish activity.

If salmon provided a means of livelihood to Eyak, it was not its reason for living to judge from the description of the community given by Presbyterian Minister Sheldon Jackson in 1894. He used Eyak to illustrate a "horrible example." He described it as having "25 white men, 25 native women, and 25 stills capable of producing 2,500 gallons of liquor, mostly consumed by Natives. They had no other visible means of support, although during the canning season the men did catch fish."

The transformation of Eyak began in March of 1906 and was described by a participant, Mr. Udo Hesse, in a letter to the *Cordova Times* editor 20 years later:

". . . on the 21st day of March [1906], the town of Cordova, Alaska, was founded with very modest and unassuming ceremonies.

"The survey party, the advance guard of the organization which was to found Cordova and commence construction of the Copper River Railroad, sailed north from Seattle on the steamer *Santa Clara*. This party, which sailed under telegraphic orders from M. J. Heney, who had just secured the right-of-way for the Copper River Railroad in

Washington, consisted of seven men, viz.: Superintendent of Construction Sam Murchison, a carpenter and surveying party of five men." The party arrived at Orca on March 13 and packed in along the beach for four miles to establish a canvas camp on the banks of a creek, which is now the heart of Cordova.

Continuing, Hesse said, "On March 21, a telegram was read (relayed from Valdez by the steamer *Elsie*) from M. J. Heney, who meanwhile had returned to Seattle from the east, containing instructions for our guidance, and the information that 'The name of the town is "Cordova."'" Immediately a large sign bearing the name 'Cordova' was prepared and conspicuously nailed to a large tree and thus the unincorporated town of Cordova sprang into existence, founded by seven men living in tents."

Exactly ten days later, on April 1, 1906, another ship landed and began discharging freight and snoose-chewing workers at the "town" of Cordova, which at this time was really the village of Eyak, now known as "Old Town." The railroad invasion had begun.

A month and a half later the first issue of the newspaper the *Cordova Alaskan* was issued on mimeograph-size sheets, and carried the story of the work accomplished in 46 days:

RUSHING WORK

The Copper River Railroad Company are [sic] *rushing the work right along. They are working about 500 men, and men are being employed as fast as they can be obtained.*

The grade between Three Tree Point and Eyak Lake is nearly completed which is nearly three miles, they are working day and night on difficult places and the rightaway gang have [sic] *the road-bed cleared for five miles ahead.*

The company's sawmill which was completed and started last week is kept running to its full capacity.

The railroad was projected to run to the great *Katalla coal fields which are only 75 miles from Cordova where thousands of acres of the very best coal in America lies. Coal experts claim it's even a far better grade of coal than is obtained in Pennsylvania, from which the whole Pacific Coast can be supplied from Cordova.*

The Copper River Railroad will be hauling coal and copper ore from this great coal and copper belt which lies in the Copper River valley, long before any of the projected railroads which are being constructed in Alaska, because M. J. Heney who has the contract to build this railroad is known all over Alaska as having built the White Pass & Yukon Railroad.

Once more Heney was making the wilderness resound to the thunder of dynamite and the ring of

steel on steel. The old Alaska Packers Association cannery building, purchased in 1905 by Heney, gave the railroad immediate buildings, a wharf, and even a small tramline to aid in the unloading of freight. The big cannery building became a temporary roundhouse.

By May 1906, the new "Orca Road" was the subject of several articles in the *Alaska Monthly*. Orca was another cannery location, about 2.5 miles north of present Cordova and still in use for a cannery. There was some confusion on the part of the magazine about the new road. There were two different stories about the same project, speaking of the "railway to be constructed by M. J. Heney from New York capital," in one, and "the interests represented by President Graves, of the White Pass & Yukon Railroad and backed, it is claimed, by Close Brothers, bankers of London and New York . . ." in the other.

But by July of the same year, there was no doubt in anyone's mind about the Copper River Railway. It was going great guns. The new town of Cordova (Eyak) was the sensation of the North. The July issue of *Alaska Monthly* carried an excellent picture of the town taken on May 19, 1906, when the town was two weeks old.

"New Railroad Town Booming," it said. "Parties who arrived in Juneau on the *Portland* say that Eyak, or Cordova, near Orca . . . is rapidly becoming quite . . . cosmopolitan. . . . The company has installed a water works system, is putting in an electric light plant and has a cold storage plant capable of holding 150 quarters of beef, in operation.

"The town, which a month ago was composed almost entirely of tents, now has a large number of frame buildings for business houses and a few dwelling houses. The business men have clubbed together and are grading the main street, so that the town is greatly improving in appearance."

The town of Cordova inherited one feature of unique convenience from Eyak—a main street tramway system. The tram was part of the equipment of the Alaska Packers cannery which the railroad had acquired. Speaking of Cordova's "narrow gauge short line," the June 16, 1906, edition of the *Cordova Alaskan* said: "Never has an Alaska town so early in its history been equipped with so rapid a system of freight transit. Received from a ship's tackle in Cordova Bay and lightered on a vessel especially designed and adapted for this purpose, the freight is unloaded on the tram road wharf, transferred to tram cars, traversing the entire length of the town [on Front Street], enabling the consignee to receive the freight at his door. The tram, which was formerly owned and operated by the Alaska Packers Association, which only recently passed into the control of the railroad, was for 19 years operated at intervals."

E. A. HEGG PHOTO. COURTESY PHYLLIS CARLSON

Top—Rock work at Mile 53, in Abercrombie Canyon. Construction work reached there in 1908.
Middle—The roadbed at Abercrombie Canyon had to be hewed out of solid rock.
Bottom—The main street in Eyak, showing the tramline; probably taken in 1906. After Cordova was built, this became known as Old Town.

E. A. HEGG PHOTO. COURTESY PHYLLIS CARLSON

ALASKA HISTORICAL LIBRARY

Driving the first spike on the Copper River Railway, August 28, 1906. (Alaska Historical Library)

The job of roadmaster for this first of Cordova's "railroads" was held by William O'Neil, and the tram was pulled by one of Cordova's real old-time characters, a mule named Maude. Maude was the object of many a joke and ribald comment by the residents of Cordova.

About 500 men were on the payroll by mid-July and that many more were already in the bustling little town. Grading crews were at work all along the right-of-way clear to the Copper River and another gang had been sent to work at Martin River, near Katalla, so that the construction could be pushed at an early date to the coal fields, which were only 75 miles from Cordova.

MOSS COLLECTION. ALASKA HISTORICAL LIBRARY

Paddle steamboat *Caswell* and barges unloading construction material; believed to be on Martin River.

Grading was progressing very swiftly due to the easy character of the country along Eyak Lake and across the level delta of the Copper River. "Their system of handling sidehills," explained the *Alaska Monthly*, "is to put in a charge of powder, blow the trees and muck loose from the surface and then level down with horses and scrapers." A sawmill was in operation, cutting the necessary piles, ties and bridge timbers. These would be needed the whole distance to Copper River, about 22 miles, where the foundation would necessarily be almost entirely pilings.

The first load of tracks arrived in July, and actual track-laying began the latter part of that month.

By September the Copper River Railway was ready for an event of some importance; the arrival of the first locomotive. This engine was a standard-gauge engine purchased from the Pacific Coast Company, and was unloaded from the big freighter *Leelanaw*. It was the only locomotive purchased by Heney for his original venture from Cordova, and was to become the most historic and beloved of all on the Copper River line throughout the years, "Old No. 50."

Steel rails for 21 miles of track and about 25 flat-cars were on the steamer. In all 2,200 tons of freight arrived on the *Leelanaw*, including 400 tons of coal.

By then the new wharf was finished at Cordova and the first steamer to land at the new facility was the well-known *Portland*.

The *Portland* was to figure in another episode that year of 1906—the famous "smallpox epidemic." Shortage of manpower was the universal problem plaguing all the lines, and it was considered good business, and great sport besides, to entice workers away from one another.

While Heney was building from Cordova and the Guggenheims and Colonel Swanitz from Valdez, another line had begun construction far to the westward from Seward across the Kenai and up the Susitna Valley. This was the Alaska Central Railroad. The Alaska Central was having difficulties, not the least of which was the worker shortage.

One day Copper River Railway workmen suddenly began quitting their work on the grade and appearing at the paymaster's window. They continued to abandon their jobs until work was almost at a standstill. The town was full of men waiting for transportation to Seward. It was found that the presence of a man from the Alaska Central, offering inducements to go to Seward to work, was the cause. Little could be done, but it was an extremely serious situation. Michael Heney was Outside in Seattle tending to the myriad details of a railroad 1,500 miles from its base of supply.

It was the versatile Dr. Whiting who saved the day, but in a most unethical manner. Dr. Fenton B. Whiting was a man of many talents, and his position extended far beyond his purview as chief surgeon of the railroad. He was a long-time friend of M. J. Heney, and had stood beside him, sometimes with a rifle, during some of the rough-and-tumble battles of White Pass days.

This present situation demanded something drastic but different. Dr. Whiting remembered an old and time-honored convict's trick used to attempt escape from prison, and he decided it was worth a try. The situation was desperate. He had a man in the infirmary with a skin affliction. He "treated" the man by annointing his skin with Croton oil, a purgative that produces a rash remarkably like smallpox. Diagnosing the ailment as the dread disease of smallpox, Dr. Whiting had the unfortunate victim confined to isolation on a boat in the harbor with a quarantine flag flying menacingly from its mast.

The steamer *Portland*, which approached Cordova, was met before it could dock and informed of the general quarantine of the Port of Cordova. Unable to dock, she sailed on, leaving several hundred frustrated railroad men waiting on the dock for passage to Seward. Those who registered an objection were invited to go out and see the smallpox victim for themselves. In those days when antibiotics and vaccinations were unknown, there were very few people brave enough to call the bluff.

Stranded in Cordova they soon spent all of their money and were forced to go back to work. The crisis was past and the victim made a remarkable recovery from his bout of smallpox.

The victim of the little drama did not even suspect the hoax until it was recounted by Rex Beach in his book, *The Iron Trail.*

The *Valdez Prospector* of November 22, 1906, reported on the hoax after learning of it from some of the men who went to Valdez after the episode. "The action of the Cordova people in holding men there until they were broke and then shipping them to Valdez lays them liable to much criticism. It is at best an imposition on the people and does not speak well for the character of the men in charge at the new railroad town." But with the shortage of workmen, all the lines were pirating workers from one another. Any trick that did no physical harm was considered allowable, and maybe even a good joke—if clever enough.

Competition was to get stiffer and more violent as the rival lines intensified their efforts, each intent on reaching the Bonanza country first. But Michael J. Heney held the Copper River route and the key to that was the Abercrombie Canyon.

12 THE BIG GAMBLE: ABERCROMBIE CANYON

WILL FIGHT RIVALS WITH DYNAMITE." That was the shocking headline of an article in the *Alaska Monthly* magazine in September of 1906. No author is given, and there can be no doubt that the situation was serious. The challenge was first printed in the *Seattle Times.*

The importance of certain narrow canyons in the railroad story cannot be overstressed as both Keystone Canyon and Abercrombie Canyon became scenes of strife.

The southern coast of Alaska is such that passage inland is limited to these two canyons, which are barely wide enough to accommodate two rail lines. Congress had provided in the Act of 1898 that "a railroad which passes through any canyon, pass or defile shall not prevent any other railroad company from use and occupancy of said canyon, pass, or defile for the purposes of its road, in common with the road first located." This did not, however, detract from the fact that the first company on the scene had a definite advantage, and in the case of Abercrombie Canyon, Heney intended to hold it.

Abercrombie was not a canyon in the true sense of the word. While one wall was a sheer rocky bluff, the other side, though it appeared to be an innocent pile of gravel, was actually the 300-foot-high face of Miles Glacier, heavily covered on this northern lobe with gravel and moraine deposit. Between the two walls roared Abercrombie Rapids.

The glacial face offered no dependable railroad footing. The sheer rocky face on the western side was the only way through, and only one line could blast out a foothold. It was here that Heney loaded his coyote holes and dug in.

There was a very good reason for his determination. Heney was engaged in a gamble. While he had Close Brothers of London financing him, he by no means had the liberal funds that he had had for the White Pass & Yukon Railroad. The Close Brothers were much more interested in a coal field railroad from Katalla to Cordova, as coal was a known commodity with known markets and little processing costs after mining. Copper on the other hand was just coming into great demand, the markets were not so obvious and the processing was complex and costly. Consequently, Heney was more or less on his own in developing the line. "Success" meant selling the route to the Guggenheims; he did not have the money to finish this road, which was to cost $20 million before it was done. Even his own fortune, earned in the building of the White Pass & Yukon, rode with the potential sale of the Copper River Railway.

If Heney could interest the Guggenheims in the purchase of the route, it would save the English company the entire expense of building and running a coal railroad from Katalla to Cordova. The Guggenheims would build it for them!

It was a good route, and a practical one, but it was expensive. Only up the Copper River could the coal and copper be joined together. Cordova furnished a deep-water, ice-free port all year round, near the coal fields of Katalla but not subject to the fierce autumn storms of that coast.

The big drawback to the Copper River route was the cost—at least $12 million more to build than the one from Valdez. Cordova offered an excellent harbor; but so did Valdez. The only reason the Guggenheims would ever have to buy Heney's route would be the bringing of the coal and copper together by rail. Coal to run the railroad, coal to smelt the copper; it was a winning combination. However, if the copper corporation fielded their own men and laid out their own survey without going through Heney, the gamble would still be lost.

Heney knew, too, that the Guggenheims were already nibbling at the bait. Even though they continued their Valdez construction, M. K. Rogers was looking over the Copper River route again. A crew of Guggenheim men had already been in Katalla sounding the harbor.

Heney had only one hole card: Abercrombie Canyon. He held the only survey that had been filed with the U.S. Land Office. Since the canyon needed extensive dynamite work, coyote holes were loaded and ready for blasting at the opportune moment—Heney was ready to "Fight Rivals With Dynamite."

An article in the September 1906 issue of *Alaska Monthly* stated, "Heney will use dynamite to fight any encroachment along the west side of the Copper River, which, engineers say, offers the only feasible route for a railroad up the stream. For a great distance the slender thread of the line will have to be blasted out of the solid rock. There is room for but one railway. Engineering facts make this certain. The construction will be costly, it is true, but more costly still—even ruinous, in fact—would be a surrender of the vantage ground now occupied by the Heney gangs of workmen.

"Across the river from the rocky cliffs there is an old moraine which offers absolutely no foothold for a railroad. The ground is treacherous in places and the high waters during the early summer months, when the glaciers melt, would sweep away any trestles or tracks laid by a rival concern.

"These facts constitute the element of property for which Heney is prepared to fight to death, if need be."

Named in the article as possible rivals were the "John Rosene Road" (the Guggenheims' Copper River & Northwestern) and the Valdez-Yukon Railroad, promoted by Colonel A. W. Swanitz, "which has a large force of men and equipment on the ground." There was one other road, not mentioned in the article, which could qualify as a rival for Abercrombie Canyon: the Alaska Pacific & Terminal Railroad Company (the Bruner Line), building from Katalla. Maps of the Bruner Line show projected extensions up the Copper River, although they did not apparently field survey crews there until 1907. When the survey crews went in, rumors of a fresh confrontation between the Guggenheims and the Bruners cropped up.

"A veritable virgin empire is the big stake in which millions of capital and hundreds of men are enlisted to make the battle until the victory is won or lost.

"Much work has been done by the Heney men in the rock-ribbed canyon of the Copper River. Five miles of track have been graded and by midwinter it is expected that 30 miles will have been completed. The entry of surveyors or workmen from any other line over that now occupied by Heney will be resisted with bands of men armed with sticks of dynamite and guns of large calibre."

The article may have been a bit exaggerated. Guns of large caliber were not needed. All Heney had to do was load the coyote holes (they had to be set off eventually anyway), wait beside them and warn any unwanted surveyors that they were preparing to blast. All perfectly proper and aboveboard; and in fact, since M. J. Heney was the first man to make application for the right-of-way, and his application had been accepted and recorded, he had every right to blast in that canyon.

Violence never erupted in Abercrombie Canyon, probably because of Heney's determined stand. It had been an unorthodox ploy, but well-timed and very effective.

As 1906 drew to a close, word was received that Michael Heney had won his gamble. The Guggenheim-Morgan Syndicate bought the right-of-way that they could have had originally if they had filed their own survey. The purchase from Heney cost a quarter-of-a-million dollars!

The Guggenheims had bought out the interests of Close Brothers of London and Michael J. Heney. They would merge the two railroads under the Copper River & Northwestern Railway. Heney was to retire from the field entirely; the contract was to be awarded to the Katalla Company with M. K. Rogers, general manager.

As the merger negotiations neared completion, work was suspended at both Valdez and Cordova. In Valdez $200,000 worth of work was abandoned, including an $85,000 hand-drilled rock tunnel in Keystone Canyon. There was bitter resentment in Valdez over the move with denouncement of the Guggenheim-Morgan Syndicate.

The port of Cordova was abandoned at Rogers' recommendation and the new Copper River & Northwestern Railway began building from Katalla where all that stood between them and success was the Pacific Ocean and the rival Bruner Line. Rogers thought that a breakwater would solve the Pacific Ocean problem. The Bruner Line was something else again.

13 KATALLA: WHERE THE RAILS MEET THE SAILS

In Katalla there was a surge of confidence and prosperity with the coming of the Guggenheim railroad. The brash young town of railroads, coal and oil soared to its zenith in early 1907. It was to be "The Pittsburgh of Alaska," the industrial giant of the North. The banner of the *Katalla Herald*, which began publication in August 1907, read: "Katalla: Where the Rails Meet the Sails."

Anywhere from 5,000 to 10,000 persons including construction workers, oil men, coal miners, prospectors, Chinese coolie laborers, Bohunks, Irishmen, card sharps and phony stock brokers, jammed Katalla in 1907. It was probably the most rip-roaring open town since Nome or Dawson, for that year. The "Katalla Madhouse," one of the most notorious saloons in Alaska, was doing a booming business.

Confidence oozed from the very ground, like the oil of the region. There was a feeling in the air that at last the railroads had found their proper terminus, and nothing could go wrong now. "The confidence that capital reposes in the future of this region is expressed in the way railroad companies are striving with one another in a race to reach the district first . . . ," said *Alaska Monthly* in August 1906.

The biggest topic of conversation in the burgeoning community was the proposed breakwater to be built by the Guggenheims. The entire success of the Katalla venture depended on this piece of construction, and there was great faith in its success.

It was magnificently conceived. The breakwater would project out from Palm Point 2,000 feet to where a water depth of 38½ feet was reached. The piers would be 1,500 feet long, large enough to accommodate three ocean-going steamers at once. It would consist of driven pilings with rocks, weighing from 10 to 20 tons each, piled on top. "And there can be no question of the feasibility of such work," asserted J. F. A. Strong, editor. Rocks for the breakwater were hauled two miles on flatcars.

"When Chief Engineer M. K. Rogers selected Katalla as the starting point of the Copper River & Northwestern Railroad company's lines into the Copper River country and the Bering River coal fields it was not until a thorough examination had been made not only of the routes to be followed, but of the harbor as well. Every step was taken carefully, methodically. The bay was sounded and measurements taken, weather and other conditions such as prevailing winds carefully noted. Mr. Rogers is no tyro in railroad and engineering problems. For years he was with James J. Hill, the greatest railroad man of today, and Marcus Daly, who not only developed mines, erected smelters but built and operated railroads as well."

Work was being pressed by the company in two directions. One spur was directed toward the coal fields, the other toward the Copper River. Work at Katalla was begun by the Guggenheims in June of 1907, and by working through the winter the coal line was expected to be completed by August of 1908.

An interesting feature of the Guggenheim effort at Katalla was the swiftness with which the work was pushed forward, and the presence, almost from the very first, of their locomotives. Work was commenced in June, and it is known that the Guggenheims had at least one locomotive in Katalla on July 3, when the battle occurred. During the year 1907, six engines of the "dinkie" (donkey) or "saddletank" type, numbered one to six, were in operation on the Katalla line, as well as steam shovels, steam dredges, self-dumping flatcars and other heavy equipment.

During August engineers were sent to the glacier area bridge site to begin the collection of data on the glaciers and the river which would be needed to successfully build the bridge at this point, and camps were established at Abercrombie Canyon.

The Bruner Line was not making quite such good progress, but it was satisfactory nonetheless. About 250 men were employed and were building the trestle to the Martin Islands, where deep water was readily reached. The terminal buildings would be on one of the two small islands with a dock projecting 500 feet. Here steamers of 25-foot-draft could load and unload at any stage of the tide, and the islands would afford them shelter. Future plans called for filling in the channel between the two islands, a distance of 1,600 feet. Then, with some further extension of the dock, "An unexcelled harbor will be had, impervious to any storm that may blow."

"Grading and pile driving are under way on both the Copper River line and the Bering coal line, the work, however, on the Copper River route being confined chiefly to pile driving in the immediate vicinity of the company's main camp, sometimes called Carbon Center. Other camps are established near Abercrombie Canyon and at the crossing of the Copper River.

"Carbon Center is building up slowly, and it now has a saloon, of which Breedman and Dietrich are the proprietors, a laundry and a barber shop."

There was one other railroad under construction from Katalla, of which little was said, mainly because it was purely a coal line—the Catalla & Carbon Mountain Railroad (the Clark Davis coal road). The terminal facilities for this railroad were to be on the Bering River flats, where a trestle three-and-one-half miles long would be necessary to reach a deep-water channel on Controller Bay. The first two miles of this trestle would be over a dry mud flat at low water. This road would be some 25 miles long.

"Clark Davis" boasted in 1906 that their road "would be the first to haul coal." In a colossal twist of fate the Clark Davis boast turned out to be correct, though the first tonnage was not hauled until 1918. This untimely delay in completion of the railroad resulted from President Theodore Roosevelt's withdrawal of all the coal lands in Alaska from entry. Indeed everything related to and connected with the

THE KATALLA HERALD

KATALLA, THE COMING METROPOLIS OF ALASKA, WHERE THE RAILS MEET THE SAILS

VOL. 2, No 1.   KATALLA, ALASKA, SATURDAY, AUGUST 8, 1908   PRICE TEN CENTS

TUESDAY'S ELECTION

Forecast of Result Well Nigh Impossible

crat and labor) 5,459; Murane (republican) 2,324; Mellen (democrat) 1,083. As will be noticed the vote polled by former Delegate Waskey (democrat and labor) and Swineford, (democrat) does not appear.

BIG VEIN OF FINEST COAL

Up on Carbon mountain, on the property of the Alaska Petroleum & Coal

Bertha By Wireless

R. D. Gray last night received an aerogram from the Bertha, asking if there were passengers or freight here for the outside. Mr. Gray replied that there were. She was then at Hinchinbrook.

FOREST FIRES AWFUL DAMAGES

(By aerogram to The Herald)
Vancouver, B. C., August 4—One

CAN'T BE DELAYED

The Development of This Great Region

RALPH E. MACKAY COLLECTION

Above—A dinkie locomotive and a dump car, part of a construction train.
Right—A very early picture of the business section of Katalla. The tramway in the foreground ran out on a short wharf.
Far right—Driving the trestle for construction of the breakwater at Katalla, July 16, 1907.

MOSS COLLECTION, ALASKA HISTORICAL LIBRARY

MOSS COLLECTION, ALASKA HISTORICAL LIBRARY

coal fields was thrown into limbo, neither closed down nor able to proceed. But each entryman, despite the fact that he couldn't be sure of his claim (even if it had been properly filed) or mine coal from it, was still required to do $100 worth of development work each year! This often took the form of "little trails that began nowhere and went nowhere, but were nice for hikers."

The withdrawal was a severe blow, but since it was supposedly temporary, its effect on railroad building was not immediately apparent. The two rival lines at Katalla continued work on their breakwater and trestles, and began laying rails, and clearing their rights-of-way. The two lines crossed at a point on Palm Point Lake.

The Bruners knew that the Guggenheims, expecting no trouble, and in a hurry to build their line, had only a preliminary survey filed on their route. They still had to file a permanent one. The Bruners planned to stop the Guggenheims.

Even though the Guggenheim workers had advanced to within 150 feet of Palm Point Lake, where the Bruners had a trestle, nobody expected real trouble. But one morning, "No Trespassing" signs appeared on the Bruner trestle. These were backed up by grim, rifle-carrying men. Not to be stopped, the Guggenheim workers continued to drive pilings.

That night the unsure calm was rent with explosions. The Bruners had dynamited a Guggenheim pile driving machine and trestle.

14 THE BATTLE OF B. S. HILL

The night the Bruners dynamited the Guggenheim line was vividly recalled by the late Jack McCord, former Kodiak rancher.

"When the dynamiting occurred, I was just a young fellow, about 22, not very important. I had a job checking supplies for the Guggenheim camp. But as checker I was in a position to see what happened better than anyone else, in the beginning.

"Our superintendent, John Krey, was a serious man with a little grey beard. When this happened the first thing he did was try to get advice from his superiors in New York. There were no communications out of Katalla, so he sent a boat called the Swan to Valdez where there was a cable.

"When the Swan came back with the answer, I was the one, as checker, who brought the cable to Krey. Krey opened it and read it right there. The gist of it was this: 'We have deposited $150,000 in the Bank of California. Go across and argue afterward.'

"So there I was. I knew that there was a lot of money on hand for this, and I knew they were going across.

"I was checking supplies off the steamer Santa Ana one day when I saw men going up to the lake. I went up to watch what was going on. The Bruners had a raft rigged up on the lake, with a cable to the mountain, and had it rigged so they could jerk it back and forth with cables from shore, so no one could approach their trestle.

"When Krey saw me, he asked if I had my work done and told me I'd better stay away, because there might be trouble. Well, I was a young fellow and I wanted to stay and see what was going on, so I stalled by asking questions.

"'What are you going to do?' I asked.

"'We're going to blow up the raft,' he said.

"We talked it over for a while, and I said I wouldn't do that if it was me, because you might cause a riot, with all the Greeks and Italians who didn't speak English and wouldn't know what was going on.

"'What would you do?' asked Krey.

"Now here was my chance. 'I'd pay Tony de Pascal to go over there and get on the raft and cut the cable.' Tony was the interpreter for the Italians.

"Well, Krey had figured on sending Black Sullivan, one of his best men, out to blow it up, but he decided he'd send Tony out to cut the cable instead.

"So Tony started out in a boat. The fellows on the trestle pointed their guns at him and told him to get away. I don't think they'd have fired; they just wanted to scare him, and they did. Tony dropped his tools and came rowing back.

"As he came ashore, I jumped in and went out. I didn't know what a job it is to cut a cable or I wouldn't have been so eager. When I got close the fellows hollered, 'We'll shoot, Jack!' I knew all these guys; we chummed around together all the time, and I knew they wouldn't shoot. No one wants to get into a fight for a corporation. So I just smiled and waved. They didn't shoot.

"This raft was jerking back and forth and I managed to get onto it, but I had all I could do to hang on and ride it back and forth. When I got on, everybody cheered, even the fellows with the guns on the trestle. They got a big kick out of watching me trying to keep my balance on that jerking raft.

"I took out my tools and started to hack at the cable, but just then it jerked and knocked me over. Then I turned to the other, smaller cable on a pulley and I managed to cut that, but it's a wonder it didn't kill me. The raft went stuck then.

"Tony de Pascal was still out for the $500 and the glory, so he started hollering and swearing and talking to the Italians, till he had a mob that was going to tackle the men with the guns.

"Black Sullivan saw trouble a-brewing, so he used his head and some good Alaskan gumption and came up to these fellows pretending to be marshal, and he placed them 'under arrest.' Then he took them out somewhere and told them to behave, and that stopped the trouble for that day.

"Next day the Guggenheims started driving pilings toward the trestle again. Then the Bruners found a new wrinkle. They had two steel rails tied together and rigged with pulleys from the hill so that they could twirl them. It was a pretty deadly device, and everything came to a standstill again.

"I was still in the limelight after the day before, and I knew they had this money in the bank for this crossing, and I began to figure how I could get my hands on a chunk of it. I was just a farm boy, but I had me some pretty big ideas. I figured that those fellows didn't really want to hurt anyone. All I had to do was offer them more than they were already getting. So I went to John Krey and asked him for the contract to cross the lake.

"'How much?' he asked, so promptly that I was kind of rocked back on my heels. Well, he kind of had me there; I didn't know how much a thing like that was worth, so I said 'Ten thousand.'

"'Not a bit too much,' said Krey, and we went off to draw up the contract. Black Sullivan was to be my lieutenant.

"After I had the contract, a fellow named Mike Sullivan—a different guy than Black Sullivan—who just came in on the *Yucatan* and knew all about poker and bluffing, came to Krey and told him he was sent by New York to settle the trouble and see that they made the crossing. So Krey sent him to me. He was just a guy off the boat, not anyone at all. But I liked his style, so I took him in and now I had Mike and Black Sullivan and myself.

"I told them my plan was simple; I'd buy the main men off. So we went down to Jack Smith's dance hall where they were all drinking and dancing. I got hold of their superintendent and Charlie Bear Claw, who had done the dynamiting, and a few more of their leaders. And after we had made a deal, we laid plans so it wouldn't look bad for them.

"First I was to storm the hill with my men and cut the cable. It would be just like T. R. storming San Juan Hill, at least it would look that way. We called it among ourselves 'The Battle of B. S. Hill.' No one was to have guns, just pick handles and clubs. And the resistance was just to be token.

"Then after we took the hill and cut the cable to the go-devil, we would take possession of the trestle. To make it look okay for them to run, we would pipe steam up under them so it would look like fire. The leader was to tip his hat for the steam.

"So it was all set. The Battle of B. S. Hill began. But just in case, I had Big Mike Sullivan with 50 men in the woods with pick handles. Black Sullivan and I led the charge up the hill.

"And it was just at this crucial moment that the fellows on the hill decided to have a little fun with me. They came out and began digging holes and packing 'dynamite' in them. I could feel my men sort of hesitate behind me. Then the cry of 'Fire!' went up.

"My ranks broke and ran.

"There we were, just a few chiefs and no Indians. Some of those guys are running yet, I guess.

"The fellows who pulled the trick were really having a ball up there, laughing. We could see they weren't running, so those of us still left, charged on up the hill.

"Ahead of us were three gangling Swedes armed with pick handles. They had wire strung across in front of them, so I offered a man $50 to cut the wire, which he did. And we got close to the Swedes and I stopped and made a little speech. I said, 'No one wants to get hurt for a corporation,' and so on, and I offered to buy them off, but they stood their ground. They struck out at Black Sullivan and hit him an awful wallop on the head. So Mike Sullivan came out of the woods with his 50 men and we finally took the hill and cut the cable which was twirling the rails.

"The upshot of it was that someone who wasn't bought off swore out a warrant and Marshal Wardell came to arrest me and my men. Big Mike saw him coming and said, 'Quick, get inside and bandage your head and groan like you're hurt!'

"So the marshal came and took a look at Black Sullivan who was really hurt, and at me, who looked like it, and he left us but he took Big Mike Sullivan in.

"That left just me, the only one left on the job. Big Mike was in the jug, Black was out of commission with a big egg on the head. And we found out that we had to complete the crossing before the ship *Saratoga* reached Katalla, because there were soldiers aboard.

"So we went to work to take the trestle. The men on the Bruner trestle were men who were loyal to me, that is, they were bought off. Only thing is, they still had that sense of humor. They were all set for some more fun at my expense, though I didn't know it.

"When the steam was all ready, the signal was given. Colter tipped his hat.

"At the signal I ran down the trestle (our incomplete trestle), which was just planks laid on top. As I ran down these planks, the men on the other trestle jerked one out with a rope they had tied to it, and I fell in the drink.

"So the 'general' went swimming, and Greeks and Italians took off with their pick handles after the Bruner bunch, retreating in a cloud of steam and hilarity, and we took possession of the crossing.

"Well, all had been more or less peaceful so far, and I went down to see Krey and collect, but he said he wanted pilings driven so he could send a picture of a train on the trestle to New York.

"So we finished driving.

"Then Krey said their bunkhouses were still on the grade on the other side and should be removed, and here's where the trouble came in.

"I figured that would be easy enough, since the bunkhouses were on the grade, but the mess hall wasn't. All we'd have to do was wait till they rang the triangle for dinner, and then sneak up while they were eating and dynamite the bunkhouses.

"Trouble is, there were a couple of drunks who stayed behind. While we were trying to get them out of the bunkhouses, I saw a couple of fellows with rifles on the other side of the lake. I thought they were ours, so I told Tony de Pascal to go tell them no rifles.

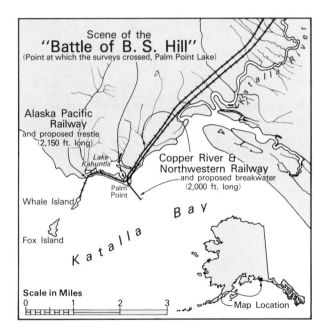

Scene of the
"Battle of B. S. Hill"
(Point at which the surveys crossed, Palm Point Lake)

Alaska Pacific Railway
and proposed trestle
(2,150 ft. long)

Lake Kahuntla

Copper River & Northwestern Railway
and proposed breakwater
(2,000 ft. long)

Palm Point

Whale Island

Fox Island

K a t a l l a   B a y

Scale in Miles
0   1   2   3

Map Location

"Tony started for them, thinking they were ours, too. Suddenly they fired, and Tony stiffened out and fell, and a bullet tore through the shoulder of my coat.

"You've heard people say their hair stood on end? That's the exact sensation!

"We weren't supposed to have guns, but I had one under my coat and I pulled it out.

"Someone hollered, 'Don't shoot, there's two more in the bushes!'

"In the meantime the fellow who shot Tony (Tony wasn't dead, but we thought he was) ran into the woods.

"Marshal Wardell came then, and I guess he wasn't relishing that man hunt through the woods for a killer, because he said to me, 'When someone kills a

man and you have him in your sights, why don't you shoot him?'

"So he sent Italians in pairs into the woods to catch him, with a $500 reward to each of them that did. When they caught him, they grabbed his gun arm in a surprise attack and some woodsmen helped disarm him. Each of the woodsmen got $500, too.

"The gunman, Joe Carboni, was put on the *Yucatan* to Valdez. While on the ship, he managed to sock the doctor on the head and knife Captain Johnny O'Brien before the mate laid him out with a belaying pin. He spent the rest of his life in an asylum. Tony de Pascal recovered and was drowned later that year in an attempt to save another fellow from drowning."

McCord was later depicted by Rex Beach in *The Iron Trail* as Dan Appleton. But according to McCord, "I'm not Appleton at all. I don't chew tobacco, I'm not a hypochondriac, and I never took a drink in my life, though I chummed around with the fellows. But I did cut the cable on the go-devil."

The Guggenheims had gone across per instructions. The time had come to argue.

15 AFTERMATH

By August of 1907 the two competing companies had their workmen far up the Copper River, where rumors of another fray at Abercrombie Canyon started to circulate.

The Bruner Company by now had two camps in the vicinity for their surveyors and locating crews. The Guggenheims had four; three crews were below the proposed Glacier Bridge site, and one was across the river at Abercrombie Canyon.

The *Valdez Prospector* reported: "Another Pick Handle Fight. Ed Meiss, who reached town yesterday after a trip down the Copper River, reports that a repetition of the 'Pick Handle Hill' fight at Katalla, is brewing near the Copper River rapids between the Bruner and Northwestern forces. The latter company has 95 men in the district where the fight is expected, and Bruner has 35. The trouble is over a strip of right-of-way along the rapids. . . ."

The charge was promptly denied by the *Katalla Herald,* which said: "J.F. Major, who is employed by the Alaska Pacific & Terminal Company was in town Sunday from Abercrombie Canyon. The company has quite a force of men clearing the right-of-way and grading in the vicinity of the canyon. . . . 'There has been no pick-handle, or any other kind of a fight between the men of the two companies at the canyon, as reported by the Valdez papers,' said Mr. Major, 'The relations between the men are entirely amicable.'"

The Bruner crossing nine days after the Battle of B.S. Hill. The Katalla line, with the work train at the right, crosses the Bruner trestle which runs out toward the inner one of the Martin Islands.

Below and right—Winter of 1910. Valdez was noted for its heavy snowfalls.

Apparently, no such confrontation occurred. But the battles already fought, and those threatened, were having their effect. Henry C. Frick, the Pittsburgh steel magnate backing the Bruner Line, was not idle. Suit was filed against the Guggenheims enjoining them—too late—from "forcibly entering, laying track upon, and crossing the right-of-way of the plaintiff company . . ." at Katalla.

Reverberations were already beginning. A dispatch from Washington, D.C., reported that Teddy Roosevelt was ready to pick up his big stick and walk softly after the Guggenheim-Morgan Syndicate.

This was the heyday of the Rough Rider; "trust-busting" was the National Political Sport, and the Alaska Syndicate of the Guggenheims was certainly fair game.

Teddy Roosevelt's "temporary" withdrawal of coal lands had been made on the grounds that certain claims, later identified as those of Clarence Cunningham and Associates, were taken out with intent to create a monopoly for the Alaska Syndicate. Horace T. Jones, a special agent, was sent from Washington to investigate the Bering River coal claims following the "temporary" withdrawal of land.

It was also reported unofficially that the Department of Justice would begin an investigation of the railroad terminal wars in Alaska. It was said that the Guggenheims were trying to prevent rival roads from constructing railroads in Alaska.

But the investigative wheels moved too slowly, for other events soon pushed the Bruner fight to the back of the public mind. Just about a month after the Katalla fights, Valdez made a strong bid for her place in the Alaskan sun. The man leading the movement was Henry Derr Reynolds, and he claimed to have a plan which, if successful, would give Valdez her All-American route, and at the same time "put the Guggenheims on the hike without delay."

Valdez, the town which had sent the startling "Annex Alaska to Canada" telegram, was still the fiery center of the Home Rule forces; nowhere was the Guggenheim-Morgan Syndicate so hated as here. And the heated oratory of Reynolds was fanning this hatred into a blaze of indignation.

The Home Rule fight was inevitably tied in with the Conservation issue, because all of the large absentee owners of Alaskan industry have historically opposed local home rule. Taxes alone would explain this phenomenon, though there was more to it than that. The Guggenheims, as the biggest absentee owner in Alaska, were the special target for Alaskan resentment, and Valdez had further reason for anger in her lost railroad.

Valdez was ready to stand up and fight and in August of 1907 she did.

16 VALDEZ: REYNOLDSITIS

Something big was in the wind. The entire population of Valdez was invited on a cruise aboard the steamer *Bertha* one lovely Saturday afternoon in mid-August. Picking up the tab for this outing was the genial host, H.D. Reynolds. Everyone who could, went.

The tour included copper properties on Prince William Sound, some of which were showing excellent promise. The Reynolds-Alaska Development Company's Iron Mountain Mine at LaTouche Island had been a sensation the previous fall. This enterprise was obviously no fly-by-night. It had installed an electric power plant, with electric-pneumatic drills. This was reportedly the first application of electricity to mining. Also the townsite of Reynolds, Alaska, was platted near the Iron Mountain property in the spring of 1907. In addition the Reynolds company had some good properties at Boulder Bay, where about 1,200 tons of ore were waiting for shipment.

The tour also included Horseshoe Bay, where Reynolds planned to build a smelter. That afternoon the Reynolds Company showed a substantial amount of achievement. The passengers were impressed.

Prince William Sound at this time of year is intensely beautiful, green in the depths, shimmering with color in the sun, with thickly wooded islands all about and snow-covered mountains in the distance. The voyage, the beauty of the sound, the comradery of the trip, and the tremendous promise of the Reynolds properties filled the group with a fresh enthusiasm.

It was time for Reynolds to present his proposition.

A mass meeting was held that evening and the town turned out in force. A great hubbub and stir was all about. The meeting opened with a prayer, led by ex-Governor John Green Brady. When Reynolds finally announced his plan for an All-Alaska railroad, it was met with roaring approval. Reynolds proposed that the people of Valdez build their own railroad—25 miles to the head of Thompson Pass for a starter. The railroad would be owned, operated and financed locally; truly an Alaska Home Railroad. Reynolds promptly put up $10,000 to get the ball rolling. Brady followed with $5,000. Cheer after cheer filled the air as others came forward to pledge, each as he was able; even a ten-cent contribution from a 12-year-old boy was accepted. By meeting's end $106,000 had been subscribed to the venture.

The idea from its inception had seemed so sound, so missionary in its zeal, that Governor Brady had lent his name as voucher for the stock. Brady was known as a man with Alaska's interests at heart. He had been a vociferous supporter of Reynolds' enterprise from the very first. He had issued an "Open Letter to

Old Valdez, as seen from the end of the wharf, with the glacier in the background. This townsite was abandoned after the 1964 earthquake. (P. S. Hunt photo)

Investors" that aroused a great cry from Alaskans, who called it "that fool letter of endorsement" and wondered if "those gosh darn bunko sharps back East had conned the Grand Old Man." Objections reaching the higher echelons in Washington resulted in Brady's withdrawing his name from the vouchers and letterhead of the company, but he made no secret of his affiliation and used his influence to raise money for the Reynolds scheme. Largely because of his championship of Reynolds' cause, he was relieved of the appointive governorship in March of 1906 (at which time it was offered to David H. Jarvis, who refused). Brady promptly became treasurer of the Alaska Home Railroad. Thereafter, he spent considerable time in the churches of the east giving stereopticon lectures and raising money for the Reynolds Company.

It is almost certain that Brady's presence among the promoters led to a great deal of its meteoric success—at first.

Saturday night's meeting had launched the Alaska Home Railroad. By Monday following the mass meeting, Reynolds had purchased the Keystone Wharf, a machine shop, a blacksmith shop, a sawmill and the *Valdez Prospector* newspaper.

Riding a tidal wave of enthusiasm, Reynolds attended the Monday night city council meeting and left with an almost blanket 99-year franchise for every street in Valdez with permission to build a wharf and railroad. In return, he was to construct a cement breakwater, and other work.

The Christian Endeavor Church, which had been the object of such pride in the 1903 Valdez edition of the *Seattle Mail & Herald,* was given outright to the Reynolds people, and it was here that they established their headquarters and bank. This bizarre development was pounced on gleefully by the opposition press, who remembered that the Brady regime had been referred to as "Jesus Christ & Company." The *Katalla Herald* gibed: "The Reynolds-Alaska Development Company, of which former Governor Brady is chaplain and which now owns Valdez, body and breeches, recently opened a bank in a church. Did Governor Brady open it with a prayer?"

Events moved along swiftly. On Tuesday the mass enthusiasm of Saturday's meeting recurred as the road construction began with huge fanfare.

"Valdez turned out en masse [Tuesday] to see the first dirt fly on the Alaska Home Railway. There was no formal ceremony. Men had been employed and spread along the surveyed line ready for work. Ex-Governor Brady stepped to the starting point and turned the first shovel of dirt. He said 'This is no time for talk. It's a time for work. . . .' Immediately the Valdez citizens grasped picks and shovels and several

hundred enthusiastic volunteers vied with each other in clearing and grading the first mile of right-of-way. Every available team in the vicinity of Valdez was pressed into service. Work was given to all applicants. With steady efficiency the work progressed and before nightfall a spendid start had been made on the long journey to the interior."

By Thursday the railway had been graded out Broadway to the intersection of the old Valdez-Yukon right-of-way. Colonel Swanitz had resigned from the Valdez-Yukon and had joined Reynolds as a consulting engineer.

The August 15, 1907, issue of the *Valdez Prospector* noted that "The town is dazed with the rapidity with which each move is made. . . . Subscriptions continue to pour in. . . . It is as though a wizard's wand had aroused the dormant energies of a mighty people. . . ."

The *Cordova Alaskan* of September 28, 1907, had a less rosy version: "After reading the last issue of the *Valdez Prospector* on the latest developments of Mr. Reynolds and his 'Home' railway, reminds us of when we were a boy and read fairy books. In one it was recorded that when Satan sheared a hog once upon a time, that he remarked, 'There is a great cry, but very little wool.'"

Actually, there seemed to be plenty of wool, all of it pulled over the eyes of enthusiastic Valdezans. Within the following week, Reynolds had acquired a bank, mercantile houses, several hotels, the Alaska Coast Steamship Company and numerous other businesses. There seemed to be no end to his grandiose schemes. His plans for Valdez as outlined by the *Prospector* illustrate the point. "Plans are underway to practically rebuild the town, but without disturbing the regular conduct of business. The residence section will be laid out in alternate blocks of houses and public squares; each house will have a quarter of a block of ground and all buildings will be of concrete, lighted and heated by electricity, with water under pressure. . . . In the business section all buildings will be beautifully designed and will have wide porch roofs covering the sidewalks. . . . The rebuilt city will have libraries, Museum of Natural History, Art Institute, Musical Conservatory, a large building for the Tillicum Club, a forum, a theatre, a school of mines and eventually a University. Thus will Alaska show to the world its inherent worth, and its people should enjoy the utmost of happiness, prosperity and contentment."

Along with Colonel Swanitz of the Valdez-Yukon Railroad another familiar name appeared on the Reynolds roster—Andrew F. Burleigh of the erstwhile Alaska Railroad Company. He was engaged as an attorney for the Alaska Home Railroad.

In early September the first locomotive arrived, and another was scheduled to arrive on the next boat, which was held up for repairs. Of all the railroads which had claimed Valdez as their terminus, this was the only one to actually produce a locomotive. It was the only one ever seen in Valdez, and it was the occasion for great excitement.

The only "annoying incident" reported—and deplored roundly—was the action of "three agitators who circulated among the men and got a number to strike on a fancied grievance. . . ." The three were spotted and dropped from the payroll, but soon after were detected attempting to "intimidate the other men who had returned to work by threats of violence when the Katalla men arrived on the scene. The matter was reported to the authorities and the three men are now reposing in the lock-up where they will have time to reflect on their error in attempting to oppose the people in their work."

The "Katalla men" referred to were several hundred men from Katalla that Reynolds was busy "pirating" away from the Katalla railroads to work on the Alaska Home Railroad. To this end he made a trip to Katalla, where he was immediately buttonholed by a hostile crowd, who demanded of the "high Panjandrum of the Reynolds-Alaska Company" an explanation of the "piracy of men from Katalla for his 25-mile electric tramway at Valdez. . . . Reynolds at first denied all knowledge of the piracy, but on being cornered said he had heard that there were two or three hundred men here who had quit work and so he had sent for them. The atmosphere by this time was getting too close for Mr. Reynolds and he beat a hasty retreat." So said the *Katalla Herald* in its edition of August 24, 1907.

The reports of newspapers other than Reynolds' own *Valdez Prospector* were mixed in their reaction to the Valdez phenomenon. Cordova, not having any railroad of its own left to fight over, could afford to be moderate: "Valdez has a case of Reynoldsitis. . . . We sincerely hope the promoters . . . are in earnest, for the more railroads built in Alaska, the better for the country."

The *Katalla Herald* was not so charitable: "HOT IN VALDEZ," it headlined: "It is 90 above in the shade at Valdez. . . . There is so much hot air in circulation that palm leaf fans are at a premium. . . . They [the Reynolds Company] say that they are 'going to put the Guggenheims on the hike without delay.' It is to laugh, but I suppose you can't blame them for feeling the way they do."

The phrase "going to put the Guggenheims on the hike," illustrates why the Alaska Home Railroad rose to such swift prominence with the people of Valdez. They were already unhappy over losing their All-American railroad when the Guggenheims moved to Katalla.

It is doubtful that Reynolds could have aroused such enthusiasm if it had not been for the "trust-busting" psychology of the times, coupled with the natural resentment of Valdez at losing the Guggenheim road. And certainly, confounding the wicked "Googies" was the real aim of the Alaska Home Railroad. Their intention of doing so was implicit, although not stated directly, in the "Platform" which was drafted by Reynolds and published prominently every Thursday on the front page of the *Valdez Prospector:*

> . . . *Object—Legitimate development of Alaska's resources for Alaskans.*
> > *Operation—In the people's interest.*
> > *No promotion shares.*
> > *No bonds or other indebtedness.*
> > *No high salaried officials. . . .*
> > *No construction profits.*
> > *No graft or incompetence tolerated.*
> > *Of Alaska, by Alaska, for Alaska.*
> > *A square deal to all. . . .*
> > > *—Harry D. Reynolds, Trustee*
> > > *Valdez, Alaska, Aug. 13, 1907*

It was a recurrent theme throughout the published accounts in the Valdez paper: "For a long time past the great corporate interests of the East have been gradually extending their sphere of influence with the obvious intention of absolutely controlling the transportation facilities of Alaska, thus gathering to themselves Alaska's marvelous mineral wealth. It is high time that the people were aroused to the danger of the situation, and Mr. Reynolds has taken the initiative and leadership in a fight of the people for their rights.

"For months past Alaskans have witnessed with sinking hearts the throttling of one independent railroad after another until today the trusts control practically every railroad right-of-way to the interior. . . .

". . . In order to forever prevent wealthy interests from securing control of the Home Railway, each stockholder will have but one vote, regardless of the extent of his holdings. . . . There will be no repetition of the humiliating experiences of Eastern minority stockholders, who must stand by helplessly while they are plundered by unscrupulous manipulators. . . .

". . . Valdez has been peculiarly subjected to the humiliating circumstances of helpless impotence in the matter of transportation. . . ."

By such gibes and inuendoes, Valdezans were gradually conditioned to the idea that they would not let the Guggenheims stop them, no matter what. And everyone knew "no matter what" meant Keystone Canyon.

By the end of August it was out in the open. The Guggenheims had posted their canyon rock work and grade:

NOTICE

The Alaska Home Railway Company, its agents, attorneys, and employees, and H.D. Reynolds, Trustee, and his agents, attorneys and employees:

You are hereby notified, that you and each of you are forbidden to occupy, enter upon, take possession of, or in any manner trespass upon the lands, premises, right of way or grade, owned, occupied, or in possession of the Copper River & Northwestern Railway Company, a private corporation; and you are further hereby notified, that any infringement or violation of the order, will be prosecuted according to law.

You and each of you are also hereby notified, that the lands, right of way or grade upon which this notice is posted, are owned, occupied, and in the lawful possession of the said Copper River & Northwestern Railway Company. Dated at Valdez, Alaska, the 28th day of August, 1907.

Valdez was jubilant.

"The Trust Squirms," crowded the *Prospector.* "Guggenheims Declare War...." After an unaccountable delay, the trust today makes its appearance with its feeble display of its familiar tactics. Anything to tie up the country and obstruct progress seems to be its highest and holiest aim...."

The Reynolds forces countered by posting their own:

NOTICE

To the men working for the Alaska Home Railway. You are working for the people of Alaska who will protect you. Pay no attention to the trust or any of its schemes to block progress. The citizens of Valdez are standing back of you. H.D. Reynolds, Trustee.

So the work was rushed right along, gradually getting closer to Keystone Canyon. Reynolds had made an effort to buy the Guggenheim rock work, but the Guggenheims, knowing the uncertainty of the Katalla venture, had no intention of giving up their right-of-way in that key spot. Reynolds asserted that the Home Railroad people "will not be bluffed..." and kept on with the work.

On September 17 the *Cordova Alaskan* carried the ominous headline: "Another Railroad Fight Brewing. That another railroad fight similar to the one that took place on July 3rd at Katalla may occur again is very evident."

17 GUNFIRE IN THE CANYON

The heart of the Reynolds venture was the 200 feet of expensive hand-drilled rock tunnel in Keystone Canyon. The success of the enterprise depended on taking over this rock work, since it was the most practical way through the canyon.

Eighty-five thousand dollars had already been expended on this rock work by the Guggenheims, and at this time they were beginning to doubt the wisdom of the Katalla venture. In July, before the appearance of Reynolds in Valdez, they had sent E. C. Hawkins to make a further study of the three proposed surveys from Valdez, Cordova and Katalla, and to make a recommendation. Mr. Hawkins was even now tramping the country evaluating all the routes.

Reynolds did attempt to purchase the rock work but failed, so now he was determined to take it by force if necessary. He, too, was going to "go across and argue afterward."

It was the Reynolds contention that the Guggenheims, by holding a right-of-way they did not intend to use, were stifling the development of Alaska in violation of the Act of May 14, 1898, preventing any one road from having a monopoly on any pass or canyon in Alaska. They insisted that the rock work was abandoned, though there is evidence that men were kept at work on it at all times up to September, and that George C. Hazelet, the Guggenheim manager in Valdez, had been sent for to return from the Interior to await Hawkins' report in case full-scale work should resume.

When the excitement began to reach fever pitch in Valdez, two deputy marshals, Edward C. Hasey and Duncan Dickson, were stationed in the canyon for the day watch. On at night were John Biggs, a detective for the Guggenheims, and Billy Quitsch, watchman.

For 19 nights and days the four stood watch, waiting for the showdown that was coming sure as winter. During the day watches at several times small parties of Home Railroad men were turned back. During these brief encounters the Guggenheims decided to erect a barricade at the entrance to the canyon, some distance from the tunnel. Says Quitsch of this endless waiting period: "We waited and kept the coffeepot going pretty well."

"On the nineteenth night I was on watch," relates Billy Quitsch, "I saw three or four men coming at three in the morning. A few minutes later five or six more came along. In another 15 minutes 10 or 12 more.

"It looked suspicious so early in the morning, so I went and woke John Biggs. I told him something was wrong, that I could see men gathering. 'Go rouse the camp' he said.

Right—The first rail for the Alaska Home Railroad at Valdez, September 16, 1907.
Below—A crowd surrounds the locomotive of the Alaska Home Railroad at Valdez, fall of 1907.
Bottom left—Copper River & Northwestern Railway cut in which the Home Railroad men were shot, showing the marshal's tent and barricade, September 25, 1907.
Bottom right—Bringing in the wounded Home Railroad men, shot by Copper River & Northwestern Railway marshals in Keystone Canyon, September 25, 1907. Home Railroad Camp No. 6 in the distance.

P. S. HUNT PHOTO. ALASKA HISTORICAL LIBRARY

P. S. HUNT PHOTO. COURTESY JEAN DETTINGER

P. S. HUNT PHOTO. ALASKA HISTORICAL LIBRARY

P. S. HUNT PHOTO. ALASKA HISTORICAL LIBRARY

"It was about a quarter of a mile to the camp. In the meantime they kept gathering out there until there were about 260 of them. We only had about 20 men in the camp.

"Still nothing happened. We waited and waited, time dragging out until about eight or nine in the morning, time for the men to go off shift.

"Dickson was going to take up position in a log cabin which had no windows. He figured it would be a good place to shoot from. 'If you get your foot into it, you might as well make it worthwhile,' he says. But I was tired; I'd been up all night. I laid down on the cot."

Meanwhile, things were beginning to stir in the ranks of the Reynolds men. Charles Ingersoll, the Reynolds attorney, had appeared on the scene and standing on a tree stump he gave a rousing speech to his forces. He told them: "The only way to get any money or anything is to jump this cut and take possession of it." Then the 260 men lined up eight abreast and began to march on the Guggenheim barricade. The only weapons in evidence were stones, clubs, shovels and pick handles.

As the men marched grimly up the road, Marshal Hasey ordered them to stop. "The way to stop us is by law!" they shouted, still advancing.

O'Neill, superintendent for the Guggenheims, made a valiant attempt to prevent bloodshed. He walked into the path of the marching men and shouted, "Go back! Go back! Someone's going to get hurt!"

At this the Reynolds men seized him and carried him as hostage ahead of them.

Deputy Marshal Edward Hasey was a man in a bad spot. He was faced by a mob, without guns but certainly not unarmed, advancing determinedly into his gun sights.

Hasey fired into the air, but the mob did not hesitate. On they came, eight abreast, becoming more angry and determined as they advanced, shouting and cursing, waving rocks and clubs which they picked up or wrenched from trees as they passed.

Hasey felt a chill sweat break out on his forehead. His hands where they held the rifle were moist and clammy. As he hesitated, a shout arose behind the barricade.

"There's some of them above us on the summer trail!"

There was no longer any choice. Hasey aimed low and fired into the crowd of men. Four shots rang out from his gun. Several men fell to the ground with assorted wounds, mostly in the knees and feet. Now the army of men stopped.

At the firing of shots, the men who had climbed around above the Guggenheim forces scrambled back to their stricken comrades, leaving behind them a bundle of dynamite with a six-inch unlit fuse. One of them remarked, "Damn fools! If you hadn't been in such a hurry there wouldn't have been any shooting!"

Back in the windowless cabin, Quitsch was aroused by Dickson who came running in fooling with his gun. The shell was stuck. As he fussed with it a shell went off, spewing gravel and making their ears ring. They went outside where another shell misfired into the gravel. The gunfire from down the canyon sounded like a whole army shooting as it echoed and re-echoed off the canyon walls.

After the Reynolds advance had been stopped, rifles were distributed to everyone. It was feared that an attempt would be made to come up over the old mountain trail and attack.

"There were a lot of Montenegro (Bohunk) fellows there. One was named Spider Leg Mike. He was the proudest of all," reminisced Billy Quitsch, "with his own 14-inch revolver and a company rifle and ammunition. We were under orders not to shoot until they came onto the railroad grade, but I have an idea he would have shot anyway. He was awfully happy.

"But they didn't attack again. Instead they sent Deputy Marshal George Dooley to bring in the other two deputies, and soldiers from Fort Liscum arrived to keep order."

Five days later, one of the wounded men, improperly cared for after the shooting, died.

A wave of outrage swept across Alaska. Deputy Marshal Edward C. Hasey was charged with murder. With him on trial in the public mind was the Guggenheim-Morgan Syndicate itself.

Nothing short of a guilty verdict would be acceptable to the public.

18 COLLAPSE OF REYNOLDS

The excitement following the shooting in Keystone Canyon reached near frenzy.

"Guggenheims Resort to Shooting Laborers," screamed the Reynolds-owned *Valdez Prospector*, first with a distorted version of the story.

Garbled accounts from the *Prospector* were widely credited: "This morning a message was received over the wires stating that employees of the Alaska Home Railway were erecting construction camps at or near the entrance to Keystone Canyon, when they were fired upon from ambush by some unknown parties. . . . Advices by phone state that a coyote hole was loaded with powder [by the Guggenheims] and would have been exploded when the main party crossed the place, if it had not been for Morrisey, who succeeded in capturing the man O'Neill, who was to explode the mine." In the wake of these stories, confusion reigned supreme, and the Guggenheims were already guilty.

Witnesses were herded together in pen-like enclosures near Valdez, and in that fiery little town there was even talk of lynching, although there hadn't been a hanging there since 1898, when a fellow named Tanner was strung up with the classic last words: "I just want you people to know you're hanging the best shot to ever come out of Montana!"

Nothing came of the lynch talk, because Governor Hoggatt had ordered the army troops from Fort Liscum into Valdez to cope with the explosive situation. The troopers discouraged any attempt at revenge, but angry Valdezans turned their wrath on Governor Hoggatt. "Guggenheim Rubber Stamp," he was called in the press.

By now there was more reason than ever for passion in Valdez; their troubles were just beginning.

"Looks Bad for Valdez," said the September 28, 1907, *Alaska Daily Dispatch* (Juneau). "Rumored Reynolds affairs to go into receivership. There has been a muttering that Reynolds has overplayed himself in Western Alaska speculation."

In October, Reynolds' bank at Valdez closed its doors, liabilities exceeding its available assets.

"The affairs of the Alaska Home Railroad company which is a Reynolds corporation, are also said to be in a hopelessly tangled condition. The workmen connected with the company were paid for work done in August but from that time to the present they have received nothing. Tomorrow will be payday and many people here are looking forward to it with no little anxiety, as trouble is feared. There are about 500 men on Reynolds' payroll and apparently no money in sight to pay them. . . ." A wire was sent to Reynolds, who was Outside on business. Reynolds replied by cable: "Draw on me," which, the *Katalla Herald* observed, didn't help put money in Valdez to meet the obligations of the company. "While Reynolds' employees have shown little disposition to become ugly, there are already murmurings and 500 hungry men are not to be trifled with. . . ."

Governor Hoggatt was still in Valdez because of the threat of trouble. An earthquake in the Gulf of Alaska severed the cable to Valdez and added to the general air of confusion. Local people were convinced that the Guggenheims were somehow responsible for that, too.

Businessmen in town were really in a bind. They had backed Reynolds from the beginning, and signs had been displayed in store windows saying: "We're behind the Home Railroad." Workmen were now appearing at those stores demanding that they make good on their implied promise.

Reynolds was quoted in the rumor mills as having said that Sam Blum, the banker, was the only smart man in Valdez, the rest being chumps. "When Reynolds formed his score or more of companies here, Blum refused to sell his bank, but he gave Reynolds an option on his mercantile business, getting $50,000 cash, through a Seattle bank. Blum has the $50,000, the balance of $50,000 not having been paid, and his mercantile business, while Reynolds has the option."

The paper observed that the comedy would be laughable if it did not threaten to become so serious.

The Katalla Company, alert to the much needed and available work force, immediately wired Valdez from Seattle that the unemployed of Valdez would be given work and free transportation to Katalla if desired. It must have been an especially bitter pill for the Valdez men to swallow, having to accept Guggenheim employment after the collapse of Reynolds. But the governor and city officials posted notices that after October 19 the city would no longer care for the unfortunate and advised citizens to take advantage of the Katalla offer.

Ingenious schemes traceable to the Reynolds conglomerate were being uncovered daily. A writer signing himself "Silex" told of an apparently widespread system of graft throughout Reynolds' dealings, especially among the contractors: "A man who runs a roadhouse on the line of construction came into town today and said that the contractors had made a deal with him to board the men for 35 cents a meal and 35 cents for lodging each day. But they stipulated that the roadhouse man was to sign vouchers showing that he was paid one dollar for each meal and a like sum for a night's lodging. By this way the contractors got a daily rake-off of $2.30 per diem per man. The contractors got their money, but the roadhouse keeper is still looking for his."

While the Reynolds enterprises were all sliding with a sickening thud toward financial collapse, and hundreds of penniless employees were walking the streets of Valdez, Reynolds was in Seattle trying to raise much needed financial backing.

Unable to raise enough money in Seattle, he went to the rival city of Tacoma with an offer to move the headquarters of his Alaska Coast Steamship Company there if they came through with enough financial backing. But the Tacoma businessmen were at least as shrewd as those in Seattle. After suitable negotiations, they bought his steamship company at a bargain price and refused to subscribe anything to any of Reynolds' other enterprises.

In a meeting with Seattle creditors, he asked for more time, saying he could easily meet all his debts if given enough leeway. The creditors reportedly "showed no disposition to crowd." They did not ask for a receivership, but they deposed Reynolds as president of the corporation, and all other officials also, except Governor Brady, who, nevertheless, handed in his resignation.

On November 3, Reynolds disappeared.

His disappearance was as sensational as his appearance had been. He was last seen in Seattle boarding a Northern Pacific train, bareheaded as always, and whistling *When Johnny Comes Marching Home.* "He didn't even bid a fond good-bye to his old-time friends before leaving," the *Cordova Alaskan* reported.

The paper reported wryly that there were a dozen or so preachers and school-marms who seemed over-anxious to contact the "Dowey of Valdez" on "important business," but that he seemed before his untimely departure to be "as gay as a boy returning home from a long school vacation. He did not say whether he would spend his next summer vacation in Valdez or go aboard and visit 'gay Paree.'"

"The whereabouts of H. D. Reynolds seems yet to be a mystery. He paid passage for himself and wife to Valdez, including the bridal suite, on the *Yucatan,* then changed his mind and headed east. . . ."

In February of 1908 they were still looking. "Reynolds, once the high panjandrum of Valdez, is billed for a second appearance in the glacier city," the *Cordova Alaskan* of February 8, 1908, reported. "Some of his creditors are prone to believe that the second coming of Reynolds is like the second coming of the Creator, very doubtful and extremely slow."

The people of Valdez had been left in a terrible financial and emotional lurch. Practically everyone had subscribed something to the venture; this money was gone, along with the wages not paid for September and part of October. Nearly every business house in Valdez was hard hit by the collapse of Reynolds' bank, even the postmaster, who had $5,000 of postal funds on deposit.

And on the Outside, mostly back east, more than 1,700 subscribers were affected by the Reynolds collapse, many of them poor parishioners, preachers and schoolteachers, who could ill afford the loss. Most of these had been led to Reynolds' shearing by the well-intentioned efforts of ex-Governor John Green Brady.

Brady was left a broken man, financially and otherwise. On the day of Reynolds' disappearance, it was reported by the *Seattle Times* that Brady was rendered penniless, that all he had left was a home in Sitka, and hardly enough money to return there with his family. He was ruined as a man to have confidence in, especially among those in the church whom he had persuaded to back Reynolds. The affairs of the corporations were hopelessly tangled, and a battery of auditors descended on Brady to assess the books. Brady still loyally insisted that Reynolds was perfectly

honest, but that he was "dangerously impulsive in his actions. . . ." Reynolds had made most of his deals without consulting with the Reynolds-Alaska Development Company. This he was not required to do, according to Brady, but the stockholders in the company were up in arms because they did not know what was going on.

Brady was the man left holding the bag. He had to work with the auditors and explain to a disillusioned and angry public; in addition, his books were thoroughly investigated secretly by federal agents, and the following tribute reported in the April 7, 1908, edition of the *Alaska Daily Dispatch* (Juneau) was given to Brady's treasury work: "During this time [the time of the secret investigation], Reynolds' books were experted and not a cent's discrepancy could be found."

With the financial collapse of the Reynolds enterprises went Brady's entire savings, the result of nearly 30 years of hard work in Alaska. Emotionally and politically, too, he was through in Alaska. He went to China as a missionary soon after the Reynolds fiasco. Ten years later he returned to Sitka where he finished out his days raising the roses he loved.

At last, in April of 1908, the creditors and government officials caught up with the elusive and silver-tongued Reynolds. He was arrested on a charge of using the mails to defraud. "It appears that the arrest was made at the instigation of the postal authorities after a secret investigation of charges brought by Mrs. T. Alexander of [Boston] [a dissatisfied stockholder in the Reynolds organization]. The specific charge was that Reynolds in his prospectus represented the realty holdings of his company as being valued at nearly twice as much as secret service men sent to Valdez found them to be actually worth. The authorities have been working on the case for months and are satisfied that they have a clear case against Reynolds."

Friends of the accused man still rallied to his support, claiming that Reynolds would have no difficulty in disproving the charges.

"'Reynolds fixed his values,' they say, 'when copper was away up and prices were booming, and these new values have been made since the copper slump and can not in justice to us be taken as fair. Reynolds is optimistic—perhaps too much so—but more than that he cannot be accused of, and these charges will fall through of themselves.'"

Too optimistic he was. He was convicted and sent to prison.

In the aftermath of Keystone Canyon, reputations were soiled, sullied and slashed. Heroes were verbally and politically beheaded right and left, and the mud and gore of battle was everywhere. And down in

Katalla one more hero was falling from grace. That was M. K. Rogers, the engineer who had selected Controller Bay as the shipping port for Alaskan coal-oil-copper. It was late September and the North Pacific Ocean was ready to pounce on the fine, sturdy breakwater on which the whole Katalla venture depended.

19 KATALLA CUT OUT

"Katalla Cut Out."

"Dangerous Landing at Katalla."

"Alaska Coast Company announced their steamers will not land at Katalla."

Thus read the descending headers of the *Alaska Daily Dispatch* (Juneau), shortly before the Keystone Canyon battle. All this was only five days after the same paper had carried a glowing account of the "Great Future" of Katalla, and reported that although the Bruner Line was not progressing as rapidly as the Guggenheim work, it was moving steadily.

What happened in the intervening five days was no news to old-time Katallans or to shipmasters on the route. The fall storms had begun ripping in from the Pacific. The first of the series carried 85-mile-per-hour winds. The *Portland* was able to land her passengers by launch, but only because of a short lull in the storm. The wind picked up again and maintained furious velocities for eight days. The *Bertha* was the only ship to follow the *Portland* that storm season.

A month later the *Katalla Herald*, which as a matter of editorial policy did not like to make too much of the storms, conceded that Katalla had had some rather drawn-out equinoctial storms. But still the paper managed to make the coverage as light as possible. "The weather, always a fruitful topic of conversation nearly everywhere, has been doing some extraordinary stunts for two weeks past. It has sounded the gamut of wetness, and the wind has been kind and generous and has added materially to the general unpleasantness."

Another month passed, a month marked by steady gales, and protest. The Katalla residents were beginning to complain bitterly about the failure of steamships to land. The second week in November found Katalla battered, bruised but unbowed. Nevertheless, there was a rustle of apprehension going through the town: "Still on the map," asserted the *Herald*, referring to rumors that the railroad might move. Clark Davis was quoted as saying, "There is no doubt there has been some radical change in connection with railroad construction but that any

other point on this coast will be the shipping point for the coal and oil of the district is patently absurd."

Both railroads worked valiantly against the elements that second week in November and progress was reported on both docks. The Copper River & Northwestern dock was seaward about 360 feet and pilings were being driven rapidly, from 30 to 50 feet a day with good penetration, 12 to 15 feet into the harbor mud. Completion was predicted in 30 days.

The Alaska Pacific & Terminal Railroad had finished its trestle to Fox Island and had laid track on top. It was working on a 100-foot dock.

That next week, the third week in November, made the difference. Sweeping Katalla with a savagery that made September's 85-mile gale seem like a summer zephyr, the wind depleted Katalla's reserves. Gone were the trestles and that impregnable breakwater.

The *Katalla Herald*, left with the job of reporting on the devastating force of that week's gale, tried not to be gloomy, but still reported, "Part of Trestle Washed Away." The story, while it made page one, was tucked unobtrusively on the bottom section of the page and read, " . . . Twelve bents of the Alaska Pacific & Terminal company trestle connecting the terminal grounds with Fox Island, were washed away during the storm of Sunday. . . ." Little was said of the Guggenheim installations, but it is known that the breakwater was scattered across Controller Bay.

The exact date of the loss of the breakwater is unknown; the *Katalla Herald* did not mention it. The *Valdez Prospector*, admittedly anti-Guggenheim, noted on September 19 that a fierce storm at Katalla had wrecked the breakwater. The *Katalla Herald*, on September 21, first referred to the equinoctial storms and made no mention at all of damage at Katalla. Furthermore, the news continued to be presented in the same cheerful vein as always, until that third week in November. It is certain that the worst storm of the year occurred in 1907, as it frequently does, concurrently with the highest tides of the year (generally in November), greatly increasing the damage done by the storm.

Archie Shiels says that the "dock itself" was almost completed when the storm was on the rampage. The storm raged for three consecutive days with the barometer falling to 27.9. When it was over, all that remained of the dock was a few stray pilings. It is difficult to conceive of work continuing on the dock after the breakwater washed out, so it seems more likely that it was lost in November, at the same time as the dock.

From that time on, things turned rather blue for the city "where the rails meet the sails."

The high tide did a lot of damage, too. This flood tide, driven by a strong southeast wind, drove up onto the main street, reaching its highest at 11:45 a.m. Monday forenoon. "The floors of a number of houses and tents on the sandspit were submerged," reported the paper. "Along Front Street water came well up to the buildings on the north side, in some cases . . . running clear across the street. No damage, however, resulted. The extension of Grey's dock, which had been badly shattered in previous storms, was finally demolished. The loss is a severe one to Mr. Grey financially and in a general way to the community."

Now it had to be recognized, even by the Pollyanna *Herald*, that Katalla was to be "temporarily" by-passed by the Guggenheim-Morgans, who would be building from Cordova. But they printed these assurances prominently on the front page:

The Katalla Terminals of the Copper River & Northwestern Railway company have not been abandoned, nor is there any intention of doing so.

The breakwater will be built on substantial lines and will be adequate to meet all demands. . . .

The work of constructing the Copper River line from Katalla will be pushed more actively than ever with the beginning of spring, and in the meantime work on the coal line will be continued.

All this means the plans of the builders of the Copper River & Northwestern, so far as Katalla is concerned, will be carried out in their entirety including the plans for smelters, etc.

And Katalla will be the place where "The rails meet the sails."

The breakwater was gone, washed out. E. C. Hawkins' report recommending Cordova as the terminus was in to the company. Mr. Rogers was dismissed. The Rosene-Rogers interest in the company had been sold, and Mr. Rosene was no longer president.

A contemporary engineer wrote of Mr. M. K. Rogers, "[He] was a very highly rated engineer and suffered greatly by the loss of the breakwater." A brief tribute. Rogers was another fallen hero.

E. C. Hawkins was hired as chief engineer, and M. J. Heney was brought out of retirement and given the contract to finish his road from Cordova, with a branch line to Katalla and the coal fields. Only the three largest of the steel bridges were to be built by the Katalla Company. Heney was to build the rest.

Cordova's one big asset, the best deep-water port in Alaska, had won the day. Cordova would be the shipping port for the fabulously rich Kennecott copper.

Katalla would be connected by a spur line *as soon as the coal could be mined.* Those fatal words, "as soon as the coal could be mined," were to be the death

knell for Katalla, as 50 years later coal was still not being mined.

At this time the name Gifford Pinchot was first being heard in Katalla. It was under his influence that the coal lands had been withdrawn, and that in 1907 the Chugach National Forest was set aside. This is discussed in greater detail later on in the book; see Part 3, "Coal, Politics and Railroads," page 109. There was confusion and some concern in Alaska, but if it was felt necessary and good, the residents were willing to go along. No one foresaw that these two weapons, the withdrawal of the coal lands and the creation of a national forest, would be used by political extremists to kill their town and its budding industries.

With events shaping up and shifting so fast, even the residents had trouble keeping abreast of the changes.

William C. Hansen, 94, one of Katalla's oldest old-timers, reflecting on those exciting days, said:

"I went to Katalla when they had the big oil boom in 1905. There was oil all over, and natural gas, too.

"There was more than one railroad started up from Katalla, and plenty of fights. There was one from Martin Islands, and the Guggenheims, and then there was a couple from Goose City [Bering River].

"They were going to haul coal and all sorts of big deals but nothing came of it. I guess it might have amounted to something if the coal fields hadn't been closed down by that Gifford Pinchot.

"They got so mad at that fellow Pinchot that they burned him [in effigy] over there. They made a big dummy of him and built a big bonfire on the beach and burned it up. Oh, there was lots of excitement.

"There were 13 saloons in Katalla then. A dollar was worth a dollar in those days too. Valdez was the main city around here. There wasn't any Cordova, just the village of Eyak.

"When the railroad started up [in Katalla] they had steamers coming in all the time. There wasn't any harbor, and always lots of storms. They tried to build a breakwater down at a place called Camp One, but it washed out, and they tried to put one in at Martin Islands where there was a wireless at the time. But they all washed out.

"The steamers would anchor up outside, and the barges would take the rails and stuff ashore. That was where I worked, on the scows taking the rails ashore.

"I had to jump overboard one time. The ropes holding the rails while they were being hoisted onto the scow broke and I saw rails coming down, so over I went. I was young and strong in those days and I could swim like a fish."

At this point in his story, Bill paused to laugh, stroking his grey handlebar mustache. "The rails crashed through the deck and down onto a big carton

Top—The storms which struck Katalla in the fall of 1907 washed out part of the roadbed. No. 5 was one of the dinkies, or saddletank engines; it was taken to Cordova and used during the construction period there.

Middle—Camp One, probably during the big storm of 1907, with Palm Point and the beginning of the Guggenheim breakwater in the distance.

Bottom—A part of Camp One, probably during one of the fall storms of 1907 that contributed to the abandonment of Katalla as a railroad terminal.

of a hundred boxes of cigars. Nobody was hurt, but you should have seen the cigars!

"Not all the railroads were real. There was one all surveyed and everything, from Kanak Island [a small sand island in Controller Bay]! That was all just a bunch of bull. Those fellows went out and sold phony stock and made some money on it, that's all it was.

"When the railroad moved to Cordova again, the barges went to work hauling all the rails piled up at Katalla back to Cordova. They carried a hundred tons of steel on each barge and I worked at that for a year."

The Rosene-Rogers interests were sold out, and the Guggenheim-Morgans bought the Alaska Steamship Company and consolidated it with their Northwestern Steamship Company, under the Alaska Steam name. In addition to smelting and copper, they were now in the coastwise shipping business, and were in an excellent position to realize handsome profits in copper when the railroad was built—if it could be built.

That solution was up to M. J. Heney, a man who was used to doing the impossible with rails.

Mr. Hawkins and Mr. Heney arrived in Katalla in late November on the steamer *Saratoga*, one of the few to sneak into Katalla between storms that winter. They inspected the damage there and laid their plans. They left the *Katalla Herald* happily in possession of interviews and assurances regarding the intentions of the Guggenheims in regard to Katalla. Then they departed for Cordova.

At the time of the move to Cordova, ten miles of grading had been completed at Katalla, eight miles of track laid and several trestles built.

20 THE WINTER OF THE PORCUPINE

The winter of 1907 was a terrible winter. Valdez was sunk in its own misery, trying to recoup its losses and find the vanished Mr. Reynolds. Cordova and Katalla were battered by storms, earthquakes and deep snow. Since the Guggenheim move Cordova and Katalla had become the staunchest of rivals, each dedicated to the proposition that the other was a flash in the pan. They spent the winter exchanging barbed compliments through the pages of their respective newspapers. The weather was too severe for any other pastime.

Cordova gloated, "He who laughs last, you know," and plagiarized the *Katalla Herald's* catch-line: "Cordova, Where the Rails Meet the Sails." The *Katalla Herald*, for its part, belittled the move and insisted that it was merely temporary, calling Cordova "One of the Termini" and "A Temporary Base of Supplies." To back up this view, they had interviews with the diplomatic Mr. Hawkins.

Cordova shot back this rejoinder: "Pity the Blind. Katalla should send for a box of Dr. Hill's famous eye-salve." With this fine medicine, they said, Katalla would be able to see—its own demise.

Katalla held innumerable protest meetings that winter over the lack of steamship service, and Cordova waxed eloquent on this: "The public meetings of the little handful of citizens of Katalla reminds us of reading the proceedings of the old-time Lime Kiln club—only the Katalla grievance committee meets oftener. Said meetings are held just after the mail steamer passes them up—long and binding resolutions are adopted, a copy mailed to one or another government department in Washington to be cast into the wastebasket. After the resolutions are signed and delivered to the postmaster, the meeting quietly settles down to a regular old-fashioned Methodist experience meeting, where each steamship company, the Morgan-Guggenheim Company, contractor M. J. Heney, the City of Cordova, and a few other men and places are each in turn roasted to a finish and shown up in the limelight of obscurity. People who attend these meetings say it is better than a circus. . . ."

Katalla, herself reeling from constant storms, found solace in the fact that Cordova had 'em too. "Blown off the Earth—What remains of the town of Cordova was practically blown down last Sunday by a gentle zephyr which swooped down from Eyak Lake. Buildings were lifted from their foundations and tumbled over like houses built of cards, according to the statements of a number of men who arrived from Cordova. . . . About the only building left was McCormack & Little's Saloon and it received a severe shaking up. No one was injured. Cordova has a population of about 15 people, but what is lacking in numbers is made up in enthusiasm for the solid 15 are expecting a boom to strike the town next."

The *Cordova Alaskan* described the same storm, which was accompanied by an earthquake: "Wind Plays Bad Pranks—First an Earthquake that threatened to cast us into eternity, then incessant rain storms that almost drove us to the limit of despair. But the culminating effort and the limit of endurance was reached and our suspenders nearly burst when, in the usually quiet hours of Thursday a.m., a fearful wind storm blowing in fitful gusts at the alarming rate of 80 miles per hour, came trooping down the valley sweeping frail tents, out-buildings, and other movable objects before it. People rushed from unsafe buildings clad only in decollete night-clothes, dogs howled a mournful wail, the night was dark like one black cat and the air was rent with the noise of the battle. Some cursed and cried and thought it was the beginning of the end, while others ventured the opinion that it was only the breath of a Katalla indignation meeting and there was nothing to it but wind."

Katalla herself admitted to a six-foot tidal wave from the earthquake, which did only modest damage. Tom White recalled the earthquake of 1899, a series of bad shocks lasting over a period of days, and followed by a hurricane.

From the arrival of the last ship, *Saratoga* with Heney and Hawkins aboard in late November, no more ships at all were able to land in Katalla for over two months. In a day without air transportation, and without any overland connections, Katalla was not only without mail, but running out of food as well. It was the winter of the porcupine in Katalla. Old Bill Hansen assured the author that porcupine meat is not half bad eating. "First you boil the heck out of it, then fry it."

The *Cordova Alaskan* reported that Katalla was living on "snowballs, love and hopes, with an occasional stray porcupine for a banquet.... The sails have not been connecting with the rails of late, so consequently the porcupine family around Controller Bay has shown a marked decrease. What do you know about that?" The *Portland* brought word that they had been unable to land at Katalla, as the launch could not come out, and that that town had had no mail since November 12. This was February 1.

The snow that winter of 1907-1908 piled deep; buildings and track work disappeared under the drifts. In December the roof of the roundhouse caved in under the weight of the snow, and other buildings threatened to do the same until they were hastily shoveled off. Rotary Bill Simpson designed a new rotary snowplow that winter and built it in the shops, to deal with the deep drifts. This deep snowfall was repeated again in the next winter, and no one dreamed of the severe consequences of these two years of unusually heavy snow. The extra snow, collected and piled up on the far reaches of Miles and Childs glaciers, was a nature-made time clock that would cause the two glaciers to begin an unseasonable advance two years hence, right at the critical time.

Plans of the Guggenheim and the Alaska Pacific companies both included work through the winter on the coal lines from Katalla, but both had to abandon these plans because of a severe financial crisis back east. On Wall Street bank failure and stock market collapse was imminent. It was the swift action and immense prestige of J. P. Morgan that saved the day. Going to Theodore Roosevelt, he gained a promise that there would be no fancy "anti-trust" reaction to his emergency moves, then proceeded to pour the extra needed money (over the protest of certain bankers) into the national economy to prevent total

financial collapse. There are accounts of this elsewhere and it is not a part of our Alaska railroad story, except in that it affected the railroad building plans of various endeavors in the North. The Alaska Pacific & Terminal, though it worked off and on after 1907, never again was able to muster the financial backing it needed to finish, and the contract already let for pile driving across Bering Lake that winter was canceled. The plans for a "Pittsburgh of Alaska" on Stillwater Creek near the Cunningham coal claims also went by the board. The withdrawal of coal lands was also having a paralyzing effect on all efforts to build; it was simply too expensive to import coal to run trains to a coal field. The irony of living in the heart of Alaska's biggest coal field without having coal enough to burn in their stoves when coal ships failed to land never ceased to annoy and disgruntle Katalla residents. Most burned oil or natural gas.

21 A TOWN IS BORN

To move Cordova," announced the *Katalla Herald* early in December 1907. "The new location is not yet known ... no one except perhaps the officials of the Morgan-Guggenheim Syndicate have any idea where the town will ultimately land—if it lands anywhere...."

Eyak, the fish canning village used by Heney for his Copper River Railway, was just too small. Most of the available land was taken up by two large tracts, one belonging to the railroad company, the other to the Russian Orthodox Church. The land that remained was inadequate and this land shortage contributed to a real estate boom that drove the price of lots out of sight.

Telling the story of the "Coming City of the North," the *Seattle Times* said that Cordova (Eyak) was having the "wildest real estate boom any of the northern cities has experienced." Lots which two months before were selling at $75 were now bringing $1,500 and were almost impossible to get, because owners would not sell. The same choice lots, it was estimated, would bring $3,000 by spring. It was a situation calling for a new townsite, and townsite promoters in early Alaska were almost as plentiful as railroad promoters. There was considerable discussion on the proposed move.

Just before Christmas of 1907, A. J. Adams and a group of engineers appeared on the scene and began surveying a place called the "Donohoe homestead," just north of Eyak.

At the same time, rumors of activity in the townsite of Nelson were once again being heard. Nelson was the terminus of the Alaska Railroad Company, which had led to the Jarvis Memorial a few years earlier. Located

The photos on these two pages show the development of Cordova from the old town of Eyak in the period from 1906 to about 1910. The photo at right was taken in October 1909.

E. A. HEGG PHOTO, ALASKA HISTORICAL LIBRARY

ALASKA HISTORICAL LIBRARY

E. A. HEGG PHOTO, MOSS COLLECTION, ALASKA HISTORICAL LIBRARY

Above—First Avenue under construction, 1908.
Above right—By 1909, Cordova had many new business buildings.
Right—Eyak, or Old Cordova, was dismantled to make way for the railway yards. The tramway tracks, used by a salmon cannery, were a feature of the old settlement.

ALASKA HISTORICAL LIBRARY

ALASKA HISTORICAL LIBRARY

Left—The paddle steamboat *S.B. Matthews,* used as a cannery tender.
Below—The first building in the new town was a saloon, the second was The Red Dragon. It doubled as a church on Sundays and a social hall the rest of the time.

ALASKA HISTORICAL LIBRARY

E. A. HEGG PHOTO. COURTESY JEAN DETTINGER

Left—Fourth of July celebration.
Below left—The Jack Dalton home.
Below—The ocean dock soon after it was built.

ALASKA HISTORICAL LIBRARY

E. A. HEGG PHOTO. MOSS COLLECTION. ALASKA HISTORICAL LIBRARY

about ten miles north of Cordova on a level piece of land at the head of Orca Inlet, Nelson offered a far better townsite than the mountainous Donohoe site, according to some. Nevertheless, Adams and his crew proceeded to lay out streets and to plat a town, the one christened "Cordova" by Heney's survey crew under Udo Hesse in March of 1906 at the Donohoe homestead.

The history of the Cordova townsite goes back to 1905, two years after Katalla was founded. Six men from Valdez were discussing the shortcomings of Katalla, and the need for a coal and oil port. One of the men, more knowledgeable of the country than the others, remarked that there was only one good protected deep-water port adjacent to the Copper River flats, and that was where the Indian village of Eyak stood. The six men decided to send several of their number to look over the possibilities. They did, and located the section just north of Eyak village. The six men were George Cheever Hazelet, A. J. Adams, John Goodell, Thomas J. Donohoe, John J. Ostrander and George Easterly. Upon arrival they found a silver salmon spawning stream, and nearby a dilapidated shack on which someone had hung a sign saying "Copper City." It may have been prophetic, for at the time the townsite was expected to be the port for Katalla coal and oil only. Valdez was expected to be the copper port.

After staking out the land, they sold half interest to Michael J. Heney and associates. This ownership was acquired by the Copper River & Northwestern Company at the time of purchase of the Copper River Railway.

Lots in the new townsite went on sale in June. One lot was donated to the Episcopal Church for construction of a seven-day-a-week clubhouse for the railroad men. Rev. E.P. Newton, who was to build the clubhouse, found himself bidding against the owner of the Northern Saloon for a pile of scarce lumber. Both men were intent on building the first building in the new town. The saloon-keeper won, and the Northern Saloon became the first place of business to open its doors. Reverend Newton's clubhouse was second; it was a railroad men's reading room and meeting place, on Sunday a church. The men took one look at the barn red building with its old-fashioned outhouse perched outside, and affectionately dubbed it "The Red Dragon." The Red Dragon may not have been the first place in Cordova, but it has been the most enduring, as it's now the oldest building in Cordova, and its original red siding has been covered with shingles of a sedate gray.

The Red Dragon served as a place to gather, read, discuss events of the day and play cards or the piano. The big fireplace cast a ruddy glow over the room, and the big easy chairs invited relaxation. On weekdays the alter was hoisted by block and tackle to the ceiling. On Sundays it was lowered and chairs were set up for church services. The Red Dragon served the religious needs of the community until 1916 when Stephen Birch, Syndicate president, donated money to build the full-time Episcopalian Church of Saint George.

Things were going along very well. New buildings were rising along the new Front Street, where the silver salmon stream had cut what amounted to a small canyon. This presented no problem; they simply filled it in and kept on building.

But not everyone in Eyak wanted to pick up and move away, and the *Cordova Alaskan* poked a bit of good-natured fun at those staying behind in Eyak, through the medium of Maude the Mule, who had pulled the tram up and down old Front Street all those years.

MAUDE THE MULE STANDS PAT

Maude, the faithful mule who has for so many days pulled the cars up and down the tram line in Eyak, or old Cordova, is quite indignant since the "guggs" laid the railroad tracks down her "short line," and refuses, with two or three others, to quit business in the swamp and come to town. The company took it for granted that Maude was a progressive beast and would come over to the new town without any "oats" being offered but they were mistaken, for Maude "stands pat." The other day as Boryer, the attorney for the company, passed her, she kicked at him and acted very "mulish." In this stand Maude has taken she has three or four followers, so Boryer is negotiating with Maude, hoping that if he can coax her over to Cordova, her friends will follow. He has promised her two bushels of oats and a stable in Cordova for her browsing ground in the swamp. Maude has taken it under advisement.

An energetic enthusiasm for building prevailed, and in just a few months, the town of Cordova took on a finished look. One old-timer, a fisherman, said that a strange transformation followed. "When I left for fishing in June, there was only one building on Main Street, the tent of A. J. Adams. When I came back from fishing in the fall, what should meet my eyes but a full-fledged city!"

With the frantic building boom, Cordova was worried about fire. An item titled "FIRE! FIRE!" in the *Cordova Alaskan* read: "There is considerable uneasiness at the present time for fear a fire will break out in the new town, while there is no means of fighting it. The construction of so many new buildings necessarily makes shavings in and around nearly every place in town and a lighted cigarette thrown among them would put the whole town at the mercy of the flames."

The papers also made the farsighted suggestion that while building was a good time to wire your house for electricity. This innovation was described as "the coming thing in home lighting."

But when the company began driving pilings toward the new ocean dock location, they ran into trouble in the form of Jack Dalton.

Back in 1906, when Michael Heney bought a half interest in the Donohoe homestead, Jack Dalton had been with the party, but it is not known if he had an interest in the site. However, either then or shortly after, Dalton filed on three mineral claims just north of the Donohoe homestead, on Three Tree Point. They were known as the Bear, Comet and Juneau fraction lode claims, and one can still see the hole in the mountainside near the old ocean dock where Jack Dalton worked his claims. These mineral claims straddled the railroad survey made in 1906 by Udo Hesse, the location of the railroad line leading to the proposed dock. Thus, the land was covered by both mineral and non-mineral entries.

When company men began laying rails to the dock, they were met at the property line by Jack Dalton, carrying a rifle.

"Where do you think you're going?" he demanded.

"Right along here, with the railroad grade," answered the crew boss.

Dalton suggested ominously that it might be a good idea for them not to go any farther, and headed for the company office.

At the office, Dalton asked for the man in charge. On being shown in, Dalton informed that gentleman that the minute the men crossed his property, he, Dalton, was going to come looking for the foreman. "And I won't stop coming till I find you," he added.

The workmen were called off, and the matter referred to the courts.

The right-of-way was completed over Dalton's vigorous objections, and the matter was threshed out in court. The case became a *cause celebre* in Cordova because of the colorful personality of Jack Dalton.

The case was not decided until late 1911 when a higher court ruled in favor of the railroad company. An earlier hearing failed to clarify the situation saying that the land was more valuable as a railroad right-of-way than as a mineral location. However, the ruling also said that Dalton's claim was valid. The higher court ruling required Dalton to remove his trestle that joined the railroad's and pay for the underpass which was built under the trestle to allow Dalton to reach navigable waters.

Thus, during the summer of 1908, the town of Cordova was born, not like Topsy, who "just growed," but a full-fledged city, built at the time of rapid

The freighter *Seward* discharging construction material at Cordova.

expansion of the railroad payroll and pushing forward of the railroad construction. These accomplishments gave the new town a boost on its way to becoming, as it was a few years later, the "Premier Copper Port of the World."

But the promoters of the Nelson townsite were not content. They devised a scheme to use Cordova's achievements for the advancement of Nelson.

22 NELSON TOWNSITE MAKES ITS BID

In 1906 the promoters of the Alaska Railroad were responsible for a bill introduced in Congress which would give them exclusive right to build, with government aid and subsidy, the only railroad in Alaska. The bill was defeated largely through the efforts of David H. Jarvis. But in 1909 the town of Nelson was back in the spotlight.

Congress passed a bill in that year to grant the townsite, about ten miles north of Cordova, to Donald A. McKenzie, ex-Governor John H. McGraw of Washington and Edwin Lewin. With appropriate ceremony, President Roosevelt signed the bill. The bill provided for the incorporation of a townsite company of 2,000 acres, to be sold by the government at the modest price of $2.50 per acre. This was spoken of as "a reward and bonus for doing the pioneer work in establishing the town." The government was to hold 3,000 acres surrounding the area in reserve for any purpose it should deem proper.

The pioneer locators of the town were said to have explored the entire coast for 200 miles before deciding upon this particular location, because they felt it alone had sufficient depth of water and area of level land to build a city to serve as coal, copper and oil port of the region.

The men claimed they spent around $50,000 in exploring and sounding every likely harbor, and looking the country over thoroughly. The spot they chose was the only place within 100 miles which had more than 100 acres of level land, and a sizable landlocked harbor with an even depth of not less than 70 feet of water. It was also, they pointed out, near the Copper River's mouth, and was expected to become the terminus of any railroad in the area (the Copper River & Northwestern was the only railroad in the area).

The promoters of Nelson apparently had given up their Alaska Railroad idea. Modestly they claimed that they would "let the world look for the gold and other minerals. To start the future metropolis of Alaska is enough for us."

The publicity the new townsite commanded was astonishing. It was heralded as the "San Francisco of the North," and was believed to fix the location of the future metropolitan center of Alaska. It was even spoken of as the possible future capital of Alaska.

"We hear little of the scheme in Cordova," commented the *Cordova Alaskan*. "But there is no denying the fact that the men promoting the proposition are strong politicians and men of influence, and the work of their lieutenants in Alaska as well as on the outside, is becoming plainly apparent."

The name of the town had been suggested by Alaska's governor, Wilford B. Hoggatt, to honor Senator Knute Nelson of Minnesota for his interest and dedication to legislation for Alaska.

They had great plans for the new town, and these were extensively discussed in the press all over the country. The first order of business was to raise the level of the land nine feet over the entire townsite. The location was in the path of an ancient glacier, and it was little better than a swamp. However, it had lots of water, and this would be used in hydraulic machines for washing down the soil from the surrounding mountainsides for the fill. It was estimated that this would produce enough fill for the entire 2,000 acres at a cost of four cents a cubic yard. The stream that meandered through town was to be straightened and made the trunk sewer line. This would cost a lot, the builders acknowledged, but it was the least they could do in the interest of the greatest, most prosperous and beautiful city in the North. They would even install coal wharves and docks before the public would be invited to build.

All this was normal promotional stuff, but what really annoyed Cordovans was that the budding new townsite, with no accomplishments at all, was using everything that Cordova had done to promote itself. The proposed townsite was making its reputation on the strength of the railroad building being done from Cordova! In the numerous articles appearing in San Francisco papers, in the *Dawson News* and others, Cordova was never mentioned. The press made Nelson look like the center of activity while in reality it was just a mud flat at the head of the bay.

The editor of the *Cordova Alaskan* was understandably annoyed by the "crust" of those printing such stories. The *Dawson News'* story had spoken of the "extensive railroad activity" around Nelson, the future metropolis and capital of Alaska, and the future center of learning. The new town had even set aside a large area of tableland overlooking the city as a site for a university. When the railroad was finished, the *Dawson News* said, the copper country would be directly connected with tidewater, and with the planned extension to the Interior, trains would be running daily from all over Alaska into Nelson.

In July 1909, Donald A. McKenzie was in Alaska to plat the town, and the promotion seemed to be perking right along. He wrote an article telling of the Hawkins Island coaling station at the entrance to Orca Bay, and the town of Nelson, which would eventually "have to become the shipping port for all the coal from the Bering Lake fields, as it alone has sufficient depth of water to accommodate large cargo carriers. The Cunningham and other famous groups of claims are in these fields. . . ." And he made friends by joining his voice on behalf of "Nelson" town to that of Cordova and Katalla in deploring the long delay in issuing coal patents.

In January of 1910, the "Nelson Townsite Bubble" was pricked. E. C. Hawkins of the Copper River & Northwestern Railway Company sent the following wire to the *Cordova Alaskan* for publication:

Replying to Cordova inquiry you may state that we have nothing to do with the Nelson townsite matters, either direct or indirect. Have no change of plans under consideration. No necessity or advantage in going to Nelson with railway or with anything else connected therewith. Would not have made heavy investments in Cordova if we believed there was any reason for changing terminals.
—E. C. Hawkins, General Manager
Copper River & Northwestern Railway

Apparently, the townsite had depended upon "selling" Nelson to the Guggenheims.

Nelson did have a post office. A. B. Cooper was the postmaster and only resident of the town. He made weekly trips to Cordova to pick up the mail for Nelson. After a few years he accepted a job with the Cordova Post Office. The Nelson townsite is still platted and eliminated from the Chugach National Forest. It is still just a mud flat at the head of the bay.

23 NAKED WITHOUT BLUSHING

It was 1908, an election year, and tempers were still high after the Keystone Canyon affair. Wickersham was running for Delegate in Congress on an anti-Guggenheim, Home Rule ticket. In Cordova, the brand-new capital city of the Guggenheims, the "Googies" were out to beat Wickersham.

The Wickersham-Guggenheim clash had its roots in the past. Wickersham had applied to the Alaska Syndicate for employment before his entrance into politics. He had written a letter to Stephen Birch, Esquire, dated at Fairbanks April 8, 1908, saying that he would accept an offer from "your allied interests to act as their General Counsel, but not in any subordinate capacity. I will accept a three-year contract at $15,000 per annum with offices in Seattle and office force and maintenance. Upon that sort of arrangement I would devote my time exclusively to their interests, and give them my best service possible. . . ."

His offer was not accepted, nor were some mining deals he had attempted to negotiate with the Guggenheims.

Very shortly after, he decided to seek election as Delegate, but he still apparently hoped for a Guggenheim subsidy, for on the eve of the election he sent a wire to his good friend from courthouse days, David H. Jarvis, who was now employed by the Guggenheims. The telegram said: "I am a candidate for Congress. Where is Birch?" An answer was not forthcoming, so Wickersham went before the convention and delivered a scathing anti-Guggenheim speech.

Wickersham also campaigned as the Home Rule candidate. But the fact was that his conversion to Home Rule coincided with his candidacy, with his sudden abhorrence of the Guggenheims and with his rebuff by the Alaska Syndicate. Just prior to his candidacy he wrote to a friend and associate, Governor Wilford B. Hoggatt, referring to those who advocated Home Rule as "good men but misguided." Wickersham generally expressed the view that it was too soon, that Alaska was too sparsely populated, and that there were "hardly 20 men who will admit that they intend to stay in the country, and if the gold fields played out, as they have in Dawson, they would quickly depart."

As the 1908 elections approached, the Guggenheim opposition to Wickersham stiffened as he became more outspoken in his campaign against them. In the popular mind, a vote for Wickersham was a vote for Home Rule, and a vote against the Guggs. In the brand-new Guggenheim city of Cordova, the Guggs were out stumping—and trumping—to beat Wickersham.

Election day drew near; feverish preparations were going on in all the railroad camps up and down the line. The Bohunks and other construction "stiffs" were being coached carefully.

In an effort to avoid skullduggery in the Guggenheim camp, Assistant U.S. District Attorney Leroy Vincent Ray was sent from Valdez to Cordova. He arrived too late.

On election day the flatcars started down the line loaded with men. Charlie Cochran, a Cordova old-timer, tells this story:

"They had an awful lot of Portuguese in those days. Some of them were sure weird-looking guys. It was the time when they were voting on Wickersham for Delegate to Congress. Well, the railroad was against him, so they brought down flatcars of these fellows to vote. In the polls, they'd ask one of these boys if he had his papers, and he'd show his railroad pass and say, 'I got my *little* paper.' And maybe someone would get up and protest the registration, but they would vote him anyway. Against Wickersham.

"Personally, I was for Wickersham, and he won."

By three o'clock in the afternoon, when the steamer *Elsie* docked with Assistant District Attorney Ray, all the flatcars had returned to the working camps with the voters. Nine hundred and twenty-five votes had been cast, over 700 of them for Corson, Wickersham's opponent. Yet the year before, Cordova could boast only a few score inhabitants. It was obvious that many—or most—of these votes were illegal, since a year's residence in Alaska was required to vote.

The *Seattle Post-Intelligencer* editorialized:

ELECTION FRAUDS IN ALASKA
"The fact that the opposition to home rule in Alaska was confined entirely to the big corporations which have investments in the territory, and to Governor Hoggatt, who, as a representative of outside investors, reflects their views, is abundantly demonstrated in the election returns so far as they have been received.

"The only precincts which have returned a majority for Corson, the Hoggatt nominee, are Treadwell, where the greatest mine in Alaska is being operated, and where the only qualified voters are the higher officers and office employees of the big corporation which owns the town and the mine, and the

Guggenheim town of Cordova. In this latter town, the terminus of a railroad now under construction, a town which but a few months ago had but a handful of inhabitants, there were 925 votes cast, 700 of them for Corson, the Hoggatt candidate. The laborers employed upon the construction of the Guggenheim road, the great majority of whom were shipped into the camp from Seattle this summer, were brought into town and voted solidly for the corporate interests. The federal laws provide that no one can vote in Alaska who has not been a bona fide resident of the territory for a year.

"Here are unmistakeable indications of a deliberate fraud practiced in the corporation interest, in order to defeat the will of the people, and to show an indorsement of the Hoggatt policy of government from the quarterdeck instead of by the people.

"The matter, it is reported from Valdez, will probably be brought before the attention of the courts. Governor Hoggatt should be called upon by the president to make an explanation and to clear his skirts of any responsibility taken by the corporation managers in the interests of himself and what he represents."

Governor Hoggatt, it was reported, declined to make a statement.

But the controversy couldn't be contained, and rival Valdez, still smarting under the collapse of Reynolds, had plenty to say about it. Snarled the *Valdez Prospector* in its editorial pages: "The [*Cordova Daily*] *Alaskan* proudly asserts that no illegal votes were cast in Cordova. Well, some men could walk through the streets naked without blushing."

And the *Cordova Alaskan* fired back with: "Well, yes. If the Valdezians keep coming to Cordova for three more months as they have in the last three, we could walk through the streets of that deserted village naked without blushing."

But the charges were not so easily brushed aside. One man, Jerry Dunn, who witnessed the election, asked for a probe into it. Dunn said that 921 votes were cast, and that 600 of them were illegal. He said when he tried to challenge the proceedings, he was laughed at.

But when the outspoken witness was placed on the stand in court in late December, he suffered a sudden lapse of memory. Under an item titled, "Nothing Done in Cordova Election Fraud," the *Katalla Herald* noted that all the witnesses lost their tongues and could not remember that the election was not according to Hoyle, "even Jerry Dunn, the most outspoken."

The obviously fraudulent nature of the Cordova elections was a colossal blunder on the part of the Guggenheims, for it made the charges leveled by

Wickersham in the next few months and years all the more believable to a public which was more than ready to believe the worst of the Alaska Syndicate.

24 UNACCEPTABLE VERDICT

The year 1908 saw the stormy trial of Marshal Edward C. Hasey, who had fired the shots in Keystone Canyon in which one man died. Hasey had been indicted by a grand jury in Valdez on five counts in connection with the shooting in Keystone Canyon. His attorneys asked for and received a change of venue on the basis that a fair trial was impossible in the inflamed atmosphere of Valdez or Seward. The trial was held in April 1908 in Juneau where the atmosphere was only slightly less hostile than in Valdez. Everywhere in Alaska people were demanding a guilty verdict. All the angers and frustrations connected with the affair, including those which normally would have been directed at Reynolds, were now channeled and focused on "the Guggenheims," and on Ed Hasey who was considered the tool of the "Googies."

The trial was set. Witnesses were rounded up. Billy Quitsch, the night watchman at Keystone Canyon at

Billy Quitsch of Valdez.

the time of the shooting, said, "I was logging up in Fidalgo Bay when a steamship began to whistle. It kept whistling, so the leader went over to see what was up. They asked if Billy Quitsch was there. They had a subpoena for me to go to Juneau for the trial. Other witnesses had been more or less corralled in Valdez."

It took a week to select 12 acceptable jurors. These men lived to regret their attempt to do their civic duty on that jury.

The case was presented in an atmosphere of muffled anger. The courtrooms were crowded and stuffy. (Full text of both defense and prosecution presentations are in the Appendix.)

The case dragged on bitterly for almost a month. The confusing stories of the *Prospector*, which had come out earlier, had stirred up intense feeling, yet when the case came up in court, the prosecution told substantially the same story as the defense, resting its case on the fact that the "right [to construct a railroad over a grade passing along the Lowe River and through Keystone Canyon] was granted by an Act of Congress passed May 14, 1898, which prevents any one road from having a monopoly on any pass or canyon in Alaska."

The defense showed that there was adequate room for another railroad in the canyon, but that Mr. Reynolds had already determined to take the Guggenheim rock work and grade by force.

Fifty years following the trial one of the jurors who still preferred anonymity said, "I've spent a lot of years trying to forget that trial. . . . I'd like to forget it." But the drama of the tale so involved him that he said:

"The Home Railroad people were desperately anxious to convict Hasey. Reynolds was a tremendously popular man and there was a lot of sentiment against the Guggenheims." (Author's note: *Reynolds, an underdog, was still popular in Alaska, then and long afterward. Many Alaskans believed that he had been the victim of "big interests."*)

"The Grand Jury indicted Hasey in Valdez and it went to the petite jury in Juneau. I was on the petite jury. The case lasted almost a month, but we brought in our verdict in an hour and forty-five minutes. We acquitted him of murder, but convicted him of assault with a deadly weapon.

"A key prosecuting witness convinced us he had perjured himself. It was the matter of the dynamite that convinced us. Testimony brought out that the dynamite was indeed carried by Reynolds' men. It was capped and fused, with only six inches of fuse.

"The prosecution witness said that they were going to set it off in the hillside behind the barricade, just to attract attention, while their men rushed the barricade.

"The 'Damn fool, if you hadn't been in such a hurry, there wouldn't have been any shooting,' remark was entered into testimony by the defense.

"On the jury was a man who knew a little something about dynamite. He said, 'If you're in rough country and carry dynamite capped and fused with only six inches of fuse, there is only one thing you can do with it. That's throw it.'

"Convinced that the Reynolds men could not possibly have had in mind a mere mountainside blast to divert attention, we brought in a verdict of acquittal of murder.

"But then our troubles had only started. Reynolds played real dirty with us. Two Pinkerton men followed us everywhere. They listened in on our conversations. Even our friends wouldn't speak to us. They thought we were bought out. 'How much did they pay you?' they'd ask.

"I never knew another man who sat on the Hasey jury to ever serve on another petite jury again. Our lives were made miserable.

"Years later one of the men who had saved for years made a trip back to London. He was accused of making the trip on Guggenheim blood money."

Marshal Hasey was sentenced to two years for assault with a deadly weapon. The sentence was considered an outrage; nothing short of a murder sentence and its attendant penalties would have satisfied the public.

Shortly after the trial, while Hasey was free on bond pending an appeal, he was discovered floating in Gastineau Channel with a lump on his head. He was fished out—still alive. Someone had struck him over the head and pushed him in. Hasey left Juneau shortly after his recovery. He served two years for the Keystone Canyon shooting, and he never came back to Alaska.

But still the public refused to forget the trial; repercussions were still recurring, and the man who kept them stirred up most was James Wickersham. Wickersham had resigned as judge in 1908 and was now running for Delegate from Alaska.

25 WICKERSHAM THUMPS A TUB

Alaskans were discontent. Their needs were not being met by Congress, which was, in effect, their absentee legislature since they had no local government. Reliant upon a distant and poorly informed Congress, Alaska was akin to the unwanted stepchild. Her needs were great, but even greater was the inaction of Congress. Alaska was desperate for the opening of the coal lands, aid to transportation, better schools and better law enforcement. All sorts of acute needs, including land surveys and rehabilitation of depleted salmon fisheries, were ignored. Heaven was high, and Congress far away.

In this unhappy and frustrated void it was easy to capture the public fancy, especially by invoking the "Guggenheim" bugaboo.

Even the collapse of Reynolds was somehow felt to be the fault of the Guggenheims. The *Alaska Record* on October 17, 1907, shortly after that affair, said, "Reynolds and Governor Brady put their trust in God, but they didn't keep their powder dry. The Guggenheims evidently watered the stock of the Alaska Home Railway and the blamed old thing wouldn't go off."

Suspicion, already simmering in those trust-busting days against Alaska's biggest trust, was raised to the boiling point by Wickersham and others who kept drumming about the threat of corporate control of Alaska, her politics, her courts, her resources.

To make it all the more interesting, Wickersham, the foe of "special interests," was trying to get special legislation passed favoring a railroad (the Hubbard Road) which he himself was helping promote. The Hubbard Road was to have its terminus in Valdez.

The Hasey trial brought with it fresh material for the growing anti-Guggenheim campaign encouraged and inflamed by Wickersham. Charges of perjury, bribery, jury-tampering and political persecution in connection with the Hasey trial were leveled against the Guggs in the public forum. The charges were made by Wickersham on the strength of an incriminating letter purportedly written by John A. Carson to David H. Jarvis, treasurer of one of the Syndicate's subordinate companies. The letter was accompanied by a bill for the entertainment of witnesses, submitted by Mr. M. B. Morrisey.

The damning letter and voucher had come to light through the disgruntled efforts of one H. J. Douglas, who had learned that he was to be fired by the Katalla Company, a Guggenheim company. He said he had taken the papers from the files.

The letter brought the wrath of friends and enemies alike down even heavier on the heads of all the jurors who served on the Hasey trial.

Then there was the matter of the dismissal of two prominent men, Sutherland and Boyce, by Governor Hoggatt. It was said that they were dismissed because of their part in the prosecution of Hasey. Political persecution, charged Wickersham.

As if this were not enough, there were charges soon brought of an attempt to defraud the government of $50,000 in connection with coal contracts at Fort Liscum, Valdez. Jarvis was again implicated. Wickersham was riding full tilt and roughshod over the Guggenheims.

No attempt was made to prosecute, even on the serious charges of jury-rigging and perjury. But Wickersham used the charges, true or not, in a vicious campaign of political persecution that made the dismissal of Sutherland and Boyce look penny-ante.

David Jarvis, former friend of Wickersham and champion of Alaska, felt these assaults upon his integrity very keenly.

Jarvis had never been a physically strong man. His friends felt that he was utterly incapable of the things Wickersham accused him of, and that he was being hounded to his death by the dismissed employee, H. J. Douglas. He was powerless to defend himself from the muckraking press, even as others were defenseless against this powerful and remorseless propaganda machine.

There seemed only one way out, and he took it. One evening in June 1911, shortly after Wickersham leveled his charges of graft at Fort Liscum, Jarvis went to his hotel room, put a gun to his head and pulled the trigger. His friends found him with a note by his side. It said, "Tired and worn out."

It would seem that all this passion and human tragedy would be enough; that things would settle down, just by sheer weariness. But they were only the local Alaskan counterpart of a much larger national scandal that was going on. Involved in this national uproar were the Alaska coal lands, and the confusion and suspicion generated by that scandal had helped to fire the many tragedies which had taken place in Alaska.

While all this was going on, the Guggenheim-Morgan Syndicate was busy—building a railroad. They had only four years to complete it. It wasn't enough time, but with the bustling energies of M. J. Heney and E. C. Hawkins, plus generous transfusions of money, they intended to do it.

BIBLIOGRAPHY AND NOTES
PART ONE

2 BEFORE COPPER—GOLD!
Abercrombie, Capt. W.R. *The Copper River Exploring Expedition of 1899.* U.S. Government Printing Office, Washington, D.C., 1900, pp. 14-15; and Gillette's Report in same, pp. 139-49.
Colby, Merle. *A Guide to Alaska.* The Macmillan Co., New York, 1939, p. 223.
The Cordova Daily Alaska. "Cordova Mourns Death of M. J. Heney," October 12, 1910, p. 1.
The Cordova Daily Times, August 25, 1916.
Graves, S. H. *On the White Pass Payroll.* The Lakeside Press, Chicago, 1908.
Hubbard, Oliver P. Testimony before the House Committee on Territories, March 28, 1910. Hubbard said: "About the time Captain Abercrombie came here [1898], by accident, almost, a man found his way over Thompson Pass, and he told Captain Abercrombie about coming in that way, and they sent out their men who made an investigation. They found it possible to build a trail. They first came to the Keystone Canyon and built a trail up over the canyon."
Whiting, Fenton B. *Grit, Grief and Gold.* Peacock Publishing Co. Seattle, 1933.

3 HI-YU CHIEF
Abercrombie, Capt. W.R. *The Copper River Exploring Expedition of 1899.* Sub-report of Edward Cashman, p. 162: "We were two days getting to Nicolai No. 2's wigwam. We stopped there about two hours. I took out the uniform you gave me to give to Nicolai and gave it to Nicolai No. 2. He wanted it very badly, but would not keep it, as he said Nicolai at Taral was 'High you Chief.' He was tenas chief. . . ."
Powell, Addison M. *Trailing and Camping in Alaska.* Wessels & Bissell, New York, 1910, pp. 78-79. "This Taral chief [Nicolai] was a man of strong character. During his active life he prohibited any direct business intercourse between the natives of the interior and those on the coast. He held the key to the interior by way of the Copper River, and as he lived on the bank of the river, no Indian dared pass. The Indians of the interior brought furs down to this dictator, and he took them to the coast traders and returned with guns and powder. They generally hammered their own bullets from native copper.
"Old Bachaneta once attempted to descend the river on a raft, but Taral Nicolai demanded that he should turn back. Bachaneta was a noted leader among the Indians at the headwaters of the river and of the Upper Tanana, but a bullet from the rifle of Nicolai caused him to seek a landing and return on foot to his home, 100 miles away. Billy Bachaneta related this incident to me, and added that if Nicolai had not died, he and his father and a few friends intended to repeat the attempt."

4 COPPER DISCOVERIES
The Alaska Monthly, Juneau. May 1907, p. 52.
The Alaska-Yukon Magazine. "Alaska Copper" by E. S. Harrison, February 1908, pp. 449, 454.

Carpenter, Frank G. *Alaska, Our Northern Wonderland.* Doubleday, Page & Co., Boston, 1925, p. 289.
Colby, Merle. *A Guide to Alaska.* The Macmillan Co., New York, 1939, p. 246.
The Cordova Daily Times. "Railroad Completed to Copper Mines," April 1, 1911.
Nelson, O. A. Personal interview.
Powell, Addison M. *Trailing and Camping in Alaska.* Wessels & Bissell, New York, 1910.
The Seattle Mail & Herald, Valdez Edition. "Copper Deposits," March 17, 1903, p. 12.
The Valdez News. March 9, 1901. Same, "The Chittyna Copper Belt—A True History of How it was Found—A Race to the Interior" by B. F. Millard, April 20, 1901.
The Valdez Prospector. "Chittyna Mines," March 27, 1908.
Wickersham, James. *Alaska Reports,* vol. 2. West Publishing Co., St. Paul, Minn., 1906, p. 134, "Copper River Mining Co. vs. McClellan."

5 VALDEZ: RAILROAD FEVER
Beach, Rex. *The Iron Trail.* First published serially in *Everybody's Magazine,* 1913. **Author's note:** The Iron Trail *has an account of a financial deal between Heney and the London Company, which involved the White Pass & Yukon and problems with the steamboats navigating the Yukon River. The Iron Trail was a fictionalized version of the real story and used many real incidents. In Beach's version, the Copper River Railway was the pawn in this game, but from newspaper accounts of 1901 and 1902 it could have been the Valdez, Copper River & Yukon Railroad that was involved. This is, of course, supposition, but as a threat to Yukon River steamboat traffic, this series of events seems to tally more closely.*
The Seattle Post-Intelligencer. August 14, 1901, p. 12.
The Valdez News. May 11, June 22, August 24 and 31, September 7, December 21, 1901.
The Valdez Prospector. May 22, June 26, August 7, 1902.

6 BATTLE FOR THE BONANZA
The Alaska Monthly, Juneau. May 1907, p. 52.
The Alaska-Yukon Magazine. "Alaska Copper" by E. S. Harrison, February 1908.
Andrews, C. L. *The Story of Alaska.* The Caxton Printers, Caldwell, Idaho, 1943, p. 213.
Colby, Merle. *A Guide to Alaska.* The Macmillan Co., New York, 1939, p. 245.
Hulley, Clarence C. *Alaska 1741-1953.* Binfords & Mort, Portland, Ore., 1953, p. 296.
Lancaster, Ralph "Slim." Conversation with the author.
Nichols, Jeanette Paddock. *History of Alaska Under Rule of the United States.* The Arthur H. Clark Co., Cleveland, 1924.
Shiels, Archibald W. *The Kennecott Story.* Privately published, Bellingham, Wash., 1967, p. 1.
The Valdez Prospector. September 11, 1902, p. 1.
Wickersham, James. *Alaska Reports,* vol. 2. West Publishing Co., St. Paul, Minn., 1906, "Copper River Mining Co. vs. McClellan," p. 134; also "Copper River Mining Co. vs. McClellan," 138 Fed. 333, 70 C.C.A.,

pp. 623, 643, 646, 660, 740; and "Copper River Mining Co. vs. McClellan," 200 U.S. 616, 26 Sup. Ct. 753, 5OL. Ed. 256.

Wickersham, James. *Old Yukon.* Washington Law Book Co., Washington, D.C., 1938, pp. 423-27, 454.

7   VALDEZ: HOME OF THE GUGGENHEIM-MORGAN SYNDICATE, 1905-1906
The Alaska Monthly. "Guggenheim Projects," June 1906, p. 78. "From Alaska Exchanges," December 1906, p. 254.
Defense testimony in the Hasey trial at Juneau.
Nichols, Jeanette Paddock. *History of Alaska Under Rule of the United States.* The Arthur H. Clark Co., Cleveland, 1924, p. 246.
The Seattle Mail & Herald, Valdez Edition. March 17, 1903.
Shiels, Archibald W. *The Kennecott Story.* Privately published, Bellingham, Wash., 1967, pp. 3-4.
The Valdez Prospector. September 4, 1902.
Wilson, Katherine. *Copper Tints, A Book of Cordova Sketches.* Daily Times Press, Cordova, 1923.

8   THE NELSON TOWNSITE AND THE JARVIS MEMORIAL
The Congressional Record. 59th Congress, 1st Session. March 21, 1906, pp. 4073-74.
Nichols, Jeanette Paddock. *History of Alaska Under Rule of the United States.* The Arthur H. Clark Co., Cleveland, 1924, pp. 266-68.

9   KATALLA: BLACK GOLD AND ANTHRACITE
Abercrombie, Capt. W. R. *The Copper River Exploring Expedition of 1899.* U.S. Government Printing Office, Washington, D.C., 1900.
The Alaska Monthly, Juneau. "Oil at Kayak," August 1906, pp. 172-73.
Alaska Sportsman. "This Month in Alaska History," April 1968, p. 25.
The Alaska-Yukon Magazine. "Oil First in Solving Alaska's Fuel Problem" by William Thornton Prosser, April 1911, pp. 3-8.
Anderson, George. Personal interview.
The Cordova Alaskan. Editorial, February 23, 1907, p. 2.
de Laguna, Frederica. *Archaeology of the Yakutat Bay Area.* U.S. Government Printing Office, Washington, D.C., 1964.
Guy, Ann. Personal interview.
Hansen, Bill. Personal interview.
Hansen, Gertrude (Mrs. Bill). Personal interview.
Jackson, Stella. Personal interview.
The Katalla Herald. "Tom White First to Find Oil—and the Fiery Consequences; Tom White's Thrilling Experiences with Fire and Crevasses," August 17, 1907, p. 2. "Tidal Wave Rushes In," November 16, 1907.
The Seattle Mail & Herald, Valdez Edition. "Controller Bay Oil Fields" by Preston H. Wilson. March 17, 1903, p. 20.
U.S. Circuit Court of Appeals for the Ninth Judicial Circuit. "Alaska Pacific Railway & Terminal Company vs. The Copper River & Northwestern Railway Co., the Katalla Company, and M. K. Rogers."

10 REENTER M. J. HENEY
The Alaska Monthly, Juneau. May 1906.
Colby, Merle. *A Guide to Alaska.* The Macmillan Co., New York, 1939, p. 227.

Shiels, Archibald W. *The Kennecott Story.* Privately published, Bellingham, Wash., 1964, pp. 5-6.
Wilson, Katherine. *Copper Tints, A Book of Cordova Sketches.* Daily Times Press, Cordova, 1923, p. 5.

11 CORDOVA: APRIL FOOL!
The Alaska Monthly, Juneau. May, July and September 1906.
Beach, Rex. *The Iron Trail* is the source for the account of the smallpox hoax, but several sources tell me that the account there is basically true. Corroborating sources include Dr. Whiting, cited below; a letter of November 1962, from Tom Kelly, an engineer on the Miles Glacier Bridge; newspaper articles cited here; and a reference to it by Udo Hesse in a letter to the editor of the *Cordova Times* in March 1926.
The Cordova Alaskan. June 16, 1906, pp. 2-3.
Whiting, Fenton B. *Grit, Grief and Gold.* Peacock Publishing Co., Seattle, 1933.

12 THE BIG GAMBLE: ABERCROMBIE CANYON
The Alaska Monthly, Juneau. "Will Fight Rivals with Dynamite," September 1906.
The Cordova Alaskan. February 1, 1908.

13 KATALLA: WHERE THE RAILS MEET THE SAILS
U.S. Circuit Court of Appeals for the Ninth Judicial Circuit. "Alaska Pacific Railway & Terminal Company vs. The Copper River & Northwestern Railway Co., the Katalla Company, and M. K. Rogers."
The Katalla Herald. "An Assured Success," August 10, 1907, p. 1. "The Alaska Pacific Co.," August 17, 1907, p. 1.

14 THE BATTLE OF B. S. HILL
The material for this account was obtained in a personal interview with the late Jack McCord.

15 AFTERMATH
The Cordova Alaskan. August 24, 1907.
The Katalla Herald. August 17 and 31, 1907.
U.S. Circuit Court of Appeals for the Ninth Judicial Circuit. "Alaska Pacific Railway & Terminal Company vs. The Copper River & Northwestern Railway Co., the Katalla Company, and M. K. Rogers."

16 VALDEZ: REYNOLDSITIS
The Alaska Monthly, Juneau. June 1906, p. 98; November 1906, p. 165; February-March 1907, p. 376.
The Cordova Alaskan. August 17 and 22, November 3, 1907.
The Alaska Daily Dispatch, Juneau. March 16, 1905.
The Katalla Herald. August 24 and 31, 1907.
Nichols, Jeanette Paddock. *History of Alaska Under Rule of the United States.* The Arthur H. Clark Co., Cleveland, 1924, pp. 112, 266, 270, 306, 307, 309.
The Valdez Prospector. August 15 through September 19, 1907.

17 GUNFIRE IN THE CANYON
The Alaska Daily Dispatch, Juneau. April 6, 1908.
Quitsch, William. Personal interview.

18 COLLAPSE OF REYNOLDS
The Chitina Leader. "Busy Life of Ex-Gov. Brady," January 4, 1919.

Colby, Merle. *A Guide to Alaska.* The Macmillan Co., New York, 1939, p. 234.

The Cordova Alaskan. October 26, 1907. "H. D. Reynolds Leaves for Home," November 3, 1907. "Reynolds Not Yet Located," November 9, 1907. "John G. Brady," November 23, 1907.

The Katalla Herald. "Reynolds' Bank at Valdez Closes its Doors," October 12, 1907; "Collapse of Reynolds' Railroad Project," October 19, 1907.

Lazell, J. Arthur. *Alaskan Apostle: The Life Story of Sheldon Jackson.* Harper & Bros., New York, 1960.

Nichols, Jeanette Paddock. *History of Alaska Under Rule of the United States.* The Arthur H. Clark Co., Cleveland, 1924, p. 307.

Powell, Addison M. *Trailing and Camping in Alaska.* Wessels & Bissell, New York, 1910, pp. 28-31.

The Valdez Prospector. September 26, 1907.

19   KATALLA CUT OUT
The Katalla Herald. October 12, November 9, 16 and 23, 1907.

Kelly, Tom. Correspondence with the author, November 1962.

Shiels, Archibald W. *The Kennecott Story.* Privately published, Bellingham, Wash., 1964, p. 4.

20   THE WINTER OF THE PORCUPINE
The Cordova Alaskan. October 26, November 23, 1907; January 18, February 1, 8 and 22, May 1, 1908.

The Katalla Herald. November 16, 1907.

21   A TOWN IS BORN
The Cordova Alaskan. December 21, 1907; January 11, August 8 and 15, 1908.

Jenkins, Thomas. *The Man of Alaska: Peter Trimble Rowe.* Morehouse-Gorham Co., New York, 1943, p. 214.

The Katalla Herald, December 7, 1907.

The Pathfinder. "Cordova, the Copper Gateway to Alaska," July 1920, p. 1.

22   NELSON TOWNSITE MAKES ITS BID
The Cordova Alaskan. March 13, April 15, 1909; January 26, 1910.

The Pathfinder, Valdez. July 1920.

23   NAKED WITHOUT BLUSHING
The Alaska Daily Record, Juneau. July 5 and 29, August 6, 1910.

The Katalla Herald. August 15, December 26, 1908.

Nichols, Jeanette Paddock. *History of Alaska Under Rule of the United States.* The Arthur H. Clark Co., Cleveland, 1924, p. 302.

The Seattle Post-Intelligencer. August 13, 1908, p. 1; August 15, 1908, p. 6.

24   UNACCEPTABLE VERDICT
The Alaska Daily Dispatch, Juneau. April 6, 1908.

Anonymous juror. Personal interview.

The Cordova Alaskan. "Hasey Found Wounded in Bay," March 22, 1909.

25   WICKERSHAM THUMPS A TUB
The Alaska Daily Dispatch, Juneau. June 22, 1911.

The Cordova Alaskan. "Early Construction Talk and Work," April 1, 1911.

Gruening, Ernest. *The State of Alaska.* Random House, New York, 1954.

Hearings, House Committee on Territories. 61st Congress, 3rd Session. "Copper River & Northwestern Railway in Alaska," March 28, 1910, pp. 203-204.

Nichols, Jeanette Paddock. *History of Alaska Under Rule of the United States.* The Arthur H. Clark Co., Cleveland, 1924, pp. 346, 348, 359, 371, 372.

The Pacific Fisherman. "David H. Jarvis, in Memorium," July 1911, p. 1.

PART TWO
SNOOSE, OVERALLS,
WHISKEY AND SNOWBALLS

PART TWO
SNOOSE, OVERALLS, WHISKEY AND SNOWBALLS
Construction of the Copper River
& Northwestern Railway

1 HENEY'S FIRST CONTRACT

Scandals and politics aside, Heney's job was to get that railroad built and he was going to do it. Katalla and her unprotected harbor were abandoned in favor of Cordova with the receipt of Heney's contract in November of 1907.

First on the work agenda was building track to Abercrombie Landing (Mile 54). Heney and his crews were to lay track while the Katalla Company was to build the three steel bridges on the line (Flag Point, Miles Glacier and Kuskulana).

Work was delegated and the *Cordova Alaskan* of November 23, 1907, reported that, "If anyone has the least shadow of doubt that railroad building in earnest has begun on this side of the line, that doubt would be dispelled should they take a trip down the line as far as the bridge that crosses Eyak River. Carpenters have completed work on Camp 2 and the camp is in full operation with 160 men. The big rock cut that was just started on last summer when the road suspended operations, is a lively scene of action, cutting through the mountainside and filling in the approach to the bridge. Farther out a big gang is clearing the right-of-way and 13 miles from town carpenters are building Camp 3. A telephone line is in and being connected to the home office."

*Opposite—***The steamboat** *S.B. Matthews* **at Alaganik in April 1906. This was one of the chief salmon stations on the river delta.**

In town 90 more men had been added to the payroll. Now there were around 450 men to keep the track moving.

While the work gangs were busy laying the line the new town kept growing. Construction was everywhere. A two-story building for the engineers and the audit division was going up as was a base hospital. A new railroad spur replacing Maude and the "slow way by tram" was added for the convenience of businessmen. Maude was retired but balked at being moved to the new town.

With winter there was no letup in the construction push, although heavy snowfall and fierce winds did slow things down. It was a hard winter, especially for Katalla. Cut off from supplies, Katalla was in trouble. In a desperate effort to bring aid to the concerned town, four men mushed overland on what became a "terrible journey." Equipped with a four-day food supply the men were forced to spend 16 days on the trail. They suffered from frozen toes, hands and faces, and "none escaped the brand of the trail."

The harsh winter caught another party out on the flats.

"J. F. Wash and Gus Boone returned from a two-week trip in the vicinity of Alaganik [Alakanik] Thursday, where they went to cruise timber and look up a location for a camp. Wash said it was the worst trip he had ever experienced in his travels in Alaska over the past ten years. The snow was soft and about four feet deep, and all the time they were out it either snowed or rained. It was almost impossible to travel with or without snowshoes. They were compelled to discard their sleds and pack their blankets and provisions on their backs. In the timber the boughs and underbrush were loaded with wet snow, making movement miserable. By hard traveling some days they only made three miles."

Just after Christmas the rails were laid through the two big cuts at the end of the lake allowing work to speed up. The rails were expected to reach the Alaganik cut by February 1. The newspaper was full of stories of "Lively times at the front," where 1,100 feet of new trestle were complete, and "Old No. 50" was making daily trips out to the end of the track. The pile driver was hard at it just a mile beyond, and "working day and night driving piles across the glacier streams and sloughs."

January was a month of severe and miserable storms, but the work had advanced to about Mile 14 with the pile driver two miles ahead of the track's end. Rumors were still around. One, emanating from an unhappy Valdez, claimed that there would be a cut in wages. The *Cordova Alaskan* reported that, "A rumor from some disgruntled source in Valdez that wages for unskilled labor would be cut from $3.50 to $3.00 a day, a reduction of 50 cents for a ten-hour work day, is not the case, although unskilled labor in the States at $1.75 per day is plentiful."

February was a significant month for the railroad. The new engine purchased from the Alaska Central Railroad arrived. "The new engine is considerably larger than old '50' and is just the size for the work apportioned to it at this time," claimed the Cordova paper. And A. O. Johnson, assistant bridge engineer, began his trek by horsedrawn sled from Cordova to the Miles Glacier, where a bridge of unprecedented size and strength was to be built across the faces of two living glaciers. This was to be the famous Miles Glacier "Million Dollar" Bridge, and it was still on the drawing boards.

"The railroad was built," said old-timer Dick Janson Sr., "by what they call 'station men.' Two or three men would form a 'companie' which contracted for different jobs at so much per cubic yard of rock or dirt moved, or in railroad construction, so much per station.

"They followed the heavy construction around the world, these station men, and they knew each other from other jobs and other places. Like on the Copper River, I worked with men from the Gillevara Ofoten, the Iron Ore mountain in Sweden, which is the world's farthest north railroad.

"A station man is a hard rock man, a rough-and-ready construction man of the old school. Hard-drinking, hard-working, swearing, snoose-spitting, he will tackle any job, no matter how tough. Like Long Carl Carlson, foreman on the south end of the Chitina Crossing—to show you what kind of man he was, several men would hook onto the heavy rails with steel tongs and carry them into place. But Long Carl would swagger up and say, 'Let's not monkey around, men,' and pick up one and pack it away on his shoulder. He was a hi-yu skookum man, Long Carl. He got his name because he was a long, lanky Swede. He came to work on the railroad at the age of 19.

"Most of the station men were Scandinavians, and they had some colorful names. Sometimes you worked with a man for years and never knew his real name. There were such handles as Pickhandle Jones, The Norwegian King, Shoot-em-up Swede, Crooked Swede, Hurry-up Jones, and the like.

There was a great deal of latitude in the matter of names. The men were of assorted nationalities, some with exceedingly unpronounceable names. If a Mr. Mxlovopovsky applied for work, the paymaster would fix a firm eye on him and pronounce, "From now on, your name is Jack Robbins." That was that. From that day on he was Jack Robbins, and off he went to work, sometimes very confused.

Another oddity of the paymaster's window was the fact that horses were on the payroll, their services bought in exactly the same manner as a man's.

All the drilling for blasting and moving of rock was done by hand. Power machinery was just coming in to use elsewhere but was not needed here where all the labor necessary was available at 30 cents an hour, or slightly more by the station.

Even so, rock work was tremendously expensive, some of it costing as much as $220,000 per mile. In one place 1,000 kegs of black powder and 35 cases of No. 1 dynamite were used to move 12,000 cubic yards of rock in one mighty roar, known as a "coyote."

O.A. Nelson said that ventilation was extremely poor in the long coyote holes. "If a man went in to work too soon after blasting, it was occasionally necessary to drag him out—dead."

Top—Railroad builders at Cordova, November 1908. From left: Front row—James English, track superintendent; J. R. Van Cleve, master mechanic; Sam Murchison, superintendent of construction; Michael J. Heney, contractor; Captain John J. O'Brien of Alaska Steamship Company; E. C. Hawkins, chief engineer; Alfred Williams, assistant chief engineer (on step); Dr. F. B. Whiting, chief surgeon; P. J. O'Brien, bridges. Back row—Dr. W. W. Council, assistant surgeon; Archie Shiels, supply; Bill Simpson, steam shovel; --- Robinson; two unknowns.
Middle left—$3,000 worth of powder in one blast.
Middle right—A steam shovel at work, somewhere on the Copper River & Northwestern Railway line. The company had four Richmond shovels, all acquired in 1907.
Bottom—Heney paychecks were issued in amounts as little as 25 cents.

RALPH E. MACKAY COLLECTION

COURTESY JEAN DETTINGER

MOSS COLLECTION. ALASKA HISTORICAL LIBRARY

No.   9156   PAY CHECK   P.R.No. 15

M.J. HENEY, CONTRACTOR.

Cordova, Alaska

FEB 20 1910

Pay to   Mike Graham   or bearer $ 25 Cents.

Only 25 Cents   Dollars

For Services during Month of   JAN -- 1910

M.J. HENEY, CONTRACTOR.

NOT OVER TWO DOLLARS $2S

To The Canadian Bank of Commerce,
Seattle, Washington.

By_____
                          PAYMASTER
Countersigned:_____
                          ACCOUNTANT

STEVE SHELDON MUSEUM. HAINES

2 THE STEAMBOAT CHITTYNA

The year 1907 at Katalla had been extremely costly, but it had not been entirely wasted. For all that year supplies were taken upriver to the crucial Glacier Bridge site.

Teams of men under the direction of Assistant Superintendent "Big Mike" Sullivan crossed the river and began the heavy rock work in Abercrombie Canyon.

So far nothing had been "easy" in the building of this railroad, and a seemingly simple task of moving freight up a river was no exception. To move freight on the Copper River meant to haul supplies up the river in shallow draft rigs pulled by ropes from shore. Tom White, the oil discoverer, headed this important segment of operation. For this work, he established a base camp on Kokinhenic Island on the Copper River flats, and hired every shallow draft rig that would float, including Indian canoes.

This cumbersome method of moving supplies allowed the establishment of four wall tent camps that first summer that were equipped to last through the winter.

At this point in 1907 when extraordinary feats were becoming the norm, the 70-ton river steamer *Chittyna* was moved from Valdez over the Marshall Pass and down the Tasnuna River to the Copper River.

The *Chittyna* was hauled overland in bundles on huge freight sleds. The largest single piece was a 5,700-pound boiler. There was no road to follow. No highway or broken trail—only frozen rivers and the mountains. At the confluence of the Tasnuna and the Copper, the steamer was assembled and put into service on the upper Copper River.

George Hazelet was in charge of getting the steamship in, and he hired Andrew J. Meals and his son George to haul the heavy parts over the Tasnuna Pass to the mouth of the river for assembly.

George Meals took the boiler in. He recalled that, "I worked freighting and packing from 1903 to 1910, mostly in the Copper River and Slate Creek, so handling heavy stuff was in our line.

"I started hauling for the Copper River & Northwestern Railway in the fall of 1905 and winter of 1906 to Keystone Canyon. . . . I got paid by the pound and some by the day or trip.

"Well, in February 1907 the riverboat *Chittyna* arrived in bundles, also some 20 or more horses [arrived]. They started moving in and breaking trail."

Breaking trail over ice and snow required patience, imagination and strong horses.

A man on snowshoes would lead a soft-shod horse over the light snow to pack it down. The main body of horses followed the lead horse to further pack the

trail. The sleds came last. The lead horse was used only for a short distance and then returned to the string because breaking trail was grueling work.

(*Sharp-shod* horses wore shoes with protruding sharp nails for traction. *Soft-shod* horses had neither sharp shoes nor snowshoes. Snowshoes had been used effectively by Jack Dalton and by Abercrombie. Abercrombie noted that the horses appreciated the snowshoes, because without them they fell through and wrenched themselves badly.)

The first sleds, loaded with the bundles of parts for the steamship, broke the trail for the largest sled-load of all, the boiler.

"I left March 12th with the boiler," Meals said. "It weighed 5,700 pounds. Had a heavy sled made for it. I didn't like the hitch but the boss thought it was okay. In making turns the horses would be pulling on only one tug and throw the sled off the trail, which it did before we got off the streets, and upset. I told the boss it was the hitch but he said it was the drivers. Took some time and work to get back on the trail, so I asked him to go aways with me.

"Didn't get very far till we were upset again. He told me I was right and to put on a hitch that would work. I put an evener and each horse on a ringtree so the pull came on both tugs. No more trouble till we reached Tasnuna."

No more trouble till Tasnuna! That was a 79-mile journey over trackless wilderness with a huge sled carrying a nearly three-ton boiler, through Keystone Canyon on the frozen river and up to the summit of Marshall Pass, 1,700 feet high, in the dead of winter! Here the climb to the summit was a series of sharp turns or "switchbacks" because of the steep grade involved. There was no road other than the trail established by the freighters themselves in hauling freight to the gold "diggings" in the Interior.

"Going up the switch[back] I used a block and tackle in order for the horses to stay on the trail, chain to a tree and as they made a turn, throw the cable off the block. That would give them a straight pull. Used six horses on the cable and one in the staves. Took three or four days to reach the summit.

"Going down the river in places had to rough-lock [hitch ropes to the trees, hauling back on the sled] to keep it from breaking loose and running over the horses pulling it.

"Once on the ice we made good time and overtook the rest of the outfit."

Most of the parts were now at the mouth of the Tasnuna ready for assembly.

The steamship was double-decked, 110 feet long, 23 feet wide, with a draft of only 22 inches of water fully loaded. It was built by Joe Supple of Portland, and assembled under the direction of Captain George Hill.

STEVE SHELDON MUSEUM, HAINES

Left—The steamboat *Chitina* pushed ashore by a small ice jam, May 22, 1909. She was pulled off undamaged.

Below—Freighting up the switchback toward Thompson Pass on the Valdez Trail. The rigs in the lower photo have reached the summit.

GUY F. CAMERON PHOTO

GUY F. CAMERON PHOTO

In May some missing parts came, and Meals was asked to take them in. But he waited for June and breakup's end.

"Some of it was too heavy to pack, so dry sledded it to the river and got some Siwash to boat it the rest of the way. . . ." The missing part was a steam winch weighing 3,900 pounds. It had to be taken on sleds drawn by ten horses, because it was too heavy for wagons. You can bet the "Siwash boat" was no Indian canoe; more likely an exceedingly stout raft.

Although it was believed the steamer would easily run in 30 inches of water, she had equipment for getting over sandbars.

The *Railway & Marine News* in describing the steamer's ingenious equipment claimed that, "In order to get over the worst places a capstan, operated by steam power, will be placed on the forward end of the cabin. This derrick is intended simply to handle the spars, putting them in place for operation. Should the boat get stuck on a bar, these spars are used to help the boat over in exactly the same manner as a person lying on his face on the floor might hitch himself along with his elbows. This, together with the action of the wheel, forming a heavy suction to draw the sand from under the hull, enables these boats to actually pass over bars which have several inches less water than the boat draws. Then, too, all the main timbers, together with the planking, are made in one continuous piece by attaching the butts together by

straps so that the hull can actually conform itself, to a certain extent, to the contour of the bar."

The ship's reassembly was completed in July. On July 27, 1907, after a successful trip from the mouth of the Tasnuna her arrival in the Copper Center was reported. Here she took on a load of wood and started back down the river. By August she had felt out the river bottom and was navigating the Copper and Chitina rivers above Abercrombie Rapids for a distance of 170 miles.

3 HEADED FOR THE COPPER RIVER

Spring 1908 brought the first big push of the construction. It was estimated that by mid-April, 3,000 more men would be on the payroll, and the audit division was preparing for the expected work load. There were reports of more new engines on order, and J. R. Van Cleve, master mechanic for the Alaska Central Railroad, was hired as master mechanic for the south end of the Copper River & Northwestern.

The first construction goal was to reach Rapids Landing and link up with the steamer *Chittyna*. To do this a locomotive had to cross the Copper River twice: once at Flag Point (Mile 27) and again at Miles Glacier (Mile 49). At Miles Glacier the train would have to cross tracks laid directly on the ice. Mile 27 could be crossed, as soon as the rails reached that point, on a temporary pile trestle.

The tough job of taking an engine across the river at these two points was given to a tough man, H. R. "Rotary Bill" Simpson. Rotary Bill had been master mechanic with Michael Heney on the White Pass & Yukon Railroad. He was now put in charge of the north end of the construction, as master mechanic.

Since the primary goal of the season's construction was to lay tracks to Miles Glacier by October, it was imperative to reach Flag Point (Mile 27), the first crossing of the Copper River, as quickly as possible. Almost 22 miles of pile-driven trestles separated Eyak Lake from the Copper River. The trestle went down rapidly and was slowed only by the cuts at Alaganik.

It was only a matter of time until Rotary Bill and his crew could reach Flag Point and make the first crossing of the Copper River.

The Alaganik rock cut was completed in early May and once more the rails had "clear sailing" toward the Copper River.

On July 4, 1908, the first train crossed the Copper River. The railroad was becoming a reality. The *Cordova Alaskan* waxed whimsical: "Crossed the Rubicon. M. J. Heney, the railroad builder, has crossed the Copper River with his iron horses and is

K. KENNEDY PHOTO. ALASKA HISTORICAL LIBRARY

Steamboat landing above Abercrombie Rapids on the Copper River.

now laying track on the island. Following up this island, for a distance of five miles, he makes another leap to the other side of the river and from there hastens to the coal fields. It is the marvel of men familiar with railroad construction to note the progress being made by Heney and his bunch of hustlers. If someone doesn't head him off down at the coal fields, he'll scare old Juneau to death by running an engine into the place some time in the near future. That would be a shame. Twould, really."

The "Crossing of the Rubicon" was accomplished by a temporary trestle which ran parallel to the Flag Point Bridge, which was still under construction.

Now the attention was on the Katalla Company. It was responsible for building the Flag Point Bridge. The company was also responsible for the Miles Glacier Bridge and the Kuskulana Bridge on the Chitina River.

Work on the Flag Point Bridge was completed on August 10, 1909.

Of the three bridges, the Miles Glacier Bridge was the most crucial. The future of the Copper River & Northwestern Railway depended on its success.

4 BRIDGES ON THE LOWER COPPER

Destined to be called the "Million Dollar Bridge," this thin link between the Miles and Childs glaciers represented success or failure to the entire Copper River & Northwestern Railway venture—there was no other way across. And they had to get across because until the bridge was completed work above the glacier area could only proceed at an iceworm's crawl.

Because Heney's original survey and suggested routing over the river had been rejected by competent engineers as impossible, certainly unfeasible, the entire Copper River route had been rejected and forgotten, until Michael Heney's quarter-of-a-million-dollar "April Fool's joke" revived it.

But now that Heney was at the Copper River & Northwestern Railway's helm it would be done. All that his crew had to do was to build that impossible bridge; build it on time and build it strong. That was it!

The Miles Glacier Bridge would have to be stronger than any bridge built up to that time as it would stretch across the faces of two active and treacherous glaciers. And there was the river to face.

The Copper was everything that ornery rivers are noted for, and then some. Besides icebergs, rapids and shifting sandbars there was the "Copper River wind," a force to be reckoned with as it coated everything in its path with sheaths of solid ice. Railroad legend

holds that the force of this wind was so great that when the railroad was running, a chain was fastened to the entrance to the Flag Point Bridge (Mile 27), and if the chain stuck straight out in the wind, the trains didn't cross.

The blue-white snout of Childs Glacier extended farther into the Copper River than it does today. Bergs crashing from the 300-foot-high face of this active glacier kept the men lining the boats upriver in danger of their lives as the great bergs sloughed off, sending tidal waves of extremely destructive force across and down the river.

But it was Miles Glacier, on the upriver side of the bridge, that created the greatest frustration for the construction crews. The tidal waves from this glacier, washing downstream with the current, were known to demolish the "dolphins" for the ferry landing (a dolphin is a bundle of six to eight pilings lashed together at the top for greater strength than single pilings. Usually used where boats land, to cushion the landing.) Within minutes, the crews would be back at redriving these dolphins, as the ferry was the main method of transporting men and material across the river. Sometimes, within minutes, the dolphins would be washed out again.

Miles Glacier was a sheet of ice larger than all the glaciers of Switzerland combined, and it covered more than half of the lake that now lies in front of it. This was the glacier described by Abercrombie as "a sheet of ice as far as the eye could see."

In the geologic past the two had formed one great ice mass covering the Copper River valley and adjoining coastal area.

Miles Glacier caused additional construction problems with massive icebergs. One berg was recorded in 1908 as 50 by 100 feet, 8 feet out of the water and moving at 7.2 miles per hour in spite of the fact that it was dragging bottom. It was not an unusual iceberg. A means to protect the bridge pier from the onslaught of 1,000-pound ice chunks had to be devised.

The bridge site was a busy place. Due to the time limit imposed by Congress, work had to go on simultaneously above, below and on the bridge. All this investment in time, money and labor, and no one could be absolutely sure that the bridge could be built at all! Pessimists confidently predicted the first spring breakup would take it along the same route as the Katalla breakwater.

In 1907 and 1908 while the rest of the railroad crew was intent upon building the line from Cordova to Miles Glacier, bridge foreman A. C. O'Neel took soundings, recorded temperatures, ice conditions, breakups, river rises and falls and noted the size of bergs from Miles Glacier.

When the bridge site was selected in the summer of 1907, the first meteorological soundings were also begun. Assistant bridge engineer A. O. Johnson was sent to the glacier bridge site in February of 1908 to continue this work. At that time the track ended at Mile 9, so Johnson sledded in with horses and equipment. The equipment made the last two and one-half miles of the journey over the ice to the bridge site via a cable and the steam winch on the drill Johnson brought. Johnson then proceeded to make test borings, lay out base lines and set permanent markers. He also prepared an accurate set of maps of the river bottom.

The problems facing bridge construction were dealt with as matters of fact, as illustrated by the following engineering report excerpt. "Data extending over a number of years in reference to the weather, amount of water carried by the Copper River, and rainfall on its watershed, was not available on account of the newness of the country. The earliest obtainable data being August 1907.

"Maximum fluxuation of the river was found to be 24 feet," a sizable rise and fall, "the greatest flow of icebergs occurring during the high water in July and August. Observations taken during 1907 showed icebergs passing the proposed bridge site projecting 20 feet out of the water. This would require the bottom of the lower chord to be not less than 35 feet above high water. Observations which we took in 1908 gave a current velocity of 9.7 miles per hour, with the water six feet above low water mark. The bed of the river and the bars are composed of boulders from one cubic foot to ten or twelve cubic yards in size."

His findings reflect the abrupt change in climate between the lower part of the river and the upper. In 1908-1909, the lowest temperature at the glaciers was 22 degrees below zero, while 20 miles away at the river mouth, Flag Point, it was only eight degrees below zero. At Cordova, 27 miles to the westward, it is doubtful if the temperature dropped to zero in that same year.

Wind velocities in the Copper River were recorded at a startling 81 and 96 miles per hour.

By the end of 1908, after observing the ice flow all summer, O'Neel had laid his basic plan for the Miles Glacier Bridge. The bridge was to consist of four spans, two of 400 feet, one of 300 feet and the critical span, span #3, which crossed the swiftest water and straddled the greatest ice flow, was to be 450 feet. The critical span was originally designed to be erected by cantilever methods in two parts; half of the span supported by span #2 and the other half by span #4. The two parts would connect in the center upon completion. However, the cantilever procedure was abandoned as slower and more expensive, and the

450-foot section was assembled as a simple truss span upon falsework through the ice. The decision as to whether to erect cantilever or upon falsework was delayed as it depended greatly upon weather conditions at the time of erection.

The third span was the key to the bridge, and the greatest gamble.

Engineer O'Neel wrote: "We decided that we could safely erect spans #1 and #2 between April 1st, when the wind and general weather conditions would not be very severe, and the breaking up of the river. Span #3 could possibly be erected in the same way, but it was uncertain. Span #4 could be erected on falsework at any time except during high water."

Because the piers had to be sunk deep into the river's bottom, they would be built on pneumatic caissons, air-tight underwater construction chambers. Open at the bottom to permit excavation, they sink gradually as river bottom material is dug out. Water is kept out by air pressure. At the proper level, the caissons are concreted in. The bridge piers are then built upon them.

To protect the bridge from the anticipated battering of icebergs, Mr. O'Neel designed detached icebreakers which resembled eccentric pyramids. Pneumatic caissons were used as a foundation for these also. A protective barricade of steel rails bedded in concrete was to surround the icebreakers and piers.

Underlying all plans was the rapidly diminishing time allowance. The bridge had to be completed during 1910. In the meantime the uncompleted bridge could not be allowed to cause a work stoppage on the other side. Goods had to pass the bridge site, but because of the heavy ice flow a temporary pile trestle (as had been done at the other bridge sites) could not be driven.

It was a problem to which O'Neel gave much thought. Until the bridge was built, it remained a severe bottleneck difficult to get supplies past.

5 UP THE UNTAMED RIVER

The supplies had to keep rolling—winter or summer, spring or fall, materials for the bridges and rock work had to move upriver. And because the Copper River was not navigable below the glaciers, everything was moved by hand and would be until the tracks were laid that far. "Grub," tents, picks, shovels, horses, steel caissons, power plants, steam points and pipe—all the gear necessary to build a first-class, heavy-gauge steel bridge, proceed beyond it, and supply the work camps—had to be brought up the river in barges or canoes, all towed by hand. Men toiled up the jungle-thick tangle of underbrush at the river's edge, pulling the boats or sledges while one man stayed in the craft to keep it offshore in the current. Some of the men had to wade in the glacier-chilled water to hold the boat off the rocks or snags. Tough western horses taken upstream to help in the moving of cargo above the bridge had to be moved up through the lower Copper in small flat-bottomed boats with one horse per boat. To drag these upriver required up to 20 men for one horse! Occasionally the horse could walk along favorable stretches, but most of the time he had to be towed. In rough spots, progress by this method was hardly over a mile a day.

It was cruel labor, performed in the most beastly weather through almost impossible underbrush and it was slow going.

The jungle-thick growth comes from the incredible rainfall of this region. The verdant coastal strip is one of the wettest spots on earth; rainfall in wet years approaches—and sometimes exceeds—200 inches. More than 16 feet of rainfall! It has been known to pour nine inches in a single day, after which it can settle down to a steady downpour of several inches per day for weeks. Dozens of trestles crossed dry beds that became, in rainy periods, raging torrents that savagely tore out new channels, ripping the pilings out and depositing them in some hapless fisherman's net out on the Copper River flats.

But with a will and a way and a bawdy song, somehow the goods moved up.

"There were hundreds of us," said an old-timer who wished to remain anonymous, "and it was pretty much the same with all of us.

"By the spring of 1908 the road had been built about 20 miles from Cordova but the builders were having trouble so in desperation they sent for me. The call was really not so personal; the company simply put an ad in one of the Seattle papers saying that anyone who wanted to work on a railway in Alaska and had $15 for steerage fare to Cordova would get the proper consideration in the matter on arrival.

"I met the qualifications, so I got a ticket on the old *SS Northwestern*, which was notorious for not sailing but for rolling its way through the billows.

"When I got to Cordova they gave me a pick and shovel and pointed in the direction of Kennecott and said, 'Dig,' or words to that effect. Well, I wrought mightily for a while, but I guess at times I straightened up and gazed sort of wistfully in the direction of the mines. The company decided my talents were not being used to best advantage.

"They could see I was a born leader, so they made me an ax man who went ahead of the construction, surveying and laying out the route. I was to dash ahead cutting down brush, trees and devil's club!

"The company supplied us generously with everything that we needed in the way of tents for shelter and food to eat and boats and pack sacks to move along with. We did not have much in the way of fresh stuff such as people nowadays demand, but we were tough and we knew it and we just had a whale of a good time.

"Down in the lower Copper where we worked the first summer it rained and blew most of the time and of course the tents leaked some and fire wood was wet and we worked in hip boots, rain coats and rain hats most of the time. We moved camp every few miles as we worked along up the Copper River. We moved our equipment and supplies up river by piling it into a riverboat and "lining" it up.

"Riverboats are long and narrow and rather deep. Lining a boat means fastening 100 feet of rope on the bow of the boat by a 'bridle' and putting a man in the stern who is supposedly good at keeping the boat out in the channel or off the rocks and around the eddies. More probably it was one who was too lazy to pull on the rope. Then all the other men, from one to 15, get on the rope and walk along the riverbank and pull the boat along.

"Progress along the river was slow and sometimes monotonous, and to relieve our spirits we often indulged in some sweet little ditty, for instance:

Home, boys, home; it's home we ought to be,
Home, boys, home; in God's countree,
Where the rains don't fall, and the winds
don't blow,
And we'll come back to the Copper in a
pig's ————. . . .

"There were a lot of verses to this, but some of them were a bit indelicate.

"One of the best men we had for steering a boat in the stern was a curly headed fellow by the name of Homer Hadley. He was a jolly fellow, a good engineer, and a good man to have in any camp. He invariably smoked a big Wellington pipe. One day the boat was rounding a point where the river was swift, when the current caught it and the boys pulling the boat didn't ease up enough on the rope and the boat rolled over in the river. Everything went in the river including the fellow steering, Hadley. But pretty soon he bobbed up about 100 feet downstream and being a fair swimmer he made it to shore. He still had the pipe in his mouth, but it will have to be admitted the light was out."

All that summer of 1908 the rails reached out up the Copper. By contract Heney had to reach the glaciers that fall so a train could cross the ice. Then he could finish the rail to Abercrombie Landing in the spring to join the steamer *Chittyna*. Supplies for all the

Below—Building one of the steel bridges on the railroad line.
Bottom left—E. A. Hegg was best known for his photographs, but the sign on his tent at Tiekel shows he also engaged in other enterprises. It advertises "Cigars, Fruit, Books, Papers."
Bottom center—The *Saratoga* was a unit of the Northwestern Steamship Company, which became part of the Alaska Steamship Company, and helped carry materials to build early Cordova and the railroad. She was wrecked on Busby Island in Prince William Sound on March 20, 1908.
Right—A construction scene during the building of the railroad.
Bottom right—A steam shovel at work in Abercrombie Canyon.

COURTESY PHYLLIS CARLSON

RALPH E. MACKAY COLLECTION

RALPH E. MACKAY COLLECTION

MOSS COLLECTION. ALASKA HISTORICAL LIBRARY

STEVE SHELDON MUSEUM, HAINES

P. S. HUNT PHOTO, FROM THE RALPH E. MACKAY COLLECTION

E. A. HEGG PHOTO, COURTESY PHYLLIS CARLSON

STEVE SHELDON MUSEUM, HAINES   STEVE SHELDON MUSEUM, HAINES

E. A. HEGG PHOTO, ALASKA HISTORICAL LIBRARY

Top—An excursion party from Valdez inspects the new Copper River line on May 31, 1908.

Middle left—Lunchtime on the grade near Tunnel Point, May 13, 1909.

Middle right—M. J. Heney's Camp 18 along the Copper River, September 29, 1908, above, and Camp 49 on the rail line, May 5, 1909, below.

Bottom—Bridge building on the Copper River flats, August 21, 1908.

construction camps could then move more rapidly. The hookup with the bridge site was essential as it provided O'Neel with his lifeline and building materials. O'Neel had to be ready to build when the ice was ready—he couldn't wait on supplies.

As freezeup approached, it appeared they could not reach the glacier camp, so the last four miles of track were laid on a temporary foundation on the ground. They reached the glacier crossing, Mile 49, in October.

By that time the weather was becoming too severe to continue and most construction was closed for the season. However, some activity continued at the bridge site. Because O'Neel hoped to begin sinking two of the caissons simultaneously through the ice in March to avoid the icebergs and waves common during the summer, crews were kept at the Glacier Bridge camp all winter. Supply trains for the bridge camp also kept rolling during the winter.

6 WINTER, 1908-1909, OR: THREE WEEKS IN A SNOWBOUND CABOOSE

Before winter set in, a full-scale camp had been erected at Childs Glacier; one of the main construction camps on the Copper River & Northwestern. Here were snug wooden barracks and cabins, a commissary, and the necessary power plants, compressors, for the difficult work ahead.

(Jack McCord from the "Battle of B. S. Hill" was in charge of the commissary. He was now being called "Lightfoot Mac, the Copper River Scout," and by all accounts was living up to his colorful personality.)

According to O'Neel, all of the heavy equipment was as self-contained as possible, so that foundation work for this temporary but necessary machinery could be kept simple. He rested the big compressors and other heavy equipment on foundations made of 12- by 12-inch timbers, drift-bolted together and placed directly on the ground. The only precaution taken in placing the equipment was to excavate any "filled ground." This assured that the big machinery rested on level solid ground. He reported almost no trouble from vibration, although the machinery ran almost continuously for nine consecutive months.

The plans for the bridge had jelled at last. The site was moved 300 feet upstream. The new crossing took advantage of an ancient glacial moraine which had left a gravel island in midstream. O'Neel planned to utilize the moraine for the placement of the second pier. Three piers would have to be built and caissons would serve as foundation material.

It was another severe winter with deep snows, alternating thaws, rain and more snow. In February, just a month before work was to begin on the Miles Glacier Bridge, disaster struck. A huge lake, imprisoned on Miles Glacier, broke loose and devastated the valley, flooding the country down to Flag Point. The last four miles of railroad track were torn out and piled with ice and drift.

The flood washed out O'Neel's plans right along with the track, for now it would be impossible to repair the track and reach the glacier camp before April or May.

The disaster occurred on February 10, and A. O. Johnson and another engineer, E. Mullett, immediately "mushed" out to Katalla, where there was a wireless to send the news to Cordova. Johnson and Mullett told of flooding for an estimated 20 square miles. Bridges and trestles washed out while ice and drift debris piled in fantastic disarray over the tracks. The water level rose steadily for 52 hours until a maximum of 21 feet increase in water level was reached. Damage, not counting the delay, was estimated at $1 million.

The time loss was ultimately the worst of it because it pushed the work on the bridge, and ultimately the work on the far end of the line, into the next two winters. This meant that because of the Congressional time limit men would be forced to work in actual temperatures of 40 to 60 degrees below zero with accompanying winds frequently in excess of 60 miles per hour. The chill factor of such a combination is difficult to describe, and beyond imagining.

But it had happened. Trains left Cordova immediately for the area.

A supply train with two locomotives (Nos. 20 and 21) and a rotary snowplow left Cordova for the bridge site. They were caught in a blizzard near Hot Cake Channel, where an earlier group had been stranded for three weeks with nothing to eat but hot cakes. The crew of this train was better off; they were stranded for a like amount of time, but they had a carload of food, a warm caboose and each other for company.

Just how the men spent their time while they were snowed in was told by one of the men in the lobby of the McCormack Hotel in Cordova as he sat in the barber chair getting his hair "made civilized" again.

"We started out on the 17th of February at 4:45 a.m., expecting to get to Miles Glacier that night, but we didn't make it. We struck some pretty deep snow out from Round Island [just above the Flag Point Bridge], and from there on it got deeper. The Copper River wind was blowing about 55 or 60 miles an hour and the snow was drifting bad.

"Finally the rotary ran out of water so we had to stop and siphon water to her from the engines. They

Top—Snows piled deep on the Copper River line. This locomotive is nearly buried in the stuff, with only her steam domes showing.
Middle—Digging out a snowed-in train.
Bottom—A snowslide at Station 2770, May 5, 1909.

Little No. 3 is one of the seven Dickson saddletank dinkies acquired early in 1907. At the right is No. 20, a Rhode Island class 2-8-0 manufactured by the American Locomotive Company in 1907 and acquired by the Copper River line in November of that year. The road had four of these locomotives, with consecutive serial numbers. (E. A. Hegg photo, Alaska Historical Library)

couldn't pull the train and push the plow, so they cut off and plowed on up to Hot Cake Channel bridge, which was only about eight telegraph poles and a half away, and left the rotary on the bridge and went back for the train. The engines got back to the train all right, but they couldn't move it, and after we had tried a while we tried to get to the bridge with the engine, but the snow had drifted so bad by that time that we couldn't move, so there we were. There was a carload of grub in the train and a cook stove in Wales' caboose, which made things look brighter.

"How did everybody take it? Well, I'll tell you. The super was along, you know, and he took it pretty bad for a while, but finally he says, 'Hell, it ain't no use looking sour about it, is there?' We said 'no'; so he was right jolly after that.

"Wales, he was along. He was the 'con' on the rotary outfit, and kind of acted as secretary to the super. Wales was considerably overworked. Ernie Warriner, better known as the Smiling Kid, was braking for Wales, and done the porter work in the caboose. He was fireman for the heating stove, and talked of how he would like to be promoted to firing a donkey [engine] in the spring. Frank Townsend, the rotary engineer, read the blood and thunder stories in the Blue Book magazine to his smoke agent Fred O'Neil. You know him? Tennessee, the old Copper River scout and giraffe hunter? Well, he'd come down to the caboose every day or two and talk and josh, but he'd look kind of blue at times. They say he is kind of sweet on a Cordova fair one, which was the reason for his indigo spells.

"Dan Barrett, the hogger on No. 20, never said much. Fact is, he couldn't for chewing tobacco and trying to oil his engine; but his fireman, Price Nettleton, better known as the Society Kid, was complaining all the time about missing all the shows and dances in town. Little Tom Thumb-erly was running the "21," and sat in the caboose telling about the things that happened out around Kamloops. Charley Stevens, the kid-gloved fireman, was firing for Tom. "Steve" just smoked cigarettes and kept his face pointed toward Pike Street, Seattle.

"The Copper River winds didn't have any effect on Clyde Dunlap's flow of hot air. He could peddle it right against the wind. He was the rotary pilot.

"We had a change of weather about the ninth day out. It got worse . . .

"Jimmy Arnot was braking on the smoky end of the local. He's only about 25, and it's scandalous to hear him talk about railroading back in 1889. Walter DeLong was the hind shack on that layout. He didn't have much to do and he did it well. Tommy Brady, known as the Harp, the man with the silver tongue and the velvet voice, was the local's brains, and we all agreed that he was the smoothest man at peddling hot air that we ever knew. When he would start to throwing out his warm zone in that caboose, the thermometer would rise two or three degrees.

"After a while the snow quit drifting a little and we got shoveled out and went on to the glacier and back to town. We were a pretty tired, bewhiskered looking bunch when we got in after twenty-two days on them flats."

Although it had been estimated by some that it would be July before the damage was fixed, another temporary track was laid on the uncertain new ice. On March 22, 1909, a track was laid across the Copper River on the ice and the first train was taken across.

The *Cordova Alaskan* carried the story: "Copper River is Conquered. The track is clear. Today at seven minutes past two, the iron horse neighed across the lake at Childs Glacier and "Rotary Bill" smiled. He is the hero who has conquered the Copper River and opened the road for traffic. Now watch the freight go to the front. In one afternoon the train can take more freight to Abercrombie Canyon than can be taken over the Valdez Trail in six months. The greatest obstacle to reaching the end of the road was the overflowing of the track at places where it was not raised to grade last fall. Had it not been for this ice the train would have been to the canyon in less than a day after leaving the dock here."

Almost the first piece of freight taken up Abercrombie Canyon by this route was the steamship *Tonsina*.

On July 2, 1909, the steamship *Tonsina* joined her sister steamer *Chitina*. (The newer spelling of Chittyna, which had been adopted for the river and the town, was now taken for the steamship.)

The *Tonsina* was assembled and launched at Rapids Landing, the steamship slip at the upper end of Abercrombie Rapids. The *Tonsina* was a bit larger, measuring 120 feet. The new vessel was built by G. H. Hill. She had two 300-horsepower engines with oil-fired boilers to turn a 16½-foot paddlewheel on the stern. Her skippers were Captain Pinkerton and Captain Bailey. She was built to carry the passengers that the Copper River & Northwestern was to bring that summer. The 14 staterooms each featured two berths. The entire steamship was equipped with the most modern systems available. Electric lights and steam heat were found throughout.

Another smaller sternwheeler, the *Gulkana*, was placed in service on Miles Lake supplying the service for the missing bridge link that summer of 1909. On July 29, it was announced that the Copper River & Northwestern was a common carrier for freight and passengers with service from Cordova to Rapids Landing, where connections could be made with the steamships now plying the upper river. Passenger fare to Rapids Landing was $8, or $11 round trip.

The keel and framework for another river steamship had already been put down by builder Thayer. It was to be named *Nizina*, and was in service that same summer. The total cost of building these three steamships was $215,000.

The steamboat *Nizina* docked at Camp 55 on the Copper River.

These steamboats kept busy the following summer, too. One of the workers in an advance camp recalled that, "The three sternwheelers, the steamboats, plied the river very busily all the summer of 1910 from Tiekel to Chitina, a distance of 30 miles. They hauled up great quantities of supplies and equipment, particularly bridge material for the Kuskulana Bridge at Mile 146. But not only for that one. There is a total of over eight miles of bridges on the Copper River & Northwestern route. The crossing at Chitina originally called for a steel bridge, too, but the company decided on a wooden trestle, letting it go out with the ice each spring and redriving it. It was originally thought that there wasn't enough copper to justify the expense, but more copper turned up than expected, and the steel bridge would have been the cheaper structure in the long run.

"The steamboats also brought up lumber and hardware to build the town of Chitina, and another town sprang up overnight.

"The men who operated the steamboats the three seasons on the Copper River were all mighty good steamboat men from the Mississippi. They knew steamboats and the Mississippi River all right, but they had to learn about the Copper. This river flows so fast that it moves tremendous lots of sand and small boulders down toward the ocean in high water. For this reason it is continually changing channels, which chase back and forth from one side to the other.

Where there was a deep channel one day there could be impossibly shallow water the next. The steamboat men found that due to long and toilsome experience on the river, some of the Indians had acquired an uncanny sense of the channels. They seemed to feel which channels would keep on deep, and which would fade into shallow water where the steamboat would ride onto a sandbar and get stuck so high and tight it might take hours or even days to get off.

"For this reason they hired some of the husky, intelligent Indians to sit in the pilot house and make the best guesses they could. It appeared that their guesses averaged somewhat better than the white man's. These Indian 'piolets' were treated with great consideration and respect, and Tony Pete and Sport MacAllister were wondrous proud as they sat in the 'piolet house' and told the white captain where to go."

7 SINKING THE CAISSONS

Midway through April the focus was again at the glacier bridge site as work began on the crucial sinking of the caissons.

A better method of getting supplies to and from the three piers was needed. Generally, a trolley system would be utilized immediately but two construction firms had claimed that the trolley could not be built saying that there was no carrier made that would operate over such a long distance (1,800 feet). But O'Neel's crews thought differently and utilizing their different talents they built the trolley that couldn't be built. The heaviest load carried by this cableway was the man lock, which weighed two and one-half tons.

Other building included: two 60-foot towers, one on each bank; double 60-foot towers on the edges of the crib above the first caisson to carry the compressed air pipe; and above it a 1- by 12-inch plank footbridge suspended by cables.

Now there were several ways to cross the river. There was the footbridge, a hair-raising walk high over the Copper River. There was the ferry *Gulkana*, or the launch that scuttled back and forth, usually skirting the glacier cautiously. There was a scow drawn back and forth by cables on a steam winch and there was the cable trolley.

Because the river was showing signs of breaking up, only the first caisson was begun on ice, out of the path of heavy ice drifts. On May 4th it was ready for sinking. No time was lost in the race against the anticipated breakup. With both air compressors working at full tilt to maintain the vital air pressure, men worked at excavating while caulking the still not air-tight caisson chamber. The river began to break

Heney's construction crews push the Copper River & Northwestern Railway along the bank of the Copper River, Mile 125 to Mile 134, August 1910.

E. A. HEGG PHOTO. ALASKA HISTORICAL LIBRARY

ALASKA HISTORICAL LIBRARY

E. A. HEGG PHOTO. ALASKA HISTORICAL LIBRARY

COURTESY JEAN DETTINGER

RALPH E. MACKAY COLLECTION

up three days after crews began sinking the caisson. On May 9th all ice was out of the river, but it was still too early for the glaciers to begin discharging icebergs. By June 16th when the glacial ice began, the "cutting edge" of the first caisson was ten feet below the bed of the river.

The caisson was landed on solid hardpan 36 feet deep in the river's bottom on July 14th. The first pier, built on this caisson, was completed August 24th, "without any serious accidents," according to O'Neel.

The battle against the ice was so constant and so generally accepted that little extra attention was given to particular incidents. At one time ice destroyed part of the concrete forms and at another time it completely demolished the tower on the edge of the crib, which had carried the vital air to caisson #3 which was being sunk at the time. Fortunately the cable had been transferred "minutes before" to a new tower supported by cables from the unfinished pier. Although tragedy was averted by mere minutes, these ice incidents were hardly considered worthy of mention.

Caisson #3, which had been started in June, was situated on a sandbar. But the river began rising and covered the bar before the caisson was completely caulked. Fortunately the caisson was anchored to shore by long cables so the men were able to finish the caulking. When all was ready the air was turned on and the lowering of the caisson began. But at that moment a huge iceberg at a point three miles away split from the face of Miles Glacier. Its impact with the Copper sent a powerful wave crashing downriver with a destructive force that completely knocked the caisson off its cribs and carried it downstream where the anchor cables pulled it up against a derrick, which it demolished. When the caisson finally rested against the wrecked derrick, it was six feet downstream, held by the cables, and 18 feet inshore. It was hauled back, jacked into position and sunk without further mishap. Sinking began July 29th and was finished August 24th. The cutting edge was 50 feet under the bed of the river!

Now they could finish pier #3. They built a trestle out from the north shore where the current was light, and on that far shore they set up another rock crusher and concrete mixing plant to speed the work along. The boulders and rock taken from the river banks (where abutments were being built) were crushed for use in the concrete. Because winter would be upon them before the concrete work could be finished, large covering sheds were erected over big piles of sand and crushed rock for the winter's work. After freezeup and snowfall, it would be virtually impossible to obtain these things. By this time, a fair-sized camp had sprung up on the north shore of the river.

Pier #2, the middle pier, was saved for last to avoid summer's high water. It was placed on an artificial island built from gravel in coal sacks. The coal sacks were hauled into position and dumped from the cable trolley; it took 12 days of dumping to make the island. The river was 14 feet deep at this point. The building of the island would have been impossible during high water as the current would have swept the sacks away.

The last pneumatic caisson began sinking on September 27th and it was landed on November 2nd, at the same depth as caisson #1, about 36 feet. After the first ten feet, the excavation was through cemented sand, gravel and boulders.

Men in the caissons flirted constantly with death. Theirs was no safe and sane job. They lived with the possibility of the bends, caused by decompressing too fast; of the lifelines being cut by any one of a dozen catastrophes; and any number of unforeseen accidents.

Although they had a well-equipped plant to supply power and compressed air, extra boilers were kept fired at all times to maintain the lifeline to the men far below the river bottom in case of accident.

A workman on the banks might at any time be witness to a sudden disaster or near-disaster. "One time I was working up there," related old-timer Charlie Cochran, who worked on the ferry landing at the time, "when a scow broke loose from a cable across the river, threatening to cut the air lines.

"It was winter, but they had the ice cut away from around the bridge some way. The pneumatic caissons were going, and they had pipe lines, air and steam, and cables from pier to pier, and a catwalk suspended from the cables, too, weighted with rocks.

"This scow was being hauled across by cable; the cable being taken up by a pile driver on a float. They were about halfway across when the cable broke and the scow drifted free.

"There were whistles tooting and men were getting out of the caissons as fast as they could, risking the bends to get out because the scow was drifting down onto the bridge and might cut the air pipes to the caissons. There was a steam launch working on the river and it was trying to stop the scow, too. It looked bad for awhile, but then the scow drifted down against an icebreaker and that stopped it. When it eventually worked free from there it drifted harmlessly down onto a sandbar."

With the opening of the railroad to traffic, excursions to the glacier bridge became extremely popular. Sometimes tourists were treated to unexpected drama on the footbridge.

In describing the footbridge Charlie Cochran said, "It was quite a contraption, that catwalk. It was stretched across on a couple of cables, and that old

Copper River wind would blow until even the rocks weighting it down didn't help much. There were just a few planks crosswise between the cables, that's all there was.

"Lots of men walked across the catwalk all the time, but I only got on it once. I swore I'd never get on it again. It was a time when they were taking a man out of the caisson with the bends. I walked over to see what was going on. Some places you could hang on because the cable was high enough, but in other places it dipped too low, and you were just out there with the wind and the help of God."

There is a previously unpublished story of a hair-raising event that occurred that year on the footbridge. The two accounts differ in some small details, but in general they agree.

Tom Kelly, an engineer working on the caissons, tells what happened that day on the footbridge. A group of financial people from New York was visiting the bridge site. They had with them "a very attractive magazine writer, a lady with red hair, and wearing a gorgeous green 'princess' dress. It was because of her that a near catastrophe happened that day. A. C. O'Neel, Dr. Whiting, Douglas the auditor, the lady, and another man were walking south to the main camp over a slender cable footbridge. . . . There was a very stringent rule that people on the walkway should never be closer than ten feet. On that day the gentlemen were escorting the lady over the works and were returning, with the lady in the middle. Making conversation they gradually 'bunched up.' I happened to be visiting the north caisson, whose crew I had saved from a blowout a few nights before, and talking to Hanson. . . . We were talking about how our 'top brass' were 'fussed' by the red-headed girl when it happened. A cocky young 'peavy man' named Harris, from Tacoma, was coming north toward us. Instead of waiting for the bridge to clear, he came on and met the group about halfway. They leaned sideways to let him pass and over went the footbridge!

"I scampered down, yelling to hang on, with Hanson at my heels. 'What do you want me to do, Mr. Kelly?' he yelled. I replied, 'Throw Harris overboard, and then help me!' He booted Harris out of the way and then, straddling the air pipe and using our arms as uprights, we took hold of the hand ropes, and with scared people helping to climb up on the pipe we slowly righted the footbridge, but we made the lady and the men travel on their hands and knees to the south pier."

"It is also worthy of note," said Mr. Kelly, "That the incident was never publicized in any report. If Mr. O'Neel and Dr. Whiting were lost that day, the story would have been tragically different. I am not sure whether Rex Beach was there that day or not."

Charlie Cochran, who was not so well acquainted with some of the people involved, and was farther away on the sidelines watching, had it as a party of women. He told it this way:

"These women got on that walkway, between the piers. Well, these ladies all got on the same side of that thing and it tipped on them. Luckily they were where they could hang on. They stood there screaming while they hung on for dear life, looking at the river far below. There was one great big fellow, a huge brute he was; who walked across that catwalk all the time. He walked out onto it and his weight uprighted it; he must have weighed 275 pounds. Then he reached over and picked up those women like so many sacks of flour and set some on one side and some on the other.

"The women were good sports about it, though. They laughed and took it all in good spirits."

With a locomotive across the river, construction above the bridge went full speed ahead that summer of 1909; by fall they had reached Tiekel River, at Mile 101. A great deal of the upper river work was hard rock work; blasting tunnels and cuts out of solid rock.

8 SNOOSE, OVERALLS, WHISKEY AND SNOWBALLS

Heney's first contract, to Rapids Landing, was completed October 30, 1908. His second contract was for the line to Tiekel at Mile 101.

Tiekel lies on the Copper River 100 miles from Cordova at the point where the Tiekel River empties into the Copper. At freezeup time when construction ended in the fall of 1909 the track had been laid to Tiekel. The going had been rough as some of the most expensive rock work in railroad building lay between Rapids Landing and Tiekel. Practically the entire line north of Miles Glacier involved heavy excavation. A total of 5,680,000 cubic yards was moved, of which 3,140,000 cubic yards was solid rock. Explosives alone cost $375,000. Over 1,200,000 yards of gravel were excavated by steam shovel at a cost of $290,000.

The heaviest rock work was in Woods Canyon just below Taral. Here it was necessary to blast off thousands of yards of solid rock. All this heavy blasting had far-reaching consequences. One time during exceptionally high water a blast sent tens of thousands of tons of rock into the deep, narrow river channel. The rock and debris sent a wave raging down the canyon with such force that the river's three sternwheelers, which had tied up to avoid the swift waters, were picked up and slammed down with such force that several holes were knocked in the hulls requiring extensive repairs.

Problems, hard work and danger were constantly with the builders of the railroad. So much so that many felt that whiskey and snoose were the only real comforts that construction work offered. It was commonly said among the railroad men that the Copper River & Northwestern Railway was built on "snoose, overalls, whiskey and snowballs."

All during the work of driving the line to Tiekel Michael J. Heney was there, urging the work on, working as hard as any of his men. He was a familiar figure, well-known and liked but, following a shipwreck he was in, the extra strain of severe overexposure showed in his face, though never in his spirit. According to some Heney contributed to the theory that the railway was partially built on whiskey when he placed a case of whiskey in the bushes at the north end of the tunnel at Mile 89. He told the men that the whiskey was theirs as soon as the tunnel was finished. The bore went through in record time.

There was only one strike ever recorded on the Copper River & Northwestern Railway and it was a result of a supply shortage of one of the real essentials of construction life—snoose. Heney ended the big "snoose strike" by rushing a whole freight car loaded with the stuff to the scene.

9 WINTER, 1909-1910: NEITHER SLEET NOR SNOW, NOR COPPER RIVER WIND . . .

Things were progressing well. Heney and his men were pushing the track through and the glacier bridge was gaining a foundation. By freezeup in 1909 two piers were complete and the third caisson was sunk at the bridge. The abutments were done. But there still was more to do and it would have to be done in the bitter cold of winter. One pier had to be finished and the two detached icebreakers built before the last gamble, the erection of the steel spans on falsework through the ice, could begin.

The disagreeable winter work, O'Neel said, could have been avoided if the track had not flooded out that previous February. It was imperative that the bridge be finished during 1910. So, despite the added cost and inconvenience, work was continued around the clock throughout the winter.

It was a severe winter. From September 26th to April 1st it was a battle against cold and wind. The wind blew at a velocity of between 60 and 95 miles per hour "for the greater part of the time," and temperatures were very low.

Preparations for winter were paying off as there was enough sand and crushed rock under cover to complete all the concrete work.

The unusual climate called for an inventive approach to work problems. For the concrete work on pier #2, they built a housing completely around the pier (these piers had, at their greatest part, a diameter of 86 feet); this was to cover the concrete. Steam pipes were wrapped around to keep it from freezing. The concrete was mixed on shore with water at 110 degrees F. The sand and rock were heated to a temperature of about 100 degrees. The concrete was then hauled on the cableway to the pier, where by the time it was dumped it had cooled to about 70 degrees.

Because of the great flow of drift ice around the bridge, detached armored icebreakers were necessary at two of the piers. The caissons for these were constructed and sinking begun in September, about the time the weather turned cold. These icebreakers were sunk to a relatively shallow 20 feet below the riverbed. The water level was considerably down by the end of September when this work began, so that the caissons and cofferdams were out of water on a sand and gravel bar. As the work commenced, the weather turned cold and the winds began their incessant howling. With plunging temperatures and high winds, the "chill factor" was extremely low. To be able to work at all, huge windbreaks were erected around the work-site, and frequently they were blown down. It was difficult and trying work to put these windbreaks back up, and frequently impossible until the wind let up. But the workers were unable to continue without this meager protection, so it had to be done. Building and caulking of these two icebreakers was begun on September 26th, and it was February 10th before the last one was landed.

The last icebreaker, due to the design of the caisson, refused to sink below 19½ feet into the gravel below the riverbed, despite a downward force of 1,410 pounds per square foot, and despite the fact that they had excavated two and one-half feet below the cutting edge. The caisson simply would not sink farther. It was concreted in at that level. This icebreaker was later washed out by a spring breakup and had to be replaced.

Further difficulties were experienced with the cofferdams, but before the middle of March everything was in readiness for the last big gamble; the erection of the spans. This work was set to begin early in April, when the weather should be less severe. The steel spans were to be erected on falsework put through holes cut in the ice, and then driven into the river bottom. This work, being done in winter, would escape the flow of icebergs from Miles Glacier. Between April and the spring breakup would determine whether or not the Copper River & Northwestern Railway would be finished on time, and probably whether or not it could be finished at all.

But the battle for the bridge was not the only one that winter. Once the Copper iced over tracks were going to be laid directly on the river's ice to speed the flow of freight past the bottleneck created by the unfinished bridge. But the unpredictable weather and glacier overflows kept the ice covered with slush and water, so that even the big brawny horses could not cross. There had to be a solution. And there was. So the resilient crews designed and built a flat-bottomed boat-sledge to be pulled across by cable. It was not as efficient as a train, but it was better than nothing, and the supplies must move up.

Here Rotary Bill Simpson and his train took over. The snow piled deep on the tracks that winter; underneath the deep drifts, the track was coated one to two feet with ice. Rotary Bill's train consisted of two engines, a rotary snowplow and a string of coal cars. The rotary had no power of its own for locomotion, only for snowplowing. The train pushed it, the engineer relying on signals from the rotary pilot. It is said that Rotary Bill, when doing this nerve-wracking winter work on the rotary, would chew through the stem of the pipe clenched in his teeth, in less than a month.

This particular trip was especially harrowing. Rotary Bill and the two locomotives started out to go the 50 miles to Tiekel. To break the ice from the tracks, Rotary Bill would signal for full power, hitting the hard coating with the blades of his plow, then back off for another smash. If not done just right, this would put the train off the track.

The first day the train made one and a half miles. Then it disappeared and was not seen or heard of for 31 days when it reached the end of track at Tiekel. During that month Rotary Bill had covered 50 miles and had been off the track about 1,500 times for an average of 30 times to the mile!

Out beyond Tiekel where the men awaited spring in their tents, arguing their "socialistic" theories, hundreds of horses and bobsleds had been taken so that freight could still move after the steamboats were laid up for the winter. There was a long haul by sled on the river ice to the various camps spread out over the next 80 miles.

But here again the river behaved with stubborn contrariness; overflowing, freezing, thawing, piling up windrows of broken ice and slush. It was incredibly hard to get horses and bobsleds through, and sometimes impossible.

Through it all, the advance camps were supplied and set up, and 3,000 men were ready and waiting for the spring work to begin.

Keeping the men supplied meant providing them with "food, snoose, powder, snoose, drill steel, snoose, shovels and other hand tools and snoose," according to an old-timer who waited out the spring in an advance camp.

He recalled that, "During the winter of 1909-1910 our party was camped in our tents about 20 miles up river from Tiekel at the lower end of Woods Canyon. We had not much to do that winter but to get our firewood and wait for spring. But the company kept us there so we would be sure to be ready when the rush of work started up in April. We seem to have been a good-natured lot and kept enough outdoor activity that no bad cases of cabin fever developed. We burned candles and made our beds of spruce boughs. We read a lot by candle light and we also had a lot of good-natured, rousing arguments such as only a lot of young people who are sure they have a solution for all social ills can have. Some of us were extremely radical, bordering almost on Communism. Some of us advocated such extreme things as labor unions, the eight-hour day, the graduated income tax, workmen's compensation and direct primary. I do not recall that anyone had the temerity to suggest such wild things as social security, employment security, paid vacations or public welfare."

10 CALLING THE COPPER'S BLUFF

By April 1910, the steel work on the bridge was ready to begin. The temporary foundations for at least two of the spans were to be pilings driven through the ice and into the river bottom.

The third span was critical. This was the longest span, and the one bridging the greatest flow of water and ice. Mr. O'Neel debated long and hard about this span. Should he build on falsework through the ice? It was a decision to make later. If he elected to build the third span on temporary pilings, it would represent a tremendous gamble against the river, the elements and the unknown time of the spring breakup.

He could not know that high in the huge glaciers a time clock was ticking away, set to go in spring—before the breakup. The extra snow received during the winters of 1907 and 1908 was bearing down in the far reaches of the glacier canyons. A ripple of latent energy was even now moving down the quiet, winter-locked tongues of ice.

December brought a preview. A warm spell came. It lasted two weeks; rain fell in steady torrents, and Miles Glacier began to move. Its forward movement heaved and buckled the ice as far as one-half mile below the bridge, piling up huge rafts of ice which acted as dams. Childs Glacier was also on the move, creating new ice dams below. The water began to back up behind these blockades threatening at any time to break loose and repeat the February 1909 flood.

Counterclockwise from above—A deep rock cut at Mile 120, August 8, 1910. The Irish Prince, Michael J. Heney. Train crew with locomotive No. 50, one of the first big engines on the line. A train at Mile 101, Tiekel. A temporary construction office in a tent along the railroad line, perhaps at Tiekel.

But it was just a warm spell. The weather changed, the glaciers became quiet and the workers breathed easier.

In January the driving of falsework for span #1 began. One-inch steam jets were used to thaw holes in the ice, through which the pilings were inserted and driven a short distance into the river bottom. The ice then froze around these pilings, locking them firmly in nine-foot ice jaws. It was excellent underpinning on which to rest the heavy spans.

In mid-March, while still awaiting delivery of the steel for the bridge spans, the three-bent traveller was built. The traveller was a huge erection device which straddled the work, traveling on tracks on pilings alongside the actual construction. With it the huge steel beams could be lifted and moved about like a child's playthings.

"This traveller," said O'Neel, "was planned having sufficient clearance to erect span #3, should we be fortunate enough to be able to erect it on falsework." The final decision on that would have to await the arrival of the steel for its construction.

So far, none of the bridge steel had arrived. Storms along the main rail lines back in the States had held up the delivery of the crucial construction material for two months!

Chafing and cursing at the delay, O'Neel and his men sweated out delivery of the span members. Without it, they would have to give up the big gamble. Old Man Copper River would win for this year, perhaps forever. Finally on March 17th, almost spring, word came that the first shipment of steel had left Seattle. The bridge builders cursed. Less than two months to go. It looked as though the entire year was lost. The cost of the loss was incalculable, as this would be the third of the four years allowed by Congress, and the line was less than half complete. It was done to Tiekel, Mile 102, with the bridge link missing. Further construction depended heavily on the delivery of materials by train, and trains could not cross the glacier bridge until it was finished.

But then spirits again rose as the trains began discharging the precious cargo on the south bank of the river. With soaring hope came excruciating doubt as the remaining time was measured against the pile of steel on the shore. A thorough inventory was begun. Great care was used in checking, for if one single bolt was missing, its replacement was 1,500 miles away.

April Fool's Day came, and because of the ice jam in front of Childs Glacier, the prankish river started to rise. It lifted the ice, and with the ice rose also the falsework for spans #1 and #2, which were locked in the nine-foot-thick crust. Men were sent down with ice chisels and steam points and set to clearing ice away from the pilings before they could be jerked out of the river bottom and borne downstream. "A large force of men were required in this way night and day to prevent the ice from freezing to the pilings and lifting the falsework as it rose. Even with the greatest watchfulness, the falsework would rise several inches in places, when all work would be concentrated on those points. In some instances, it would not settle to its original position and the blocking under the steel had to be changed. . . ."

On April 5th the last of the steel for the first span was there, and the gamble was engaged. Work began swiftly. All the men worked in a single shift now, from seven a.m. to eleven at night. For meals they rushed to the mess halls, bolted their food and scrambled back to the work. The first 400-foot span was finished in 13 days, despite the ice thawing and necessary chiseling. During this time the steel for the second span had arrived, and its erection began the very same day the first one was finished, April 18th. This 300-foot span was finished in six days flat.

It was not until May 6th that the steel for span #3, the critical 450-foot span, was delivered. On this same day the ice dam broke and the water level fell five feet without any damage; the ice holding the falsework settled down with no downstream movement.

It was as if the Copper River, knowing that the big decision was to be made, was luring O'Neel into a false security.

Plans for the important third span had originally incorporated the cantilever method of construction. The two halves of the span were to be finished and then lowered to meet in the middle, where they would be fastened together. These two cantilever halves would be fastened to pins at the ends of spans #2 and #4 which would be the anchor spans, their weight counterbalancing the unsupported weight of the half-spans until they were joined.

This was the certain method. It was also more costly and would consume a great deal more time than building on falsework.

There were a number of considerations. O'Neel said that, "The reasons for the importance of erecting this span on falsework were: If it were erected cantilever, the bridge could not possibly be opened for traffic earlier than September 1910, and all of the construction material and supplies for the remaining 100 miles of road, to be constructed, would have to be transferred across Miles Glacier Lake by a small barge carrying two cars at a time. For a large percentage of the time there would be so many icebergs in the lake from Miles Glacier that navigation would be impossible. These icebergs would be continually damaging the ferry slips and approaches, requiring constant renewals and frequent cessations of navigation. Taking these interruptions into consideration, the capacity of the ferry would not be sufficient to supply the necessary construction material.

"When the ice went out of the lake the ferry slips and approaches would be entirely destroyed and have to be renewed at a cost of $46,000. The probabilities were that the ferry could not be put into operation until nearly the middle of July, when the first material to be transferred would be span #4, one-half of span #3 and one-half of the erection device, a total of about 2,100 tons. During all this time construction on the upper 100 miles of the road would be very greatly impeded if not at a standstill.

"The direct saving in the cost of the bridge alone, by erecting span #3 on falsework, would be approximately $240,000."

Mr. O'Neel did not mention the cost if ice took the third span out. If he decided to build on falsework, this possibility could not be even considered.

A. C. O'Neel, as bridge builder, had a big decision to make. How much time was left? Two weeks? Almost certainly. A month? Maybe. The ice was very firm now and nine feet thick. In 1908 it had only been five feet thick and had gone out on June 6th. A month and a half? Hardly.

Men waited. Finally O'Neel emerged from his tent and went over to talk to Charlie MacDonald, foreman. Charlie left that conference roaring orders in a voice that at one time could be heard in the highest skysail of a full-rigged ship.

The decision was made. The chips were down and they were going to play their hand for all they were worth.

Still, O'Neel was covering his bets too. He decided as a matter of precaution to fasten the south half of the third span to the anchor device on span #2. The north half of the cantilever could not be so connected, because its anchor span, #4, had not been built yet, and would not be until after breakup.

The Copper, as if it had a devilish mind of its own, was still playing its games with the builders. While they were getting ready to connect the south half to the anchor span, another ice jam broke in front of Childs Glacier, and the river ice moved downstream, carrying the falsework with it. The end to be connected went downstream with this movement until it was 13 inches out of line, and had to be hauled back. This was done with hydraulic jacks, which lifted the steel until the connection could be made with the erection device. Then the cantilever was called into play, and with the help of block and tackle, the steel was hauled back into line. New pilings were driven above the old, and the span lowered onto them for the remainder of the construction of this half, which finished without further trouble.

Meanwhile, O'Neel, with one-half of the third span completed, had to decide whether it was safe to do the other half on the falsework, as planned. The ice had been capricious so far, but there seemed no reason to believe that anything more unusual than these ice jams and small movements in the river cover could be expected. The ice appeared completely firm and showed no evidence of rotting; therefore it could not go out for some time yet. It was May 11th; surely there was plenty of time to finish the second half of span #3, with the crews working long shifts. They set to work with a will.

Two days later the Copper River played its "hole card." Miles Glacier began to move. This movement of the glacier was completely unexpected, because since 1907—in all the observing and measuring of the ice and the river—there had never been any sign of wintertime movement—nothing before spring. But now, ice four miles square and nine feet thick was being pushed forward against the bridge by the power of a tremendous glacier.

Although the first day's movement was only two inches, it was gradually increasing each day, an inexorable force against which every resource must be bent. The nine-foot crust of ice was too thick for saws, so long ice chisels were put to the task. Two shifts of 30 men worked constantly to relieve the pressure by cutting ice from behind the pilings. More than half of the steel for the second half was already in place, so it would take longer to remove it than to finish the span; there was no choice but to fight the relentless advance of Miles Glacier.

More trouble. "At about nine o'clock of the evening of the 14th, two loading beams at the top of the traveller were broken by a lower chord section fouling when the lift was being made." Repair work was prompt and desperate. It was done by eight o'clock the next morning, and work went on without pause. "From this time on the same shift of men worked continuously on the erection until midnight of the 16th, when this span was completed and swung. . . ." (From engineer's report, "Bridge Across Copper River Near Miles Glacier, 1910.")

Forty hours straight without a break, save for meals! No sooner was the last bolt driven home and the steel swung onto its resting place on the pier, than the big traveller was gotten safely to the third pier. By the forenoon of the next day the ice had moved so far that the falsework pilings had been pushed from under the bridge and a great portion of it collapsed. Although the ice did not actually break up for another week, this forward movement was just as deadly, and the bridge had been finished just hours ahead of a movement too swift and steady to battle. Only by scant hours had the big bridge been saved! Even the

Below—Camp Tiekel at Mile 101.

Above—The bridge under construction on April 19, 1910.
Right—One of the company steamboats, perhaps the
Gulkana, approaches Miles Glacier.

Left—Construction at The Million Dollar Bridge below Miles Glacier, May 1910. The third span has been completed in the nick of time, hours before the ice going out carried the falsework away; some of the wreckage lies beneath the finished span. The traveller is on the north pier, waiting for construction of the north span to begin.
Below—Bridge caissons were sunk 60 feet below the riverbed here.

Above—Building the bridge across the Tiekel River.
Left—A pile driver at work on the crossing of the Tiekel River.

pile drivers had to be abandoned on the shattered and crumbling ice.

In the months ahead, when reams of words were written of this tremendous feat, and the praises of O'Neel and E. C. Hawkins sung in lyrical prose, these two men told the simple truth, that they could not have accomplished it without the exceptional devotion of the men who worked on the high steel in every kind of weather, sometimes in cruelly long shifts without a break. No sacrifice seemed too great for these men to make, and no engineer, no matter how brilliant, could have done it without their superhuman efforts. "It was the most amazing exhibition of loyalty, efficiency and endurance that I have ever known." (Also from engineer's report.)

The big bridge was safe. Five million pounds of steel now rode safely on the sturdy armored piers while the great icebreakers below parted the ice and sent it safely past.

There was a feeling of relief bordering on anti-climax in the words of the engineer's report: "Span #4 falsework was completed, pony bents were erected on it, a track lain across and daily trains were operated over the bridge beginning with June 1st [1910]. . . . Span #4 was commenced June 10th and completed June 19th, without any noteworthy incidents."

11 THE ICE ADVANCE

After the tremendous battle they had waged to build the bridge, it would seem that there had been enough drama—too much to suit the bridge builders. But it was not over. Upon completion the big bridge was threatened again, this time by a wholly unexpected and unprecedented advance of the ice.

From the northern margin of Childs Glacier an ice tongue licked out and advanced to within 1,500 feet of the bridge. Cold weather brought it to a welcome halt.

O'Neel records that the ice broke out of the river on May 23rd, and that Childs Glacier, which had advanced quite a distance during the winter, immediately became very active. However, except for the northern margin which was not undercut by the river the glacier was cut back to its former position on the bank. The northern portion began moving forward again in June, gaining speed in August. After August it continued to advance, but more slowly, until freezeup in October.

In August during the fastest forward movement a team of glaciologists from National Geographic Society, under Ralph Stockman Tarr and Lawrence Martin, arrived to study the phenomenon. They were in Alaska making a general study of glaciers along the southern coast, and were in time to observe, measure and comment on the spectacular "surge" in Miles and Childs glaciers.

The advance of Childs Glacier was obviously undercutting the opposite bank, tearing out a new channel for the river. Where there had been a well-worn path along that bank, all was now fallen into the river, and trees and brush on the inside of the trail were now overhanging the water, ready to be washed away with the next big "slough."

This central portion of Childs Glacier, though it advanced quite rapidly, even forcing the river into a new channel, still was equipped with a "self-governor," the undercutting action of the river. Therefore, its total advance is unknown. This constant eating away of the glacier's face kept its advance to a minimum, and when the water was high, even resulted in a slight recession due to greater sloughing of the ice. It was the opinion of the glaciologists that, without this undercutting action of the river, the glacier would have completely overridden the railroad and obliterated it, bridge and all.

However, the northern lobe caused the greatest consternation, for here the ice was on dry land. Not being undercut by the river, it began a spectacular and hair-raising advance on the glacier bridge. Its measurable surge in June was better than two feet per day, in August over three feet per day and by mid-August it climaxed to a startling gain of *over eight feet per day!*

The normal distance of this ice lobe from the bridge was about two-thirds of a mile, a position it had held for so long that small alders had taken root and had begun to grow. But in 1909 and the winter of the completion of the bridge, it had begun a very slow but steady forward march. By the time of the beginning of the big surge, it was about one-third of a mile from the bridge. Now began the steady, relentless advance, several feet of gain every day. The forward edges now became giant plowshares, mowing down mighty trees, digging up rocks, stumps and anything else in their path. The scientists would take photographs from a vantage point and the next day the spot would be covered with ice, 300 feet thick. And still coming.

On June 3, the glacier had moved within 1,775 feet of the bridge; on August 17, to 1,624 feet; on October 5, when the freezeup stopped its advance, it was 1,571 feet from the bridge. The bridge itself was 1,550 feet long. The ice was just about the length of the bridge away from it, and towering 200 feet above it.

Glaciologist Tarr said: "What the glacier might do before the spring of 1911 was of great interest. It might continue to advance. . . . The bridge cost $1,500,000 and is the key to the new 20-million-dollar railway to the copper mines. It is absolutely certain that no corps of engineers living could save the bridge and railway if the glacier should advance that far. . . ."

On the other side, while not so menacing in appearance, Miles Glacier had also surged. That the glaciers could easily move forward enough to endanger the bridge and the railroad was a known fact. When Abercrombie first passed this way back in 1884, there was no lake at all; Miles Glacier covered it all. In 1885, Allen had made the specific statement that, "The most southerly part of [Miles Glacier] is one mile or less from the most northerly part of . . . [Childs Glacier]." There had been a glacial surge in 1885 that took the glacier within 400 feet of where the bridge now stood. On his return to the glacier area in 1898, Abercrombie had expressed great surprise at the change in Miles Glacier, observing the new lake there, and pointing out that the glacier had receded in the direction of Mount Saint Elias at least five or six miles in the intervening 15 years.

Now the glaciers were on the march again. What would happen in 1911? It was a matter of grave concern to the bridge engineers and glaciologists alike.

Actually, the ice did gain some in 1911 during the month of June, bringing the ice lobe to its closest approach to the bridge, a distance of 1,475 feet. Then it began to recede.

The scientists, searching for a clue to this sudden significant advance in the glaciers, came up with several possibilities. Study showed that the amount of snowfall in 1907-1908 was 433 inches at the bridge site and 410 inches in 1908-1909. Measurements taken during the following winter seemed to indicate that normal snowfall was less than half that amount.

Miles and Childs were not the only glaciers on the route of the Copper River and Northwestern that the builders had to contend with. At Heney Glacier and again at Grinnell Glacier, the rails were laid across abandoned moraines very close to the glaciers' snouts.

But these were nothing compared to Allen Glacier. Here, for five and one-half miles, the railroad was laid upon the glacier itself. Ballast, ties and rails were laid directly on the ice of the glacier's tongue, which extended along the very edge of the Copper River. To go around would have involved heavy rock work costing hundreds of thousands of dollars and the building of two additional bridges across the Copper. The tongue of Allen Glacier was heavily overlaid with gravel and mud. Small alders and underbrush grew upon it. The builders mistakenly stripped this overlying material. Left in place it would have acted as insulating material. As it was, there was a great deal of shifting and slumping at first because of the

increased melting of the ice after removal of the vegetation. To compensate for the loss in insulation it was necessary to place tons of gravel on top of the ice to rebuild the insulating cushion. This stretch of track, because of its constant forward movement, had to be replaced and reset frequently. Trackwalkers had to walk the rails each day, and trains crossed slowly and gingerly, but it caused little trouble other than the need for constant maintenance. There was a minor glacier surge in Allen Glacier in 1912, which caused some difficulties, but the trains kept moving.

After the completion of the Miles Glacier Bridge, construction materials for the rest of the line moved up swiftly and easily. All along the unfinished portion of the railroad, it was necessary to distribute materials and supplies far ahead of the end of the track, because it was planned to finish, whatever the consequences, in the winter of 1911. It was a dreadful decision, to finish this section of track in midwinter, but there was no other way—the allotted four years were almost up.

12 THE LAST BIG PUSH

The railroad was completed to Chitina, Mile 132, on September 12, 1910. The tough Abercrombie and Woods Canyon rock work was now done. Trains ran regularly on the five-and-one-half-mile ice tongue of Allen Glacier, and at last the new town of Chitina had been reached. Chitina was to be a "junction" town; the main line was to be run north to Fairbanks and/or Eagle, while the copper spur turned eastward here and ran along the north bank of the Chitina River.

COURTESY PHYLLIS CARLSON

Laying track at Mile 118 in 1910.

About one-half mile above Chitina, another crossing of the Copper River was to be made. A steel bridge was planned for here, but to expedite the completion of the important copper spur, a piling trestle was driven across, and allowed to freeze into the ice for the winter. It would naturally go out with the spring breakup, but it could be redriven by the "B & B" (bridge building) gangs.

Tentative plans for this crossing were discussed off and on for a number of years, but the company finally abandoned plans for a steel bridge at the Chitina Crossing due to the stormy political situation.

The winter of 1911 saw the completion of some of the most difficult work of all on the Copper River & Northwestern route, due to the bitterly cold weather in which the men had to work. The big push was on to finish, and nothing, not even sub-zero weather, was going to stop them now. It was hoped to start hauling copper in the spring of 1911.

In a little less than a month after passing through the town of Chitina, the rails had reached out to Mile 146, Kuskulana Canyon. Here another of the three difficult and expensive steel bridges built by the Katalla Company was to be erected. It was another situation where everything stood still until the link was done. Only the material which could pass up the Chitina River by horsedrawn sleds on the uncertain ice could pass.

Kuskulana's gorge was 238 feet deep, with extremely swift water in the chasm. The bridge must be built cantilever; there could be no falsework for this type of bridge.

It consisted of three half-camel back spans, and was 525 feet long. Its three spans were 150, 225 and 150 feet long, respectively. Most of the work was done in the bitterest part of the winter, with temperatures plunging down to 50 and 60 below zero. Two months were consumed in its construction; as far as is known, it is the only bridge of its class ever built in the dead of winter in Alaska, and the engineers afterward expressed the hope that it would be the last, as "the many difficulties attending steel construction in midwinter are too great to be again considered." The men, working in this cruel weather, were so bundled up they were described as looking like so many "wooly bears on a bridge."

Acetylene lights were used for the work, which, being in midwinter, had to be carried on through many hours of darkness. The lack of electricity was a great handicap, O'Neel felt, and he planned on installing a light plant before beginning work on the Chitina Crossing Bridge.

After two months of this struggle in the cold, the bridge was completed on New Year's Day, 1911, "amid the screeching of whistles, popping of guns and lusty yells of the steelworkers." What a New Year's celebration! They were through with the almost inhuman cold; just a bit of finish-up and most of the steelworkers could board the train for a cozy ride back to Cordova and the Outside. Very few of the veterans of the Miles Glacier Bridge had signed up for the Kuskulana, so the work was done mostly by men who were new to Alaska and unfamiliar with the climate.

"The swinging of the Kuskulana steel bridge is the second of the 'impossible' bridges on the Copper River & Northwestern line of railway. The building of the bridge itself was no difficult feat, but the fact of its having been done in the dead of winter with the thermometer often ranging 40 degrees or more below zero, is a most creditable task which the 'wise ones' claimed was impossible, and throws Supt. O'Neel and his able corps of assistants once again in the spotlight," wrote the editor of the *Cordova Alaskan.*

ALASKA HISTORICAL LIBRARY
The high steel bridge across the Kuskulana River.

With the completion of the bridge, much of the equipment used in its construction was stored nearby, because it was felt it would be needed for constructing the Chitina Bridge when the time came.

There was the usual quota of joshing. An article in the *Chitina Leader* said that "The train crew at the front expressed the desire that 'Deacon' Jones, watchman at the Kuskulana Bridge, wouldn't cuss so hard as the train pulls over the crossing. It's new yet, and no telling what effect that blue stuff the 'deacon' belches out might have on the structure. The boys say that the 'pious' old watchman had such a grouch on the other day, he had to take two buckets and go clear down the Kuskulana gorge to get water to cool off."

The local papers were hard put to find enough superlatives for the work accomplished that winter. Veteran black powder and dynamite man Paddy MacCormac finished an exceedingly tough piece of "station work" on the tunnel at Mile 131, just below Chitina, where trains had been using a particularly nasty switchback. This tunnel was not a hard rock station, but was composed of frozen muck and loose material. Several station gangs had already given up on it. The company was forced to offer bigger money for its completion, and Paddy MacCormac then successfully completed the cut through the "big mud hole," as it had come to be called. It was said to be "one of the toughest station contracts on the Copper River & Northwestern."

The *Cordova Alaskan,* January 7, 1911, reported: "Locomotive engineer Jack Compton and Fireman Jack Courtney, on the 4-spot, with conductor Frank Clarkin, had the distinction of being the first train crew to pass the big tunnel and cut."

The news writers had to dredge up a fresh stock of felicitous expressions in describing the Gilahina Bridge at Mile 160, just 36 miles from Bonanza Landing. This bridge was a wooden structure, built by bridge foreman Pat O'Brien for the contractor. This trestle bridge was 880 feet long, 80 to 90 feet high, and required a half million board feet of lumber. "Call it what you will," said a railroad official, "the work is nothing short of marvelous, when weather conditions are taken into consideration. For the past two weeks the thermometer has been ranging between 30 and 60 below and at times during the extremely cold hours, trouble was experienced by the carpenters in driving the bolts, which split the heavy timbers like a cake of ice." In order to drive the pilings, holes had to be blasted first, for it was impossible to drive them in the frozen ground. In early February this bridge, the largest and most difficult of the wooden ones between Chitina and Bonanza, was finished in record time. It was laid down in eight days, trains being able to cross on January 28, 1911.

There was no slowing of the momentum as more records were set. In the month of March a blizzard piled wet, heavy snow on top of the winter's accumulation of light, powdery snow, creating avalanche conditions. For miles the track disappeared under huge piles of snow, some up to 49 feet deep. But in spite of the uncooperating winter, the train made it through to Chitina in five days. The heaviest drifts were between Abercrombie and Woods Canyon, where it took 24 hours of steady work to clear the drifts down to a height the rotaries could handle. Mr. Barry, a railroad official, commented, "The Copper River & Northwestern now holds the world's record over all the trunk lines for cutting through snowdrifts. Our rotary cuts 14 feet 7 inches, and as some of the cuts were from 40 to 60 feet in height, we had to put the men on the drifts and cut benches with the shovels, throwing it under the hood of the snowplow so the rotary could handle it and the river side of the cuts had to be shoveled down before the plow could throw the snow out. . . ."

Early March. Now the completion was near. Every day the mileage of track laid was faithfully reported, and the paper announced, "Road to be Completed Next Month," on the same day the record snow clearing was reported. By March 22, 1911, the railroad was within a few miles of the Bonanza Mine. "The Copper River & Northwestern Railway had its tracks laid to within five miles and 600 feet of the Bonanza Mine, Kennicott, at noon today, according to Chief Engineer E. C. Hawkins, who says the road will be completed by April 1st."

They beat that date, too, for the road was completed on March 29, 1911.

13 THE COPPER SPIKE

The railroad was done! Four years of grievous and epic work, much of it done in the dead of winter, most of it against physical odds almost impossible to recount; it was all in the past now. Just a few more rails, and the driving of the last spike. Alaska's only successful, standard-gauge private passenger railroad was built, as far as it would ever be, though plans were in the mill for more.

Most railroads are traditionally finished with a golden spike. The Copper River & Northwestern was to be completed with a symbolic copper spike.

Joe Redmond, chief blacksmith for Michael Heney, and one of the men with the original Heney enterprise, fashioned the spike from copper taken from Chititu Creek near the Bonanza Mine. Mr. Redmond made the spike from heated "copper float."

Redmond, completely taken up with his unusual assignment, went further. He also made a copper horseshoe pen holder. This special desk ornament was to be given to Mr. E. C. Hawkins as a personal memento of the Copper River & Northwestern.

Now all was in readiness. On Monday, March 27, 1911, the first through train left Cordova. In Superintendent Van Cleve's private dining-sleeping-observation car rode Van Cleve; E. C. Hawkins; R. J.

Laying track at the end of the railroad, Kennicott, March 29, 1911.
(E. A. Hegg photo, Alaska Historical Library)

Barry, general freight and passenger agent of the new railroad; E. A. Hegg, photographer; and Will A. Steel, editor of the *Cordova Alaskan* and the *Chitina Leader*. At Chitina they were joined by J. C. Martin, manager of the Orr Stage Lines.

The train moved on up the line, overnighting at Kuskulana camp, Mile 146, and the next day on to Kennicott. They arrived within a quarter of a mile of the end of track, but here they had to stop and wait another day. The pile drivers were still driving a 256-foot trestle and track-laying across it could not be done until next day, Wednesday.

On Wednesday morning, March 29, the tracks were laid across this last trestle. The party had lunch before the completion, but it was easy to see that the spike-driving would take place soon.

It was a lovely day. The temperature seemed like a special balm to the men who had worked all through that terrible winter. It was 38 degrees above zero.

After lunch, the last 800 feet of steel was laid. At 3:30 p.m. the final ceremonies took place.

E. C. Hawkins, chief engineer and general manager of the Katalla Company, conducted the ceremonies. The spike was driven in alternation by E. C. Hawkins and Sam Murchison. As the spike settled home, all the engines blew whistles and there was a general round of congratulations and excitement.

The copper spike was afterward drawn, and inscribed with the words "Native Alaska Copper" on one side, "Copper River & Northwestern Railway" on the second side, "Kennecott Mines, March 29, 1911" on the third side, and the fourth left blank. It was placed in a cabinet bearing the plate, "From E. C. Hawkins to S. W. Eccles, president, Copper River & Northwestern Railway." It was sent to Mr. Eccles in New York, making the journey in the safe aboard the steamer *Northwestern*.

In spite of the air of general festivity that marked the driving of the copper spike, there was an element of sadness, too. All through the ceremonies, faithful old engine No. 50, Michael J. Heney's first engine, had stood nearby, with a large number of bewhiskered, snoose-chewing construction workers clinging to her from various vantage points. On the front of the engine was prominently hung a portrait of the contractor, Michael Heney, the "Irish Prince." Prior to driving the spike, Hawkins had called for a moment of silence in honor of Heney. The workers doffed their battered headgear and bowed their heads in silent tribute. For Michael J. Heney was dead. He had died the previous winter, a victim of the years of hard living and work on the raw frontier. He did not live to see his greatest achievement, the Copper River & Northwestern Railway, completed.

Heney died in time to escape the knowledge that the great All-American route he had begun would never be more than a mining road. For in the year 1910, everyone still believed that the coal fields would be joined with the rich Kennecott copper. Smelters would spring up in Katalla, that promising industrial city of the North; there was no need to ship the ore Outside. A bright new future was ahead with completion of the All-American route to the Yukon River. As late as 1917, maps of the Copper River & Northwestern Railway showed the projected route to Fairbanks, with spurs to Bering River and the Matanuska coal fields.

But it was not to be. Some of the greatest battles of all were yet to be fought, and they would take place over coal. For now the Copper River & Northwestern Railway and the Guggenheim-Morgan Syndicate were caught up in a sordid squabble not of their own making. It was a battle over Alaskan coal, and its effects were to be disastrous.

BIBLIOGRAPHY AND NOTES
PART TWO

1 HENEY'S FIRST CONTRACT
The Alaska-Yukon Magazine. "Viewing the Copper River Spectacle," June 1910.
Cochran, Charlie. Personal interview.
The Cordova Alaskan. October 26, December 14 and 21, 1907; January 11 and 18, February 1 and 29, 1908.
Engineers Report. "Copper River Bridge near Miles Glacier," 1910, p. 1.
Engineers Report. "General Description of the Construction of the Flag Point Bridge Across the Copper River, Alaska," 1909.

2 THE STEAMBOAT CHITTYNA
The Katalla Herald. August 10, 1907. "Work in Canyon," August 17, 1907.
Meals, Owen. Personal interview.
The Valdez Prospector. June 20, August 1 and 25, 1907.

3 HEADED FOR THE COPPER RIVER
The Cordova Alaskan. December 1907 to July 1908.

4 BRIDGES ON THE LOWER COPPER
The Technical World. "It Had to be Done" by Carlyle Ellis, March 1912.

5 UP THE UNTAMED RIVER
The Technical World. "It Had to be Done" by Carlyle Ellis, March 1912.

6 WINTER, 1908-1909, OR: THREE WEEKS IN A SNOWBOUND CABOOSE
Alaska Sportsman. "This Month in Alaska History," July 1966, p. 25.
The Cordova Alaskan. February 6 and March 22, 1909; April 1, 1911.
Engineers Report. "Copper River Bridge Near Miles Glacier," 1910.
The Katalla Herald. "Glacier on Rampage—Big Damage to Copper River Road," February 20, 1909.
The North Star, Cordova. "What Railroad Men Did in the Blockade," March 13, 1910.

7 SINKING THE CAISSONS
Cochran, Charlie. Personal interview.
Engineers Report. "Copper River Bridge near Miles Glacier," 1910.
Kelly, Tom. Personal interview.

8 SNOOSE, OVERALLS, WHISKEY AND SNOWBALLS
Burns, Frank, of Cordova. Personal interview.
The Cordova Alaskan. "Railroad Completed to Copper Mines," April 1, 1911.
Nelson, O. A., of Chitina. Personal interview.
The Seattle Post-Intelligencer. "Seattle Kid Finds Life Rough on Copper River Rail Iron Train" by Berne S. Jacobsen, October 29, 1958.
Shiels, Archibald. *The Kennecott Story.* Privately published, Bellingham, Wash., 1964, p. 7.

9 WINTER, 1909-1910: NEITHER SLEET NOR SNOW NOR COPPER RIVER WIND . . .
The Alaska-Yukon Magazine. "Winter's Crucial Battle on Copper River," June 1910.
Engineers Report. "Copper River Bridge Near Miles Glacier," 1910.
The Technical World. "It Had to be Done" by Carlyle Ellis, March 1912.

10 CALLING THE COPPER'S BLUFF
Engineers Report. "Bridge Across Copper River Near Miles Glacier," 1910.

11 THE ICE ADVANCE
Tarr, Ralph Stockman, and Martin, Lawrence. *Alaskan Glacier Studies.* The National Geographic Society, Washington, D.C., 1910, pp. 395-433, 445.

12 THE LAST BIG PUSH
The Cordova Alaskan, January 2, 7, 25 and 26, February 4, March 2, 1911.
Nelson, O. A., of Chitina. Personal interview.

13 THE COPPER SPIKE
The Cordova Alaskan. March 27 and 31, April 1 and 11, 1911.

PART THREE
COAL,
POLITICS
AND RAILROADS

PART THREE
COAL,
POLITICS
AND RAILROADS

1 COAL AND SMELTERS

It is our intention, as future conditions warrant, to extend our line until we have an American railway of standard gauge reaching from the Pacific Ocean to the Yukon River.

—S. W. Eccles, President
Copper River & Northwestern Railway Company

(Letter to the Commissioner of the
General Land Office, Dec. 14, 1908)

Coal was the key to Alaska. Coal was the source of power to run the railroads and to smelt the copper. Coal was heat. And coal provided fuel for ships of the U.S. Navy. Without coal, Alaska was effectively locked up.

Coal was the reason, the only possible reason, for the Guggenheim move from Valdez to Katalla. The Valdez route was cheaper, easier to construct and shorter. But, it tapped no coal.

J. P. Morgan is said to have declared emphatically that, "We must bring the coal and copper together!" He was right. The future growth of Alaska and of Morgan's own economic interests there depended upon coal, as well as copper.

Opposite—**Along the right-of-way, somewhere between the Pacific Ocean (Where the Rails Meet the Sails) and the Yukon River. The Yukon River objective represented considerable ambition.**

But the history of coal land legislation in Alaska is a history of blunder. Alaskan newspapers declared that if the coal laws for Alaska had been written by the residents of an insane asylum, they could not have been worse, and probably would have been better.

In the years before 1900, there was no law by which coal land could be acquired in Alaska. In 1900 a coal land law was passed, but it specified that only surveyed lands could be located, and at that time few surveys had been made in the District of Alaska.

This legislation created such an uproar that in 1904 Congress passed another law to open the coal lands. But caution predominated and the law was ineffective as only 160-acre claims could be made. Only four claims could be combined for a total of 640 acres. Though it was common knowledge that such small claims were not feasible to mine, the law precipitated the "coal rush" of 1905, during which most of the locations in Alaska were made. Due to the economic restrictions of these small sites there were many sub rosa agreements for combining coal claims after patent. These agreements were technically against the law.

The Bering River coal field was the first to be discovered, and almost all of the nearly 1,000 Alaskan claims were made in this field. The Matanuska coal field had just been discovered and hardly prospected when, in November of 1906, President Teddy Roosevelt by executive decree withdrew all the coal lands in Alaska from entry. "It is not wise," said the

President in his Sixth Annual Message on December 3, 1906, "that the nation should alienate its remaining coal lands. I have temporarily withdrawn from settlement all the lands which the Geological Survey had indicated as containing, or in all probability containing, coal. The question, however, can be properly settled only by legislation. . . ."

The unexpected order was issued with great suddenness—word of it was received at the land offices by cablegram. The *Alaska Monthly* magazine, which carried a glowing feature story on the coal fields of Alaska in its December issue, was forced to add a postscript: "Coal Lands Withdrawn From Entry."

All coal lands in the District of Alaska were withdrawn from filing under the coal land law, but it was not clear whether it applied to public lands only (lands not yet located), or to *all* coal lands.

"If the order applies to public land only (that which has not yet been located) then it leaves those who already have 'vested rights' a complete monopoly of the coal industry in Alaska . . ." according to the *Alaska Monthly* magazine article. But if it also referred to those who had located and performed all the acts necessary as required by law, how could the government set aside these claims, except for fraud? If the order was issued to prevent monopoly, as was claimed, why weren't *all* mineral lands withdrawn? Why just coal?

The only plausible explanation obtainable was that the Eastern "coal trust," fearing loss of their Pacific Coast markets, had engineered the withdrawal. Indeed, there was great fear in the East of the promising new discoveries in Alaska.

The work stoppage meant more than a lot of unhappy miners. It meant the curtailment of railroad building in the area. And it meant that the railroads would be kept from using this ready source of fuel in Alaska.

It is important to remember the direct connection between coal availability and railroad building, for this relationship is at the heart of the Alaskan railroading story.

"If this cablegram means all it says," continued the *Alaska Monthly* magazine article, "it is the hardest rap that Alaska has yet received for it will stop all the railroad building now going on to the westward. The government not only has refused to grant assistance to railroad building in the way of subsidy, but it now removes the chief incentive that is prompting private capital to proceed further with their gigantic undertakings. Already millions of dollars have been invested in railroad surveying and construction and scores of men have spent several of the best years of their lives in the development of one of Alaska's future chief industries, and now they are left 'holding the

sack' by this order to 'withdraw from filing and entry' all coal lands."

Coal there was in Alaska, good coal, and plenty of it. In 1907 when M. K. Rogers was chief engineer at Katalla for the Copper River & Northwestern Railway, he spoke of the "Vast Coal Deposits" of the region and estimated that there were 500,000,000 tons of coal in the Bering River field, and that it "should be worth a dollar a ton to Alaska."

"Mr. Rogers has visited the coal fields a number of times and has given the coal section a critical examination," said the *Katalla Herald*. ". . . In his office he has a chunk of the finest Anthracite coal, which he himself packed out from the Cunningham properties a short time ago . . . the immense tonnage should be an eye-opener to the people of the Pacific coast . . . and probably accounts for the rushing completion of the company's coal road."

Nineteen hundred and seven, the year following Teddy Roosevelt's withdrawal of coal lands from entry, was a busy year for the development of mines already located. Everyone still believed in the government's promises, and the withdrawal, while it would stop new entries, was not believed to abrogate agreements already made. Most of the claimants had already paid the required $10 per acre ($1,600 per claim) purchase price according to law. Only in cases of fraud could the money be confiscated—they thought.

Erickson & Borland had the subcontract in 1907 to finish the coal road for the Katalla Company. Pilings were to be driven across the shallow Bering Lake to reach the fields. The work was to be done during that winter, "even if we have to change the weather," asserted Mr. Rogers. The average depth of the lake was nine feet, and the job was not considered difficult; after completion, two-thirds of the distance was to be filled in, leaving the western end of the lake open for navigation.

Navigation was important as one of the most thriving and promising mines, that of T. P. MacDonald, was located on the north shore of Bering Lake. Mr. MacDonald's mine needed no railroad. He could load his coal directly onto small scows and ship it to Katalla or Martin River for offloading onto steamers. His development was far ahead of the others for this reason, and was watched with great interest because it was an indicator of progress in coal development.

The *Katalla Herald's* issue of September 21, 1907, claimed, "Coal Mine a Good One. T. P. MacDonald's coal mine on Bering Lake is looking better all the time. The tunnel is in a much better grade of coal, and it is confidently expected within a short time the solid portion of the vein will be reached.

"The coal that has been mined up to this time has been ground up and mixed with shale and dirt, but the last quantity showed a marked improvement, being cleaner, lighter and better. . . . The Katalla Company is taking a barge load every other day, and it gives excellent satisfaction. 'We will soon be in a position to supply the local demand,' said Mr. MacDonald, 'We will bring down one thousand tons for domestic use in Katalla. . . .' "

By October, when the equinoctial storms were beginning, MacDonald had "Plenty of Coal Awaiting Shipment." The tug *Imp*, which was to take the scows out, was laid up for weather, so things were held up, but it was reported that MacDonald had succeeded in striking a vein of coal 11 feet wide. "The coal comes out in lumps, crumbles on exposure to air, but gives excellent satisfaction as a steam producer. MacDonald, now in Seattle, is expected to return on the *Santa Clara* and work will begin on a larger scale," reported the *Katalla Herald*, October 13, 1907.

To add to the excitement over coal, a sample taken from the MacDonald mine was burned in the battleship *USS Nebraska* in 1908. The report was so favorable that it sent Alaskans into a fever of prospecting and development work on their claims, despite the now two years of withdrawal.

Coal for the West Coast markets, coal to run the trains, coal for the U.S. Navy, and primarily, coal for smelting. A. H. Brooks, head of the Geological Survey in Alaska, devoted an entire booklet in 1911 to "Alaska Coal and Its Utilization." In it he spoke at length of the stagnation in coal development in Alaska resulting from the government's policy of coal land withdrawal. The booklet also stressed the excellent coking properties of coal from both the Bering River and Matanuska fields and listed probable markets.

The possibility of smelting with Alaskan coke was also explored: "Coke undergoes little direct competition with fuel oil. While there has been no marked increase in coke consumption for a number of years, yet such an increase is soon to be expected. Copper smelting on the west coast, *notably in Alaska* (author's italics) when the Copper River district has been rendered accessible by railway, will undoubtedly increase the demand for coke." There was apparently no doubt in Mr. Brooks' mind that Alaskan coal would undergo a natural vigorous growth with the completion of the railway. He did not foresee the political upheaval ahead.

Although Brooks was concerned primarily with the smelting of copper, he discussed the possible smelting of iron.

That a copper smelter was actually planned is beyond doubt. It is referred to constantly in every story of the region. Archie Shiels, Heney's close friend

and associate, wrote that, "The Syndicate, of course, had many mining engineers out in the field, searching for new properties or looking over the claims of others who might want financial aid for their development.

"It soon became apparent to the Syndicate that there were many properties in the vast interior region that could be profitably worked if there were a smelter closer to them.

"Mile 40 on the Copper River & Northwestern Railway was a large, flat country. Here the Syndicate surveyed a townsite for industrial use, including a smelter. From this townsite the Bering River coal fields were but 60 miles distant, so a survey was made for the purpose of determining the best route to bring that coal to the main line at or near the townsite. Coal and ore could then be brought to the smelter at a cost that would enable all, or most, of the 'low grade' properties to be profitably worked."

Smelters were not the only reason coal was so important to the Guggenheims.

Coal was an absolute necessity for the planned operation of a first-class freight and passenger railroad to the Yukon River. This northern extension, as indicated previously, was still planned when the copper spike was driven home in 1911. The Copper River & Northwestern Railway was to be the much sought after All-American railway. In fact, Mr. Law, an attorney for the company, testified at a House of Representatives Hearing in 1911 that preliminary surveys "had been made up as far as Fairbanks." Eagle had also been suggested as a possible northern terminus.

2 BALLINGER-PINCHOT CONTROVERSY BEGINS

Just when it seemed that the Copper River & Northwestern Railway would be able to overcome any difficulty hurled her way, she was stopped short by a governmental controversy raging thousands of miles away. In Washington, D.C., the Ballinger-Pinchot Controversy was drawing the future of Alaska's coal industry to an abrupt halt. The coal lands were being withdrawn—first, temporarily and then, permanently. As a result of this loss of available fuel, the much dreamed of and planned All-American route would never be. The railroad wasn't the only loser. Alaska was. In the years 1907 to 1911 the Ballinger-Pinchot Controversy blazed as a national scandal of paralyzing proportions. In its wake progress stopped and the lives and reputations of hundreds of innocent people were ruined.

The loss to Alaska was incalculable. Gone were the All-American railroad (it would cost the taxpayers more than $70 million to build it themselves); the planned smelter, stoked on Bering River coal; the one-half billion dollars in copper ore intended for the smelter; and the development of low grade copper ores which were now uneconomical to mine. Before its end the controversy would kill the coal and oil industries of Katalla and the Bering River, and strangle the copper and gold mining industries of the area. Four ghost towns would be included in the legacy of the Ballinger-Pinchot Controversy, and also the election of a President of the United States.

The Ballinger-Pinchot holocaust was kindled in the forest reserves of Alaska and stoked to white-hot heat on Bering River coal.

The moving force behind the controversy was the chief forester under Theodore Roosevelt, Gifford Pinchot. Pinchot was a violent and flamboyant character with a flair for publicity. He was an extremely popular political figure in those "trust-busting" days, and was considered the chief architect of the "Conservation" policy under Teddy Roosevelt. During the formation and strengthening of the brand-new Forestry Department, Pinchot revealed himself as a natural and formidable propagandist with a goal he believed justified any means of attainment. He wanted to cancel all the Bering River coal claims and to inaugurate a leasing system controlled by the Forest Service. His first move was to persuade Theodore Roosevelt to create the Chugach National Forest in Alaska in 1907. The eventual boundaries included almost all of the coal lands in the Bering River area.

The immediate effects of the forest withdrawal on Alaska were to place the coal lands under an additional layer of official red tape and to further tie up approval of the coal spur of the Copper River & Northwestern Railway. An early diary of Forest Ranger T. M. Hunt, of no exact date, but circa 1910, says, "It was noted in conversation with Mr. Hawkins that the right-of-way for portions of the line from Katalla to the coal fields or from Katalla to the Copper River & Northwestern Railway on the Copper River have *not been* (italics by Mr. Hunt) approved although the maps of definite location have been filed for several years."

Gifford Pinchot did not like Richard A. Ballinger, former mayor of Seattle. Ballinger seemed to have a knack for getting in Pinchot's way. Innocently enough, Ballinger accepted an appointment by Teddy Roosevelt in 1907 to be commissioner of the General Land Office, a post he held for one year. His next contact with Pinchot was as Secretary of the Interior. Pinchot, a Teddy Roosevelt man all the way, was enraged when President William Howard Taft elected to replace Garfield with Ballinger. Taft was already

under suspicion of being "anti-Conservationist" by Pinchot.

When Ballinger first served in public office as land commissioner, he worked hard to clarify the legal tangle surrounding the Bering River coal claims. He had several investigations mounted into the Bering River coal lands to clear them up quickly where possible so that those claims made in good faith and paid for could go to patent. This was against Pinchot's plan. So when Ballinger was appointed Secretary of the Interior, Pinchot's main motive was to discredit him and remove him from office. He did this by zeroing in on the alleged involvement of Ballinger in the fraudulent Bering River coal claims of Clarence Cunningham and Associates.

In 1903 Clarence Cunningham, a mining engineer and prospector, organized an association to acquire coal lands. There were 27 members in the original association who entered into agreement, as recorded in Cunningham's journal in 1903:

"Am entering into verbal agreements with the subscribers . . . whereby each of said subscribers shall have one claim of 160 acres recorded in his name, and will own same individually until such time as title can be secured for same. After this is done each subscriber agrees to deed his interest to a company to be formed for the purpose of developing and marketing said coal, and receive stock in the company in payment for the same. . . ."

At the time of this agreement, there was no law against such a procedure. In fact, the transaction was void since there was no law to obtain title.

The law of 1904 allowed combinations of up to four claims, or a total of 640 acres. Cunningham, unaware of all of the provisions of the law, also failed to comply with other provisions, but the only evidence of intent to defraud was in the signing by the participants of the affidavit required by the law of 1904. The law required that an applicant file "in good faith, for his own benefit, and not directly or indirectly, in whole or in part, in behalf of any person or persons whomsoever." Even if the oral agreement of the parties had been abandoned, as Cunningham later asserted, fraud would not have been committed.

But the oral agreement had not been abandoned, and Cunningham perjured himself twice on this matter. That the agreement was still in force is shown by the fact that on July 26th, the Guggenheims secretly took out an option on one-half interest in the claims. Later that year it is alleged that they picked up that option. The deal supposedly included the organization of a $5,000,000 corporation with $250,000 of working capital contributed by the Alaska Syndicate. The Cunningham claimants were to have half the stock. Clearly, it was no penny-ante bargain,

RALPH E. MACKAY COLLECTION

RALPH E. MACKAY COLLECTION

Clockwise from above—Mile 6 out of Cordova and the start of the 11-mile tangent across the Copper River Delta, the longest stretch of straight track on the road. Locomotive No. 102 and its tender. The Copper River & Northwestern Railway's fleet of four rotary snowplows. Crossing the Lakina River trestle at Mile 74, 1915.

P. S. HUNT PHOTO. FROM THE RALPH E. MACKAY COLLECTION

but to say it would give the Guggenheims a monopoly was sheer unadulterated nonsense, for the Cunningham claims were only a very small part of the Bering River fields, and were located in the very farthest reaches of the field in the shadow of Bering Glacier.

Nevertheless, the combination was against the law as it stood, and constituted a fraudulent deal.

The fraud was not apparent, and was not discovered until January of 1908 when the journal entry was found.

Pinchot said that Ballinger was aware of the fraudulent structure of the Cunningham claims from the beginning. Pinchot claimed, ". . . it is altogether incredible that Ballinger could have escaped knowledge of the Cunningham claims, their importance, and their fraudulent character. Unquestionably he brought that knowledge with him to Washington when he became Commissioner. . . ."

But Ballinger had acted in good faith. Upon his appointment as commissioner, investigations were made by special agents Jones and Love, and finally Louis R. Glavis. The first two investigators found evidence of fraud, but not in the Cunningham group. Three reports were on file in the land office from Jones and Love. None cast doubt upon the Cunningham group. In fact, they were reported favorably, though the reports called for "particularly necessary" investigations into certain other specified claims.

In December, following the Guggenheim-Cunningham negotiations, ex-Governor Moore of Washington called on Ballinger to ask the cause of the delay in the issuance of coal patents. Moore was one of the Cunningham claimants. In the file Ballinger found the three favorable reports, and the claims were ordered "clear-listed" or ready to patent. As a last-minute measure, it was thought a good idea to notify Glavis, the special investigator who had just left for Alaska to begin his investigations. Glavis wired back that the claims ought not to go to patent yet, and Ballinger suspended the clear-list order.

In 1908 Ballinger returned to his private law practice. During the year he worked on various matters for land interests in Seattle. He also prepared a document for Clarence Cunningham, who was concerned over the discovery of the journal entry. Cunningham had an affidavit prepared by Ballinger in which he stated that the agreement had indeed existed at the time the entry was made, but that pursuant to provisions of the 1904 law, it had been "entirely abandoned." Ballinger showed the affidavit to Secretary of the Interior Garfield, who said that he did not think it would make any difference, and had the affidavit filed.

However, Pinchot claimed: "As attorney for the claimants, Ballinger knew about the Morgan-Guggenheim option, and he knew this statement to be false. Nevertheless, he himself made a trip from Seattle, for which he was paid by the claimants, and put the affidavit before . . . Garfield. . . ." Pinchot made the preparation of this legal form seem highly incriminating.

When Ballinger became Secretary of the Interior in 1909, he found that Glavis was still working on the Alaska coal cases. In 1907 Glavis had said that his investigation would be completed in a few months, but his funding had run out. Soon afterward a new appropriation allowed the continuation of the Alaskan investigations, which by now included the Cunningham claims. Ballinger's first action was to order expedition of all the Alaskan cases. He then determined that since he had worked briefly on the Cunningham affidavit he was to have no further connection with Alaskan coal cases and that Assistant Secretary Pierce was to have full power and jurisdiction over them. The record shows that this order was scrupulously followed.

On June 29, 1909, Governor Moore wired the Department of the Interior a strong protest regarding the incredible delay on Alaskan coal lands. The Cunningham patents had been pending for *five years* when this wire was sent. Governor Moore stated that he did not think it fair that the government had had the use of the $52,800 paid by the Cunningham claimants for all those years. He noted that apparently there was still no effort being extended to get Alaskan coal lands to patent.

H. H. Schwartz, one of Ballinger's assistants, investigated the file on the Cunningham claimants, and decided that there was enough evidence to show that the claims were not made in good faith. He then wired special investigator Glavis to prepare a report immediately and to begin hearings to clear the matter.

Glavis at first refused, then stalled, claiming that he needed more time. Glavis had had, not counting the interruption for lack of funds, more than two years in which to complete his work. "It was my conclusion," Schwartz said, "that Mr. Glavis was over cautious, and I knew from my 12 years' actual experience in the field investigating cases of this character, that there was no necessity for investigations to be strung out indefinitely. . . ." During these two years, every assistance was placed at the disposal of Glavis. Any further loose ends could be picked up during the time consumed by the hearings.

When Schwartz insisted on the hearings, Glavis called in the Forest Service and Gifford Pinchot.

In his letter to the Forest Service, Glavis held out the tempting motive of power to Pinchot: ". . . Another point involved, to which your attention is called, is that the entire field has been withdrawn from entry.

Therefore, should these filings be canceled, there would be no opportunity for other filings to be made. This would enable the Forest Service to secure legislation which would enable it to control the output of coal in a similar manner to that which they are now disposing of the timber. . . ."

With the entry of the colorful and dramatic figure of Gifford Pinchot, the gun-totin' Forest Service head, the Bering River coal situation simply blew up. From that time on there was no thought of justice, no attempt to sort out honesty from fraud; there couldn't be in the violent storm of conflict that raged over the next two years.

Gifford Pinchot's propaganda machine was a smooth-running gristmill that ground its enemies very fine. President Taft had had the temerity to remove Pinchot's friend Garfield from the office of Secretary of the Interior. Now this machine was turned on the man selected to replace Garfield: Richard Achilles Ballinger.

In Glavis, Pinchot had the perfect tool: an Interior Department employee willing to point an accusing finger.

Pinchot moved into action. The opening gambit was to lay the matter before President Taft. If Taft removed Ballinger and replaced him with an Interior Secretary more to Pinchot's liking, then everything Pinchot wanted could be accomplished without struggle.

Glavis, under Pinchot's direction, prepared a 50-page report for submission to the President. In his report Glavis accused Ballinger of knowing that the Cunningham claims were fraudulent and, further, of trying to get them to patent without proper investigation—perhaps in collusion with the Guggenheims.

In a further effort to prejudice the President's viewpoint, Pinchot wrote two personal letters—one of introduction in which he stated he had "known [Glavis] for several years." In the second letter he told President Taft that the Forest Service had taken action to prevent the Cunningham claims from going to patent.

Neither statement was true.

Taft noted that all the accusations in Glavis' letter were one-sided and that no apparent effort had been made to discover the opposing viewpoint. Taft contacted all the accused parties and asked them to submit their own statements of fact for his consideration immediately.

The resulting testimony, along with supporting documents, was several thousand pages long. It was considered by the President at some length. His conclusion was that Ballinger and his staff were not guilty of any wrongdoing.

As a last-minute thought, Taft asked the Attorney General for his opinion. The Attorney General's opinion was couched in far sterner language than the President later used:

"The insinuations or charges of improper action on the part of Secretary Ballinger are, in my opinion, entirely disproved. . . . Glavis' 'report' and summary abound in contradictions and misstatements. They omit to a degree that amounts to absolute suppression, letters, telegrams, and other documents. . . . His action in appealing to the Forestry Bureau . . . was a breach of all proper discipline. . . . Glavis' actions appear to have been founded upon a wholly exaggerated sense of his own importance, and a desire for personal advancement rather than on any genuine desire to protect the interests of the Government."

This was substantially the same conclusion President Taft had reached, but for diplomatic and political reasons he toned down the language in his letter of exoneration, written to Ballinger on September 13, 1909. This letter was smeared by Pinchot in the press as the "Whitewash Letter." It was far from a whitewash letter; it was a sweeping indictment of Glavis, and a clean bill of health for Ballinger. Pinchot was not mentioned because, as the President wrote to the forester, he hoped not to bring Pinchot into it at all.

The letter dealt with each accusation separately, showing how each one was too flimsy to be considered. Glavis was accused of "having suppressed data which, if included, would have given a different significance to documents quoted by him."

Said Taft: ". . . the case attempted to be made by Mr. Glavis embraces only shreds of suspicions without any substantial evidence to sustain his attack." The letter authorized Ballinger to dismiss Glavis for "filing a disingenuous statement, unjustly impeaching the official integrity of his superior officers."

Glavis was fired. Ballinger was cleared. One would have thought that would be the end of it, but Pinchot had other ideas. He still wanted to get rid of Ballinger and gain control of the Alaska coal lands.

Now Gifford Pinchot moved into the public arena, all guns blazing. He urged Glavis to publish a rehash of his accusations in *Collier's* magazine. It was entitled "The Whitewashing of Ballinger," and contained a new wrinkle: in addition to the charges made to the President, it implied that Ballinger, as land commissioner, had "urged Congress to pass a law which would validate fraudulent Alaskan claims."

The article was only the first of a long series, and Pinchot's version of the story dealt with a supposed conspiracy between Ballinger and the Guggenheims to defraud the Forest Service of valuable coal lands. This in spite of the fact that the Forest Service was really hardly involved at all! The story was pressed home by two competent writers, Norman Hapgood and Mark Sullivan, through magazines and newspapers of national circulation.

"Are the Guggenheims in charge of the Interior Department?" demanded a typical headline, under a picture of a giant corporate hand reaching out to seize the nation's heritage. Cartoons appeared depicting Morgan and other corporation bigwigs sailing down the river dividing the nation's timber, water power, coal, etc., between them. At the helm was Secretary of the Interior Richard Achilles Ballinger.

It was necessary, for this propoganda attack to be effective, that the public fully believe that "the Guggenheims" were out to completely control Alaska. For this purpose, no charge was too outrageous to make, and on several occasions (the rigged Cordova election, the Keystone Canyon fight), the Guggenheims had alienated Alaskan sentiment to the point where they played directly into the hands of the Pinchot faction.

The secret deal between the Cunninghams and the Guggenheims to mine coal gave Pinchot all he needed to tear the Interior Department apart, and the Taft Administration too, if necessary.

Pinchot, aided by Alaska's delegate James Wickersham and a corps of unscrupulous writers for the muckraking press, mounted a blistering campaign against Ballinger. The charges were so blatant and widespread that it was only a matter of time until the entire business came to the attention of Congress. Ballinger himself urged a hearing to clear his name.

In January 1910, a Joint Committee of the House and Senate was appointed for the investigation with Senator Knute Nelson as chairman. The committee was to investigate both the Interior Department and the Forest Service. The first investigations were done, but somehow forestry never came under scrutiny.

Glavis' charges, made through *Collier's* magazine, had raised the threat of lawsuit; it was said that Ballinger would sue for libel in the amount of $1,000,000. *Collier's* hired Louis D. Brandeis as attorney for Glavis. Brandeis was one of the most astute lawyers of his time. He converted what was to be an open fact-finding hearing into a vicious prosecution of Ballinger in an effort to keep Glavis from a lawsuit.

During the preparations for the hearings, Pinchot was making great political hay of the developing controversy. He was deliberately furnishing misleading information from government files to the newspapers to further his own cause. He had no intention of letting Ballinger slip from the noose he was so carefully laying out.

President Taft issued the order that no one concerned should try to contact any member of Congress in his own behalf, or even respond to a request for information without clearing it with his own department head first.

In open defiance of the order, Pinchot wrote a long letter to Senator Dolliver, and Dolliver read the letter on the floor of the Senate.

The Dolliver letter was read on January 6, 1910; on the morning of January 7, papers reporting the incident declared that Pinchot was "Defying the Lightning—Probably Will be Removed by Taft."

Taft had no choice. Pinchot was fired as Forest Service chief on that same day. It was apparently what Pinchot wanted. Wrapped in the cloak of Teddy Roosevelt Conservationism, he roundly condemned his former chief for not having done it sooner.

In the meantime, the Joint Committee had begun its investigations. The hearings dragged on in an atmosphere of scandal and suspicion for four months.

Red herrings and scandalous accusations—almost all of them based on the flimsiest kind of evidence—were scattered liberally along the way and kept the headlines blazing. It was a time of heartbreak and hate and the country was paralyzed with it. Almost nothing could be accomplished during this period, nor for almost a year afterward. Reputations and lives were torn asunder and anyone who tried to do anything in Alaska was suspected of being in collusion with the "Googies."

When the majority opinion of the Joint Committee of Congress was in, it did as Taft had done before: It exonerated Ballinger. The majority report read: "Neither any fact proved nor all the facts put together exhibit Mr. Ballinger as being anything but a competent and honorable gentleman, honestly and faithfully performing the duties of his office with an eye single to the public interest."

But the finding was ignored.

Pinchot's charges had been pressed home so vigorously, on so many fronts, and with such effectiveness, that Ballinger stood convicted in the public mind.

Much of this was due to the skillful work of Louis D. Bandeis. Brandeis showed himself the master of the art of the red herring. Many matters that had no actual bearing on the case were used to muddy the waters and confuse the issue to the detriment of Ballinger.

Ballinger never had a chance. He resigned as Secretary of the Interior in 1911, and went to his grave in 1922, still under the cloud raised by Gifford Pinchot.

Taft, of whom Pinchot has written: "He was self-indulgent in many ways. He hated to pull against the stream. For him the Indian Heaven where rivers ran uphill on one side and downhill on the other, so that one could always travel with the current, would have been Heaven indeed," proved himself on the contrary a man of great courage by standing firmly by Ballinger all through the latter's political persecution, and then through his own.

To a friend he wrote: "I am very sorry to get your letter of May 19. If I were to turn Ballinger out, in view of his innocence and in view of the conspiracy against him, I should be a white-livered skunk. I don't care how it affects my administration and how it affects the administration before the people; if the people are so unjust as this, I don't propose to be one of them. Mr. Ballinger has done nothing of any kind that should subject him to criticism. He has been made the object of a despicable conspiracy, in which unscrupulous methods have been used that ought to bring shame to the faces of everyone connected with it.

"I am sorry to differ with you on this subject; but life is not worth living and office is not worth having if, for the purpose of acquiring public support, we have to either do a cruel injustice or acquiesce in it."

3 CONTROLLER BAY RAILROAD SURVEYS

Each closure and reclosure of the coal lands, and each inuendo hurled by Pinchot against Ballinger and the Cunningham claims, had its immediate effect on the local Alaskan scene. The Bering River coal field was, after all, what it was all about. Here was a coal field believed to be big enough and rich enough for the politicians to fight over. It was Alaska's biggest coal field; nearly 700 of the 900-odd known coal locations were in this field.

Far from being in danger of monopolization, the Bering River coal field was a hotbed of competition. Claims had been taken by many hundreds of different persons, and at least seven, and possibly more, independent railroads were surveyed from the coal fields to tidewater on Controller Bay.

In 1908 the passage of the Heyburn Bill was met with a general upsurge of happiness and confidence. The bill was misleading, as where one paragraph allowed coal claimants to combine up to 2,560 acres, another paragraph reversed the move. But still it was a start. Men were being led to stake great sums of their personal wealth on the risky development of a coal mine in Alaska. To do this successfully, they needed a railroad, or several railroads, to bring the coal to tidewater.

In early 1909 when several of the "clear-list" and "expedite" moves had been made by Secretary of the

Interior Ballinger, the Katalla pioneers rolled up their sleeves and set out to build themselves a whole raft of coal railroads.

The first three railways to attempt to tap the Bering River coal field were the Alaska Pacific & Terminal Railroad Company, the Copper River & Northwestern Railway and the Catalla & Carbon Mountain Railroad.

Clark Davis' Catalla & Carbon Mountain Railroad which still retained the old-style spelling of Katalla, was begun in 1906 and was stopped short by the withdrawal of the coal lands. Davis filed a new survey in 1909.

The Catalla & Carbon Mountain survey apparently ran from Carbon Mountain at the far end of the Bering River coal fields in Cunningham Ridge to Atna, a wharf site on the Bering River. The new survey of 1909 extended from Atna to a point on Controller Bay. From this terminus a three-and-one-half-mile trestle was to extend over the shallow bay to a docksite on a deeper channel.

While Davis' route pushed to the far end of the coal field, the Kush-Ta-Ka Southern Railway branched out along the Kush-Ta-Ka Lake with arteries to Lake Charlotte and northward.

According to Archie Shiels, "The Kush-Ta-Ka Southern Railway was part of a program to connect the coal fields with the Copper River Railway."

Surveys for the Kush-Ta-Ka (a Tlingit Indian word meaning, perhaps appropriately, "ghost") were filed shortly after the newer Catalla & Carbon Mountain survey in 1909. This railway was surveyed by J. L. McPherson, who was also its chief engineer; president was Charles F. Munday. The Kush-Ta-Ka's main branch ran to a group of coal claims, which included claims of Michael Heney and his brother Patrick A. Heney. This group of claims was known as the "English group."

There is evidence on the maps of the Kush-Ta-Ka Southern Railway that the Copper River & Northwestern had surveys for terminal and docking facilities on Kanak Island, coming across from the north instead of from the west, as the other three did. Four surveys had Kanak Island in mind for docksites, while two projected a long trestle to Okalee Channel from the west shore of Controller Bay.

The Bering River Railroad had much in common with the Kush-Ta-Ka Southern. Surveys for both began in January 1909 and were completed the next month. Both also projected trestles to Kanak Island, a low sand island in Controller Bay, over almost identical routes.

However, surveys filed for the Bering River Railroad were filed March 25, 1909, almost five months earlier than the August 21 filing for the Kush-Ta-Ka. The two lines ran almost parallel courses as far as Lake

Right—The salmon cannery at Mile 52 on the railroad was nearly swept away by the 1912 flood.

Below—Chitina was where rail and road met. A branch of the Richardson Highway ended at Chitina, and the town became an important transfer point for both passengers and freight.

Above—The river steamer *Gulkana,* partly dismantled, on the shore of Miles Lake, July 28, 1914.

Right—Just south of Chitina a trestle bridge across the Copper River washed out every spring when the ice broke.

Kush-Ta-Ka, at which point they diverged. The Bering River route then ran east of the lake and the Kush-Ta-Ka ran west.

Beyond the lake the Bering River Railroad tapped four claims in the Cunningham Ridge, north and west of Carbon Mountain. The president of the company was C. J. Smith, the vice-president was H. C. Henry and the locating engineer was H. L. Hawkins. But the most memorable name appearing on the maps was that of its secretary, Clarence Cunningham.

The Controller Railway & Navigation Company, whose line terminated south of the proposed trestle for the Catalla & Carbon Mountain Railroad, completed the fourth of the survey series that year. The route was to run up Canyon Creek to the Carbon Mountain area. Preliminary surveys were begun September 21, and completed October 17, while definite location surveys were made a year later. Richard S. Ryan was president and H. R. Gabriel was locating engineer. There was to be a lot more heard of this railroad for it became one of Gifford Pinchot's "red herrings."

Projections were nice, but without the land for coal mining and terminal facilities the railroads were stymied. The coal land withdrawal followed by the Forest Service withdrawal was making life difficult for all involved in the development of the Bering River coal fields.

The miners and railroads were joined in their protest by the Cordova Chamber of Commerce in 1910. The chamber sent an eloquent appeal for action to President Taft. They reiterated the facts pointed out—that the Chugach National Forest now had the entire field sewed up, and that the coal claims had been pending for over five years.

And Richard Ryan of the Controller Railway & Navigation Company went to Washington, D.C., to plead for a withdrawal of land from the Chugach National Forest for terminal purposes.

He ran head-on into Gifford Pinchot's propaganda buzz saw.

4 "DICK TO DICK," ANOTHER RED HERRING

In response to the Alaskan appeals, President Taft eliminated 12,800 acres of land adjacent to Controller Bay from the Chugach National Forest for railroad terminal purposes on October 28, 1910.

Before acting Taft held a full cabinet discussion, and referred the question to Pinchot's successor. Chief Forester Henry S. Graves reported that he would have no objection to a withdrawal of up to 18,000 acres; however, after some discussion he recommended a withdrawal of only 320 acres, just enough for terminal

purposes for the Controller Railway Company. President Taft determined that a small land withdrawal favoring one company over others would not be justified. He felt that enough land should be eliminated to provide all the competing lines with terminal facilities if they desired. This move also had the effect of discouraging monopoly and establishing a large enough area for a railway terminal townsite. There were no trees in the entire 12,800 acres of Forest Reserve in question.

Taft issued the order, an executive decree, knowing that it would be decried and roundly condemned by the press, but he felt it to be right, so he did it.

Collier's, on target, was the first to pounce. "The Latest in Alaska; Controller Bay and its Control of the Alaskan Situation," by Mabel F. Abbott, was published May 6, 1911.

"Although the people of Alaska do not know to whom they ought to be thankful for their deliverance from the clutches of the Guggenheims, they know that theirs was a narrow escape...." Then the article added darkly, "Have they escaped? It is not yet time to sleep."

After thus invoking the spectre of the wicked "Guggenheims," Miss Abbott went on to state that there were only three outlets possible for Bering River coal: Cordova, Katalla and Controller Bay. Cordova, she said, was too long a haul, and Katalla was proved impracticable by the loss of the Guggenheim breakwater in 1907. This, according to her, left Controller Bay as the only practical outlet.

Starting from these half-truths, she went on to imply that the Controller Bay withdrawal would immediately pass into control, in its entirety, of the Guggenheim-Morgan Syndicate. This was, of course, a patent absurdity, but in the inflamed condition of the public imagination it was easy to swallow. The Guggenheim implications were not stated outright, but were driven home by the old and time-honored method of the loaded question: "The key to the situation is the ownership or control of the coal land and the water-front of Controller Bay. *If before Congress should have a chance to act the title to any of these lands should become alienated, how would that alter the situation?*" The question itself was absurd; it implied that ownership of *any portion* of the coal fields, *or* any portion of the Controller Bay elimination, would automatically put the entire Bering River coal field into "the clutches of the Guggenheims." She drove home this unstated implication with the bugaboo of the Cunningham claims: "The Cunningham claims have not passed to patent, but a strategic site has been eliminated from the Chugach National Forest on the shores of Controller Bay."

The "strategic site" on the shores of Controller Bay to which all this refers is so shallow that a three-and-one-half-mile trestle, as shown on the 1909 surveys, was required to reach a channel only 15 feet deep. And since it was a shifting channel at that, it might not be in the same place day after tomorrow. The use of the "strategic site" by these struggling little railroad companies was really the best they could make of a poor situation.

The fact was that all the companies which would use the terminal tract withdrawal would be in direct competition with the Guggenheims, a situation devoutly to be wished, if preventing a Guggenheim monopoly was really the aim.

It is certain that the Guggenheim-Morgans had no intention of trying to ship coal from the shallow, windswept anchorages of Controller Bay (though they did have a survey to Kanak Island), as a short 30-mile spur railroad could join Bering River coal with their Cordova mainline and a deep protected harbor with a dock large enough to handle three ocean-going steamers at once. They also had a coal and smelter townsite surveyed for the junction of the two lines.

But the Pinchot faction was not concerned about preventing monopoly. They wanted to discredit Interior Secretary Richard A. Ballinger, and if the President got in the way, he would be tarred with the same brush. At this point the presence of Richard S. Ryan of the Controller Railway & Navigation Company came dramatically to the public's attention.

A story written by Miss Abbott and published in the *Portland Journal* claimed that Ryan had obtained the elimination order from President Taft through the influence of the President's brother Charles, who supposedly was interested in the company. Miss Abbott proved her contention with a letter, allegedly written by Richard S. Ryan to Richard A. Ballinger, hence "Dick to Dick." The letter was found in the files of the Interior Department, according to Miss Abbott, while she was doing research for an article. The bombshell letter read:

Dear Dick,

I went to see the President the other day. He asked me who it was I represented. I told him, according to our agreement, that I represented myself. But this didn't seem to satisfy him. So I sent for Charlie Taft and asked him to tell his brother who it was I really represented. The President made no further objection to my claim.

Yours, Dick

The "Dick to Dick" message caused quite a stir, implying as it did that the President was conniving

with the Guggenheims. Most people down south were not familiar with Alaska's Controller Bay so it made a juicy scandal. It helped drive home the myth, created by Pinchot et al., that President Taft was in collusion with Ballinger to hand over Alaska to the greedy Guggenheim corporation.

But Mabel Abbott had gone too far. The letter was soon found to be a complete fraud, a hoax perpetrated by Miss Abbott whose mental stability was afterward called into doubt. But it was too late. The story had been picked up by the Philadelphia *North-American* and had spread like wildfire.

John E. Lathrop, who had originally printed the story by Miss Abbott in the *Portland Journal*, had followed the story up with articles in the *Pacific Monthly*. These made the outrageous and totally false claim that Mr. Richard Ryan was preparing to fence in the public domain on Controller Bay with barbed wire.

All the fanfare on Richard Ryan's railroad had created a potentially dangerous situation. Thanks to all the publicity and exaggerated values attributed to the coal claims, Richard Ryan was in the position to make a "killing" by selling stock to his railroad.

The *Seattle Post-Intelligencer*, close enough to the Seattle-Alaska people to know the situation, felt called upon to print a warning:

RYAN ROAD MERELY A SCHEME—

The so-called Ryan Road would reach no coal which could be shipped out of Alaska, even if it had a terminus from which shipping were possible. Like the other projected schemes in that region it has the ear marks of a plan to take advantage of the receptive condition of the public mind, a condition due to the exaggerated popular notion of the value of the Bering River coal deposits. If some cunning manipulators of frenzied finance succeeds in getting an Alaska coal company organized, the trusting public will be due for a trimming which will make all other "get-rich-quick schemes" of the last decade look like a nice little game of penny ante. This is said as a warning. . . .

The article pointed out that all the public outcry about "this group or that group or that other group" of coal claims, and the commonly assigned values were so far out of line as to be dangerous. Not one of the claims had been valued at under $10,000,000 by careless writers, and indeed, Miss Abbott (of the fertile imagination) in her supposed expose of the Controller Bay elimination, gave the claims a value of one billion dollars. All these asserted values, of course, were not worth the paper they were printed on, because no work had been done on the Bering River coal claims in order for anyone to assign a value of any sort. No one knew what they would be worth, if anything. Apart from a small bit of development mining done by MacDonald and a few others in 1907 and 1908, there actually had been no coal mined.

The truth was that coal mining was as good as against the law; the same law that said a coal mine must be opened before a claim could go to patent. The situation was becoming more and more confused and frustrating, and anyone who tried to shed any light on the matter was immediately accused of being in league with the Guggenheims.

Surprisingly, an Alaskan helped to perpetuate the situation. James Wickersham, now Alaska's Delegate in Congress, nursed the wounds from his own 1907 job refusal from the Guggenheims by fostering an anti-Guggenheim attitude. In 1908 he had won his seat going against them and he hadn't stopped. "But everyone knows," observed the *Fairbanks News-Miner,* "just where he would be today had the purchase price been paid."

5 WICKERSHAM RIDES ROUGHSHOD

Wickersham was not a man to be crossed. He came out fighting the Guggenheims hard, and often swinging low.

". . . If ever there was a criminal conspiracy in the United States to get the immense resources which belong to the people, it is that of the Alaska Syndicate in Alaska. . . ."

". . . There is one great monopoly there, the Alaska Syndicate, which is now threatening to control its resources—the coal, the copper, the fish, and especially its transportation routes. . . ."

"And . . . today the threat is not that our resources are to be leased so much as they are to be leased to the Alaska Syndicate. . . ."

These statements (repeated on other occasions with various embellishments) were all quoted from Wickersham's testimony before a House Committee on Territories in 1910, concerning "Railroads in Alaska." Wickersham at this time was busy promoting another railroad from Valdez known as the "Hubbard Road," and trying to obtain incentives for the enterprise of Mr. Hubbard without giving any of the same incentives to the Guggenheims. It made sticky going for the Delegate, but the hearing afforded him a fine vehicle for making such statements as those quoted. Although he was a voteless Delegate, his statements concerning Alaska were given great weight, and he used his prestige to the limit to

discredit the Alaska Syndicate and further the distortions being advanced by Pinchot.

The distortions and outright lies then being circulated were legion and extremely confusing to the public. Among the most repeated and damaging untruths slung against the "Googies" was the claim of "Syndicate control." The Guggenheims were accused of controlling all three routes to the Interior, as well as numerous companies. They also supposedly had control of all copper smelters on the Pacific coast, and all transportation routes. And now there was the threatened control of the Bering River coal fields.

Many of the company holdings, which were cited, did not exist. A close scrutiny of these charges reveals how much the public was misled.

Wickersham was the proponent and originator of the claim of "Syndicate control" of all three Interior railroad routes.

While arguing in favor of the Hubbard Road, Wickersham erroneously reported that, "The Alaska Syndicate is composed of J. P. Morgan, the Guggenheim brothers, M. J. Heney and S. H. Graves of the White Pass & Yukon Railroad."

Actually the Alaska Syndicate was composed of the House of Morgan, the Guggenheims, the Havemeyer financial house and Kuhn, Loeb & Company. The interests of Heney and Graves were purchased in late 1906 when the Copper River Railway was purchased by the Copper River & Northwestern Railway Company. It is likely, however, that Heney and Graves held stock in the newer enterprise.

From this questionable assertion, Wickersham proceeded to show the extent of Syndicate control. He said, ". . . There are three gateways into the interior of Alaska, and only three. There is the White Pass & Yukon route from Skagway over to the head of the Yukon River, and down that river; that is one gateway. That belongs to the White Pass & Yukon Company. The head of that company in Alaska is Mr. S. H. Graves. It is an English company; Mr. Graves is the president of it, and he is also a member of the Alaska Syndicate.

". . . The Copper River route is the second gateway into Alaska, and that is now occupied by the Alaska Syndicate with their road. . . ." This did not take into account the Valdez route, which Wickersham himself was trying to promote at this very hearing.

". . . The third gateway is from Seward. The Seward gateway belongs to the Sovereign Bank of Canada, in which J. P. Morgan & Company are partners and one-third owners. So that the Alaska Syndicate is, practically, for all purposes, the absolute owner of all three of the gateways into Alaska."

This latter assertion was so patently untrue that O. G. Larabee, president of the Alaska Northern

Railroad from Seward, fired a letter off to the Committee chairman in which he said:

"I understand the statement has been made before the . . . committee on Territories by the Hon. James Wickersham, Delegate from Alaska, that the Morgan-Guggenheim Alaska Syndicate owned this road, or had an option to purchase it or control it in some manner. Any such statement is absolutely without foundation. I wish to state here most emphatically that neither the Messers. Guggenheim nor the Morgan-Guggenheim Alaska Syndicate have any interest in this project, and have never, to my knowledge, expressed a desire to negotiate for it. This has already been stated on oath by the representatives of that syndicate. . . ."

The only one of four possible routes shown to be controlled by the Alaska Syndicate was the one up the Copper River, yet the fear of Syndicate control of all the railroad routes in Alaska continued to dominate Congressional thinking for a decade.

Concurrent with this fear of Guggenheim railroad domination, was the fear of steamship monopoly. In 1907 the Alaska Syndicate bought out a number of the leading steamship lines and consolidated them under the Alaska Steamship Company. Far from being the only line operating, the Alaska Steamship Company was in direct competition with several other lines which advertised frequent sailings.

Coal, of course, was at the heart of the accusations. Eastern coal interests greatly feared the advent of Alaska coal, and they played heavily on the fears which Pinchot and Glavis had engineered for their own purposes.

If the charges against the Guggenheim-Morgan Syndicate had been pressed merely on the ground of "Syndicate control" they could easily have been refuted as there was substantial opportunity for successful competition. Pinchot, Glavis and Wickersham were far too skilled in the propaganda arts to leave it at that. Instead, charges were made in the national press, of jury tampering in the Hasey trial; of irregularities and bribery; of coal graft at Fort Liscum. Wickersham was in full cry. A letter and voucher which had been brought to light by the auditor, Douglas, implicating David H. Jarvis and the Alaska Syndicate, was aired liberally in news columns. All the publicity was apparently too much for the honorable Jarvis. He committed suicide in June of 1911. His death and the suicide note only made the Wickersham charges more easily believed.

Now Wickersham turned his wrath on the Attorney General (also named Wickersham), who had failed to join the Pinchot wolf pack. Wickersham accused the Attorney General of "Shielding the Guggenheims" from prosecution in the jury tampering allegations.

This, too, was fully investigated by Congress. On July 31, 1911, they completely exonerated the Attorney General of the charges leveled by Wickersham.

Not a single charge made by the Pinchot faction was ever proved, yet countless lives and reputations were ruined by them. Each new accusation was thoroughly investigated by both the Congress and the President. All this delaying action was wearing Alaskan nerves thin. Six years had passed and in the coal fields hundreds of coal miners were still waiting for their coal claims to go to patent.

6 MARCH OF FORGOTTEN MEN

Something had to be done about the Bering River coal claims. Six years was a long time. And each year, in spite of government inaction, a claimant was required to do $100 worth of improvement work on his claim. Many had also paid the $1,600 purchase price of the land.

The trouble was that in spite of all the furor, the charges of graft and fraud and all the rest, there was little agreement on what the law actually meant. Consequently, no claims had gone to patent and no one owned a foot of coal land in Alaska.

One of the big disputes grew out of interpretation of the 1908 Heyburn Bill, which allowed claimants to combine up to 2,560 acres. The question of how this affected unperfected claims in the field arose. Could they be patented if, prior to "initiation of entry" they had agreed to consolidate after patent and to operate at joint expense? The legal staff of the Department of the Interior was of the opinion that they could.

The Pinchot faction immediately pounced on this legal opinion denouncing it as an effort by the Interior Department to patent the fraudulent Cunningham claims. The department in its opinion was referring solely to unperfected claims and thus not to the Cunningham group at all, but since it hadn't been spelled out properly in the written opinion, the Pinchot people had a field day with it.

A difference also arose as to the meaning of the term "initiation of entry." Did it mean "location," as Glavis would have it, or did it mean the filing of certain other papers after location had been made? These differences caused endless confusion.

In an effort to clear the air, the Attorney General took up the same question and rendered an opinion that was popularly misconstrued. While it agreed with the Interior Department's opinion regarding unperfected entries, it was generally interpreted as a negative response.

Glavis, adding to the misinterpretation, stated in *Collier's* that this opinion reversed the original "on every point" and that through his (Glavis') efforts in getting it referred to the Attorney General, he had "saved the Alaska coal cases."

He had, of course, done nothing of the kind. Instead, he had furthered the Pinchot myth of a "conspiracy" in the Interior Department to patent fraudulent Alaska coal claims, and he had created an impossible situation for the Alaska coal miner. How could a prospector and miner understand the law when even the lawyers couldn't agree on what the law said?

In all the charges and counter-charges of fraud, graft, corruption; all the bitter contumacy resulting from the Ballinger-Pinchot Controversy, the Alaskan coal miner was truly the forgotten man.

In March 1911, Richard Achilles Ballinger, unable to endure the stigma attached to his name, resigned as Secretary of the Interior.

With the resignation of Ballinger, Walter L. Fisher became Secretary of the Interior. In Fisher, Gifford Pinchot had all that he could desire. Fisher was a vigorous conservationist, who was intent on prosecuting all the Bering River coal claimants as criminals. He probably did not see it this way. His real intent was to cancel all the coal claims in Alaska to facilitate the leasing program he favored. The only way these claims could be canceled was for fraud. It was his belief that the construction of the law was such that none of the Alaska coal claimants had complied with it.

The only way out was for the courts to decide.

The first court cases were brought while Ballinger was still Secretary of the Interior. They were designed as test cases, the first being against three defendants: Archie W. Shiels, Charles F. Munday and Earl Siegley, all friends and close associates of M. J. Heney. The indictment against these three was brought on November 3, 1910, and the very next day another series was brought against a larger group which included in its number, Donald A. McKenzie, promoter of the Nelson townsite. A third series of cases named among its number, Michael J. Heney, although he had died the month before. All were for fraud. Before it was over, most of the coal claimants in the Bering River field would be indicted on the same charge.

On the day of the driving of the copper spike at Kennicott, March 28, 1911, the first of the Katalla coal cases went on trial. On the bench was Judge C. H. Hanford. The outcome of the Shiels-Munday-Siegley case was awaited anxiously in Katalla and Cordova for it would answer many of the unanswered questions for nearly a thousand Alaskan coal claimants.

A week later, on April 4, 1911, Judge Hanford handed down a decision in favor of Shiels, Munday and Siegley. Cordova and Katalla were understandably jubilant. If the decision was upheld by a higher court, it meant that the coal lands would at last go to patent, at least the ones which were not fraudulent; the Copper River & Northwestern would likely build its Katalla-Bering River spur and then the extension on to the Yukon River. The All-American railway would at last be a reality in Alaska.

The case had been referred to a higher court; in the meantime, there was great agitation for some action in the coal land matter—now. Both Katalla and Cordova initiated a campaign to send a sea of telegrams to Washington, D.C. Some of the hundreds of wires that were sent give an idea of the feeling of the towns:

We claim no protection for coal frauds, only justice.
—S. Blum & Co.

We ask for nothing but our own coal. Why delay?
—Cordova Commercial Co.

Why are we punished when the law is with us?
—E. A. Hegg

No coal this year means ruin for Cordova.
—J. H. Plant & Co.

Sealing up Alaska coal is not conservation.
—O. E. Lambert

Without coal our gold is too dear.
—Horseshoe Liquor Store

Several hundred telegrams were sent, personal and business, both from Cordova and Katalla. Not one of them was ever answered or even acknowledged by official Washington. In no reply, Alaskans had their answer. The feeling was for a demonstration that could not be ignored.

Early May 1911 found Katalla dying on its feet from federal interference and inaction. The forgotten men of Katalla had had enough. Along the streets a massed parade formed. A huge sign was carried at the head of the parade. It read:

PINCHOT, MY POLICY
No patents for coal lands!
All timber in forest reserves!
Bottle up Alaska!
Save Alaska for all time to come!

Behind the banners they carried a dummy wearing a big sign "Gifford Pinchot." The parade wound its rowdy way through the streets, chanting and shouting; along the main street and down to the beach they marched with increasing momentum and passion.

On the beach a great bonfire was built, and nearby a crude gallows was erected. When the parade reached the beach the dummy, old rags stuffed inside a miner's coat and pants, was carried to the gallows, and one of the leaders stepped to the platform.

"Have you any last words?" he demanded of the lifeless lump. A howl of laughter and ribald comment followed this, and one wag shouted, "Don't let him say anything more! He's said too much already!"

With mock severity and ceremony the stuffed head was jammed into the hangman's knot and hoisted up where it swayed in the breeze to the derisive cheers of the crowd.

Then the crowd's leader walked over to the bonfire, and in a booming voice he read a copy of President Roosevelt's "temporary" withdrawal of coal lands. That proclamation was now six years old, and still no coal land patents. The reader finished and then walked ceremoniously to the blazing fire and threw the proclamation in. More cheers and whistles.

Suddenly there was a stirring in the ranks. A man came running up carrying a toy pistol. He ran to the ragged figure on the gallows and strapped the toy pistol on. This was greeted by a roar of laughter and applause. Pinchot always wore a gun. In his autobiography he said: "At least on some of his rides and tramps, Teddy Roosevelt carried a gun. After my responsibility came home to me, I did so as a regular thing, and I was right. Thank Heaven I never had to use it." Whether he was right or not, it was considered an outright insult in Alaska that he thought it necessary to wear one on the streets of their towns.

The telegrams, and the Katalla protest parade were part of a restless spirit now moving in Alaskans, who were ready now to demand their rights. The feeling was for something even more dramatic, a protest so electrifying it could not be ignored by official Washington. Cordova was ready to perform.

7 CORDOVA'S BOSTON TEA PARTY OVER COAL

Deputy Marshal Sam Brightwell was aware of the growing sentiment in Cordova. He knew that something was up, but he could not find out what.

On May 3, 1911, Brightwell received a call from Orca, three miles by boat from Cordova. There was some trouble there so he left immediately to investigate.

Shortly after Brightwell's "convenient" departure, Richard J. Barry, general agent for the Alaska Steamship Company and the Copper River & Northwestern Railway, was sitting in his office on the ocean dock, checking some invoices. A large shipment of coal brought 1,000 miles from Canada the day before by steamship was on the dock. The ship was still moored dockside.

Barry heard an unusual noise and glanced out the window. Just someone working around the warehouse, he decided. The bay outside lay sparkling in the clear May sunshine. A beautiful day.

Again he heard it. Voices, like chanting. And the sound of many boots. Marching. The sound echoed hollowly on the wooden dock.

Barry got up from the desk and went to the window. There were hundreds of men. All carrying shovels and chanting: "Give us Alaska coal. Give us Alaska coal."

Several men had cut the lines to the ship and it was drifting free. Others had climbed onto the pile of coal and were shoveling it overboard. Soon a large force was shoveling. As they worked they took up the chant: "Give us Alaska coal. Give us Alaska coal."

Barry snatched open the door and ran outside.

"Hey, what do you think you're doing? This is company property!"

"We want none but Alaska coal!" declared one of the leaders. "Shovel away, boys!" Once more they took up the work and the chant, "Give us Alaska coal."

In vain, Barry pleaded, pointing out that it was not the government who would lose, but the company. He argued that the company had already bought and paid for the coal.

His answer was the chant, "Give us Alaska coal!"

Angrily, Barry ran inside. "Get the marshal," he snapped at a clerk. "Where's Sam Brightwell?"

"I already called. He's gone to Orca."

Barry opened a drawer and took out a pistol. He ran out onto the dock. "You fellows stop that shoveling," he demanded, waving the revolver menacingly. "This is company property!"

The clerks came running out of the office. "Now, Dick," they pleaded, "take it easy. You might kill someone with that. We can still call the police chief or the mayor or someone. Put that gun away."

Barry hesitated, looking at the gun. The men on the dock, after all, were men he knew. There was A. J. Adams, who had surveyed the townsite of Cordova, and former Mayor Will H. Chase, Councilman James Flynn and Charles Ross and dozens of his own friends.

It suddenly occurred to Barry that this was no unruly mob, but a well-organized demonstration. He shook off the restraining hands of his clerks and went back inside.

He picked up the telephone. Outside the shoveling resumed. A woman took up a shovel; she was cheered as she tried to work the blade down into the lumps. From the sidelines, the crowd, now almost 300 strong, urged the shovelers on. One of the men found an ordinary shovel too small, and he used a broad snowshovel, to the intense delight of the crowd.

Uptown, Barry's call had gone through to Mayor Lathrop. The Mayor had no power to act and passed it up to the U.S. Commissioner. Then he wired Governor Clark, who was in Washington, D.C., at the time:

> *Big demonstration at ocean dock. Crowds armed with shovels dumping foreign coal into bay. Agent steamship company was telephoned for assistance. Deputy marshal out of city on case. Have appealed to U.S. commissioner. Situation desperate.*

The commissioner then deputized Mayor Lathrop and Police Chief Dooley. A wire also went out to Marshal Sullivan at Valdez.

By the time Dooley and Lathrop arrived on the scene, the shoveling was in full swing.

Dooley stepped up and shouted, "All right, you men. Break it up. In the name of the United States law, I order you to disband and go home!"

At this a big husky Negro jumped onto the pile of coal and, brandishing his shovel, offered to do combat with Dooley, pistols against shovels. Some of his buddies quickly talked him out of this.

The quieting of the combative black man had a calming effect on the crowd. Now an impromptu "town meeting" took place as they debated whether Dooley had any authority to act. Some were in favor of breaking it up since the law was now represented. Others felt that Dooley was bluffing; his authority didn't extend beyond the city limits unless he had been properly deputized. They doubted if he had been. There was a hesitation in the crowd. They were almost ready to follow the example of the few who had resumed shoveling, when like a cavalry charge to the rescue, Superintendent Van Cleve arrived with a detail of railroad men from the roundhouse. The beleaguered Dooley heaved a vast sigh of relief as the shovelers quietly shouldered their tools and headed for home. They had made their point. They were satisfied.

The "Cordova Coal Party" was a sensation. "Cordova Has Boston Tea Party," headlined the *Cordova Alaskan*.

"Alaskan Citizens Throw Canadian Coal Overboard," sang the Associated Press wires, carrying the story all over the United States.

By the next day, there were as many versions of the story as there had been demonstrators.

An account of the affair written by L. F. Dobbs, known in Cordova as the "Whistler," read:

"I had a cleaning and pressing shop on Main Street . . . and I was working in the window, and all of a sudden a crowd was passing on both sides of the street, so I went out to find out what was happening and the crowd told me to close up and come along, as they were going to dump all of the Googie coal into the bay. So naturally I closed up and went with the Good Citizens of Cordova, and we went to work on the coal and dumped most all of it into the bay, and would have finished the job, but all of a sudden George Dooley, the Chief of Police, came running like hell from his FISHING TRIP? with one of Cap Lathrop's wagons and teams and he climbed up on the spring seat of the wagon and began making a wonderful speech and demanding, in the name of the company and the President of the U.S. that we stop throwing that coal overboard, and all of us being Good Citizens we did stop.

"And I remember very well Sam Brightwell *just* had to go down to Orca Cannery to investigate a Japanese murder. And do you know, I never did find out if Sam ever caught that murdering scoundrel; or if Dooley ever caught any fish; but George always seemed to like me pretty well and I believe if he had of had more time he would have at least given poor little ole me one for my supper after all that hard work, doing that long shore work!"

There was considerable difference of opinion as to the amount of coal actually thrown into the bay. One cynic said, "You know how much coal went overboard? One sackful. The soup's not as hot as it's cooked." Another, who was there and shoveling, said that almost a ton went over the side.

The amount of coal thrown over is not important. The important thing was that here was a demonstration which could not be ignored. Cordovans had finally made the government—and the public— sit up and take notice.

Sentiment throughout the States was generally favorable, and the parallel between the Cordova Coal Party and the Boston Tea Party was too strong to be missed. Papers all over the United States carried editorials. The *Seattle Post-Intelligencer* pointed out that while in Boston they had gone in the dead of night disguised as Indians, in Cordova they had gone in broad daylight, asking nothing but their rights.

The government was not so charitable. "An act of unmitigated lawlessness," declared Secretary of the Interior Walter L. Fisher. Governor Clark of Alaska said that while he understood the plight of Alaskans who were still waiting for action in the matter of coal

Clockwise from right— Shushanna Avenue, the main street of McCarthy. The Mother Lode Mine in winter. The Row, one of McCarthy's contributions to R&R for the miners. A territorial G.O.P. excursion to Chitina, believed to have been in 1916. The sign above the elephant says "CHITINA. To Cordova 129.4 miles. To Kennicott, 64.5 miles."

lands, "we must be patient a little longer." Official Washington deplored such anarchy, meanwhile engaging in an arbitrary sort of anarchy itself in regard to Alaskan coal lands.

In the days immediately following the Coal Party, there was great fear of further demonstrations. At least two more coal-laden ships were on their way to Cordova, and precautions were being taken in Cordova to see that no more coal was dumped. Then a few days after the Coal Party, huge boulders appeared on the railroad tracks. General agent Barry expressed the view that the boulders hadn't just rolled there, but that this was an intentional act to prevent the coal from being taken to safety. One rock required blasting to remove it from the tracks.

District Attorney George Walker and United States Marshal Harvey Sullivan were on their way to Cordova to investigate the uprising. They had announced that at least 50 warrants would be issued for the arrest of that many known participants, but the storm of protest from all over the country made them decide that a little delay would be prudent. Telegrams and letters poured into Cordova from other Alaskan cities, expressing support for the Cordova position as demonstrated by the Coal Party.

When District Attorney Walker and Marshal Sullivan arrived in Cordova, they received a far different impression than they had gained from the press coverage of the protest. Walker issued a statement: "I have made a thorough investigation of the matter and it seems that the citizens of Cordova on their own behalf and on behalf of the people of Alaska have attempted to attract the attention of the public and federal officials to the Alaska coal situation by shocking it. I know the temper of the people of Cordova and as it has been my official duty to investigate these matters I know they are law-abiding people and am proud to observe that in this exploit it was not accompanied by any personal violence or disorder and there was no loss of public or private property further than was necessary to make a demonstration expressing the motive and deep-seated hope and necessity of the Alaska coal situation." He praised the "high-class citizenship of Cordova," and pointed out that it was adequately policed, not only by federal officials, but by a "pure and patriotic public sentiment."

In the aftermath of the Coal Party, Isaac Guggenheim, on arriving in New York from Europe, was quoted as saying that his people did not own or want a foot of coal land in Alaska, but that they were ready to spend millions to build a railroad to the coal fields if the government would adopt a sane and stable policy. He remarked that the bottling up of Alaska was preventing its development, and that Europeans marveled at the treatment accorded Americans in Alaska.

8 PINCHOT VISITS ALASKA

But the positive publicity was short-lived as the favorable sentiment aroused by the "Cordova Coal Party" evaporated in a black cloud of suspicion and fear.

In June the Bering River coal claimants received letters from Secretary of the Interior Walter L. Fisher demanding that they "show cause" why their claims should not be canceled for failure to apply for patents before the deadline. But these same claimants previously had been notified by circular letter that the time allowed them to apply for patent had been extended to 1914! Now they had to defend themselves against this low form of governmental harassment.

Harassment took many forms, and in the battle for national sentiment, the Pinchot people were winning hands down.

It was time for the victors to take a "fact-finding" trip to Alaska. In September the coal and railroad areas of Alaska—Seward, Cordova and Katalla—were visited by Secretary Fisher, Senator Miles Poindexter and Gifford Pinchot. They were dubbed the "Three Guardsmen" by the *Valdez Miner*, which commented wryly that the moral of the performance by these "political tragedians" was that "while it was probable that God made the U.S., the Three Guardsmen would do a better job for Alaska."

Secretary Fisher and his party came first. They were met with little hostility other than badges worn by welcoming committee members saying: "Allow us to Mine Our Own Coal!"

Gifford Pinchot, as always, was the man to stir up the fireworks. Senator Poindexter and Pinchot stopped in Cordova on their northbound trip long enough to issue a statement saying, "Contrary to general opinion, the Conservation men are not responsible for tying up the reserves of Alaska. Since President Roosevelt sent his first message urging development in 1906, we have been trying to get Alaska opened under conditions fair to all the people. But we should not believe that development should necessarily mean monopoly."

With that and the invitation to meet with "the pioneers, the business men, the professional men, and above all the miners and prospectors ...," he departed for Valdez and Seward. His itinerary called for a visit to the Matanuska coal fields out of Seward, a return to Cordova where he would travel over the Copper River & Northwestern to Kennicott and back. From there he would take a launch to Katalla for a visit to the Bering River coal fields and Controller Bay.

While Pinchot and party were making the early portions of their trip, the volatile and imaginative people of Katalla were preparing what they considered a proper "welcome" for Gifford Pinchot. Empty buildings, of which there were plenty by now, were placarded: "Closed—Result of Conservation."

The *Katalla Herald* published the "Katalla Program for Pinchot Celebration."

Song of Welcome (????): Hail to the Chief
by the Katalla Quartette.

The conquering hero comes too late,
To view the corpse in its last estate,
With the sword of power, in the hand of greed,
Marvel not at the fatal deed,
On the storm that sweeps on the
  glacier's height,
Echoes the moan from the last brave fight.
They have blocked the trails that the
  brave have trod,
And fenced the land from man and God;
All hail to the chief of Alaska's desolation.

Platform
Pinchot et al. vs. Alaska development.
Eastern coal vs. Alaska coal.
Conservation lunacy vs. progress and sanity.
The Eastern coal barony vs. the people
  of Alaska.
Pinchot vs. (Oh, Pshaw.)
(To be followed by a banquet in the
  Chugach Forest Reserve.)

Menu
(To be cooked without wood or coal.)
1st course—Porcupine soup.
2nd course—Porcupine mulligan.
3rd course—Roast Porcupine.
4th course—Porcupine ala mode.

Grand Chorus
"An optical demonstration of the way we do,"
(by the gumshoe men).

Obituary
DIED—Alaska
CAUSE—Too much Conservation.
Funeral oration over Alaska by Lord High
  Executioner, Gifford Pinchot. (Keep your
  hands on your pocketbook.)

When Katallans got their first look at the Pinchot party, they were amazed and amused to find that the great ex-forester had hired two guides (Tom White and a Katalla Indian), two bodyguards (Jack Dalton and Bill Boswell of Cordova), and carried a .44-caliber pistol under his coat in a shoulder holster.

In addition to this menacing retinue, Pinchot brought along his own press agent, John E. Lathrop, who had first picked up Mabel Abbott's "Dick to Dick" story. Mr. Lathrop's first act in Katalla was to wire his wife and reassure her that he was in no danger. He said that his family had begged him not to make the trip to Katalla for fear of violence. The people of Katalla, though they were considerably overwrought about the coal situation, were still law-abiding citizens and the thought of personal violence had not occurred to them. They considered Mrs. Lathrop's concern over her husband's personal safety a good joke.

It would seem that the source of danger to the Pinchot party was not the people, but the elements. As if Mother Nature herself was out to express her displeasure with Gifford Pinchot, the weather turned unseasonably foul and remained so throughout their trip. At Seward the weather was so bad that Pinchot, supposedly a great outdoorsman, abandoned his plan to visit the Matanuska coal field. Senator Poindexter ignored the weather and went anyway.

As Pinchot came down from the Kennicott country by train, an earthquake rocked the landscape, and Mount Wrangell erupted. A few days later an icy lake broke loose on the Kennicott Glacier and tore out 14 bents of a railroad bridge and ripped out 460 feet of embankment. The force of the water caused the famous Kennicott "Pot Hole" to gush high in the air like a geyser.

Down in the Katalla area storms hammered the coast from the time of Pinchot's arrival onward. Pinchot's launch was weatherbound on the mud flats near Camp Seven and was two days late getting to Katalla.

When he finally arrived, a large meeting was held with the people of Katalla, where residents had a chance to "Talk plainly to Pinchot." The *Katalla Herald* reported that, "In joint debate last night, Conservation theories were knocked sky high by Alaskans—Pinchot ventured opinion on coal cases but was forced to admit he knew little about them." In the debate residents were especially critical of the Chugach Forest Reserve, saying it did not serve any forestry purpose whatsoever. Pinchot defended it on the grounds that the timber would be needed "in time" for local development.

Although the debate was heated, every courtesy was shown to the former forester.

From Katalla, Pinchot and his party set sail on the launch *Pansy* and headed for the coal country. Only "Pinchot's own crowd" were along on this trip. In the coal fields, he paid a visit to the headquarters of the MacDonald mines, the Lippy-Davis property and the Cunningham group. He saw little of the coal country itself, but contented himself with talking to the men in charge of the camps.

While there, the Katalla storms raged on, and the coal miners had plenty of time to "talk plainly" to the "Conservation faddist." Pinchot, under this concerted verbal attack, switched his tactics and came out strongly in favor of leasing the coal lands. He gave out an interview in which he stated he would make every effort to get Congress to pass such a bill.

While they were unalterably opposed to his policies, the individualistic Alaskans were intrigued by the colorful and individualistic Pinchot, who, according to the *Katalla Herald*, "packs a gat and travels with bodyguards." E. E. Ritchie, commenting editorially on the fuss made over the Pinchot visit, observed sourly that, "He is no more entitled to notice than any other tramp tourist. Still less, in fact."

When at last Pinchot and his party were able to buck the wind and rain back down the Bering River to Controller Bay, Pinchot must have been more than happy to get away.

He and his party now stopped off at Richard Ryan's temporary headquarters on Controller Bay. While here, Lathrop related the story of Mabel Abbott's visit to his office with the "Dick to Dick" story. He also had to answer some rather embarrassing questions about the statements attributed to him that Ryan was preparing to fence in the public domain on Controller Bay with barbed wire. Nevertheless, the day passed pleasantly enough, each side observing the host-guest amenities.

In an interview while there Pinchot admitted that the Controller Bay harbor was not bottled up, and that Richard Ryan's small holding along that shore was in no way a monopoly. He said the matter had been "grossly misrepresented" by the Eastern press.

Outside, the weather raged on, the wind constantly picking up in intensity and the rain driving in solid sheets before it. Pinchot and his party declined the invitation from Ryan to spend the night ashore at his place, and retired to sleep aboard the launch *Pansy*. By this time a full-fledged gale was in progress. In this part of Alaska, no wind, no matter how strong, was ever classed as anything but a "gale"; there were never any hurricanes, even when winds roared to over 100 miles per hour, as they often did. The storm this night was so violent that the 48-foot Forest Service vessel *Restless* parted her moorings and was dashed against the mud flats and completely demolished. The *Pansy* was unhurt, but the occupants spent a sleepless night, with constant anchor watches throughout the wild, black night. Next day Controller Bay was putting

on one of its famous performances for the benefit of Gifford Pinchot.

The entire party, anxious to reach dry land and the relative comfort and safety of Katalla, left the *Pansy* and began the long trek to town. Katalla people, used to such violent weather, found it highly amusing, especially in the light of the publicity given to the "strategic importance" of Controller Bay as a harbor. Commented the *Katalla Herald:* "Controller Bay in Throes of Storm—Pinchot Compelled to mush overland on return from coal lands as he cannot tread the angry waters of his much-touted Controller Bay harbor, where the seas are rolling mountains high."

Although Katalla residents found much to rejoice over in the personal discomfort of Gifford Pinchot during his visit, there was little real progress out of the trip. Pinchot did declare that the wind-swept shores of Controller Bay were not fit for any purpose, least of all politics or transportation, and he did admit that Bering River coal did not seem to be the threat to Eastern coal interests that was feared, but there was no letup in his efforts to see the claims canceled. He asserted that he did not think there was a single valid claim in the entire field, on account of the construction of the law.

The *Katalla Herald* said that, "The feeling here is that the Government proposes to confiscate all the coal lands on some technicality for leasing purposes."

They were right. That was exactly what the government proposed to do.

On December 4, 1911, the Supreme Court reversed the decision of Judge Hanford. The court now decided that a person or association, regardless, was limited to one coal land entry in Alaska. Judge Hanford had taken a different view. In his decision he had said: "Locators of coal claims in Alaska under this law [1904] have the right to use business sense, to look ahead and make arrangements for working capital and to contract in advance for transportation facilities, and to sell or mortgage their claims. By mandatory words the law prescribes that the locator who meets the requirements prescribed shall receive a patent." It was not construed to mean dummy entrymen, though. (Dummy entrymen were those with no interest in the transaction but who merely allowed their names to be used.)

Now this decision was overturned, and anyone who had "used business sense" in trying to establish the business of coal mining in Alaska was open to prosecution as a criminal. The decision upheld the indictment of Shiels, Munday and Siegley, and would also affect the other pending cases, which covered almost all entrants in the Bering River field. Hundreds of claimants would not only stand to have their claims canceled, but there was a possibility that some of them would actually go to the penitentiary for trying to mine coal profitably in Alaska! It was pointed out, however, that it was not likely that a western jury would ever render a guilty verdict in a case of conspiracy to defraud charged by the government.

It was small comfort.

9 DELAYED DECISION: AN AMERICAN DREYFUS

It was not until 1940 that it became publicly known that Ballinger—and Alaska—had been needlessly crucified upon a flaming cross of coal.

In that year Secretary of the Interior Harold L. Ickes published an official finding titled: "NOT GUILTY. An Official Inquiry into the Charges Made by Glavis and Pinchot Against Richard A. Ballinger, Secretary of the Interior, 1909-1911."

Following this, and taking perhaps a leaf from Glavis' book, Ickes published an article in the *Saturday Evening Post* entitled: "Was Ballinger an American Dreyfus?"

"When I came to Washington as Secretary of the Interior in 1933," said the official document, "I was thoroughly convinced that Richard A. Ballinger, one of my predecessors, had been guilty of maladministration . . . of more than bad administration; that he was a co-conspirator with the Guggenheims and the Cunninghams in a movement to defraud the United States of valuable forest lands." But as time went on, Ickes became aware that everything was not as he had so strongly suspected; that in fact the forests were only superficially concerned. Accordingly, Ickes decided to find out the truth, and to this end he appointed a disinterested committee to officially investigate the charges which had been pressed so rigorously against Ballinger 30 years before.

The results were startling. They showed that an innocent man had been persecuted unjustly for political ends, tried and convicted on charges which were *never even stated,* in the court of public opinion where he could not defend himself.

In 1911, the political chaos resulting from the Pinchot-Ballinger Controversy split the Republican Party down the middle. As a result, Teddy Roosevelt rallied his supporters and formed the Bull Moose Progressive Party. In the three-way election of 1912 he pulled over four million votes, not enough to win, but enough to virtually assure the election of Woodrow Wilson over William Howard Taft.

The coal fields of Alaska were at the heart of the controversy that split the party. Taft would not forget them before his term ended.

History had come around full circle. Thirteen years and a monumental amount of effort and money had been poured into the attempt. It was 1912 and fate was still working on Alaska's "All-American" railroad.

The Copper River & Northwestern Railway could not now build to the Yukon, nor could any private company without local coal. In June of 1911, shortly after the Cordova Coal Party, the company announced that the locomotives of the Copper River & Northwestern would be converted to oil-fire, thus removing the bugaboo of Guggenheim "control" of the coal lands. It also removed the possibility of a smelter for the copper ore, and decreed that all the millions of tons of high-grade Kennicott ore would have to be shipped out of Alaska. The lower grade ores would be left in the ground. It also meant that if Alaska was to have a railroad clear to the Yukon River, the government would have to build it at taxpayers' expense because the Alaska Syndicate no longer stood ready to invest its millions in the enterprise. It wouldn't be profitable without the coal.

The government began to move. That same year President Taft set aside a large area of water frontage on Orca Inlet between Cordova and the Nelson townsite for a Naval coaling depot, and the Army was preparing to construct adequate defenses to protect the copper and coal of that region in case of war. Also the Navy was preparing to conduct some rigorous steaming tests with the Alaskan coal to determine if it met their high standards as a marine fuel.

In 1913 two parties were sent out, one to the Matanuska and one to the Bering River coal field to obtain samples of coal for these tests. At the time both fields were inaccessible.

As Taft prepared to round out his executive career and leave the White House, he performed an act which was to gather momentum in the coming years. He created the first Alaska Railroad Commission.

This four-man commission was charged with the duty of studying and recommending "the best and most available routes for railroads in Alaska which would develop the country and its resources."

The members of the commission were: Major Jay J. Morrow of the Army Engineers; Alfred H. Brooks of the U.S. Geological Survey; Leonard M. Cox, a Navy engineer; and Colin M. Ingersoll, a consulting railway engineer.

These men spent five months in the field investigating a dozen ports and railway lines totaling more than 3,000 miles.

Coal, being at the heart of Alaskan politics, was the central consideration, though colonization and commerce, as well as suitable ocean terminals entered into the study also. According to the commission's report, the routes studied fell into three classifications—all related to coal:

(1) Those to the Interior without reaching a coal field (the Skagway route, Haines-Fairbanks over the old Dalton Trail, Iliamna-Kuskokwim, Valdez-Fairbanks).

(2) Those to coal fields only (Katalla and Controller Bay railroads).

(3) Routes to the Interior which tapped coal fields en route via spurs (Cordova-Fairbanks, Seward-Fairbanks, Seward-Innoko-Iditarod).

The routes in the first class were discussed. The Skagway and Haines routes were considered impractical inasmuch as they went through Canada, involved excessive mileage and tapped no coal. The Iliamna-Kuskokwim route was reported to have some limited value as there were several good harbors available for feasible short line railroad development.

The Valdez to Fairbanks route gained closer scrutiny than any in the first group of routes because "Valdez has a harbor inferior only to that of Cordova and about equal to that of Seward. There is no probability, however, of its being utilized as an outlet for either the Matanuska or Bering River coal. The commission considered the possibility of developing Matanuska coal by way of this port, but the haul involves the surmounting of two major summits (Tahneta and Thompson passes), and one minor summit (Ernestine), besides being longer in distance than the haul over the alternate route to Seward."

The commission then turned its attention to the second classification, the railroads to coal fields only. These involved the Katalla and Controller Bay routes, all of which were summarily rejected for lack of suitable harbor. They felt it would be more feasible to build a spur to the Copper River & Northwestern Railway to connect with Cordova's port. The neccessary spur was only 30 miles long and offered no major construction problems.

These observations reduced the discussion to three routes; two to the heart of the Tanana Valley (one via Cordova, the other via Seward) and the third to the Kuskokwim River from Seward.

"After its study of all available harbors, the Commission is of the opinion that the one at Cordova is, without question, the best. It has no disadvantage not possessed by all, and one great advantage possessed by no other—namely, an ample area of good anchorage. Seward is evidently the seaport for the Matanuska coal and Cordova the logical outlet for the Bering River coal. . . .

"It is evident that on the Cordova route the first investment will be less than on the Seward route; the

resulting freight rates will be lower; the terminal offers a better harbor than the one at Seward; and the tributary coal field promises the earlier development because its product can be marketed cheaper. Each of these economic features points clearly to the advisability of reaching the Tanana Valley via the . . Copper River, and *the commission therefore recommends the construction of a railway from Chitina to Fairbanks.*

"The construction of a railway through the Copper River valley to the Tanana would leave a large area unprovided for; it in no way furnishes transportation facilities to the rich agricultural land and mineral wealth of the Matanuska . . . further there is no provision for the Kuskokwim valley. Fortunately, both the Kuskokwim and Susitna valleys can be developed by a railway from Seward to the navigable waters of the Kuskokwim. *The building of this line into the Susitna valley is second only to a line to Fairbanks, and its extension into the Kuskokwim should also be provided for as soon as possible, and the Commission so recommends.*"

Thus, the Alaska Railroad Commission had recommended two "All-American" railroads, with their attendant coal spurs. The conclusion of the report emphasized the importance of these railroads and pointed to the advisability of the federal government building them:

"In conclusion it should be stated that the commission is unanimously of the opinion that this development should be undertaken at once and prosecuted with vigor, and it can not be accomplished without providing the railroads herein recommended under some system which will insure low transportation charges and the consequent rapid settlement of this new land and the utilization of its great resources."

Its job done, the Alaska Railroad Commission formally disbanded and Congress began the lengthy and heated debates on the "Act to Authorize the President of the United States to Locate, Construct, and Operate Railroads in the Territory of Alaska, and for other purposes," commonly known as the Alaska Railroad Bill.

There was some opposition on the grounds of Alaska's "worthlessness" and all the stereotyped arguments, but by and large it was felt that something was necessary.

Said Senator Furnifold McL. Simmons, D. of North Carolina: "The United States government has not only not helped the people of that country . . . and . . . its industries, but it has literally fettered and gagged the people of the Territory in their efforts to develop it. . . .

"We have practically prohibited railroad building!

"How have we done this? By the most outrageous system of discriminatory legislation that any great country ever followed toward one of its territories or colonies. . . . We have imposed an annual license tax of $100 a mile upon every mile of railway; we have withdrawn from entry all the coal and oil lands in Alaska; we have deliberately denied to the railroads that have been constructed and we deny to any railroad that may hereafter be constructed, the use of these two great natural resources for the purpose of operating their lines."

Opposition to the bill, oddly enough, came from representatives of existing, struggling and defunct railroads in Alaska. All of them urged that if only Congress would pass the legislation to make railroad building possible, the government and taxpayers would be spared the needless expense of millions of dollars.

But the political climate would not permit this. It was felt that a government line would aid in keeping transportation costs down as no private road could. After lengthy hearings and debate, the Alaska Railroad Bill was passed on March 12, 1914.

The bill authorized the President to construct a railroad or railroads "not to exceed a thousand miles, to . . . connect one or more open Pacific Ocean harbors on the southern coast with the navigable waters of the interior of Alaska, and with a coal field or fields so as best to aid in the development of the agricultural and mineral or other resources of Alaska, and the settlement of the public lands therein, and so as to provide transportation of coal for the Army and Navy, transportation of troops, arms, munitions of war, the mails, and for other governmental and public uses, and for the transportation of passengers and property."

The Alaska Engineering Commission was duly appointed, consisting of William C. Edes, Lieutenant Frederick Mears and Thomas Riggs.

In Alaska there was a surge of high elation, especially in the Cordova area. It was expected that, in light of the priority set forth by the earlier Alaska Railroad Commission, the government would buy the Copper River & Northwestern Railway for completion of the Cordova-Fairbanks route, and also the 70 miles of the bankrupt Alaska Northern Railroad at Seward for the Seward-Kuskokwim route.

So it was that, almost from the moment the copper spike was driven, it seemed that the government itself would buy the Copper River & Northwestern Railway for completion of the first of two proposed "All-American" railways.

BIBLIOGRAPHY AND NOTES
PART THREE

1 COAL AND SMELTERS
   The Cordova Alaskan. "Thousand Coal Claims Affected by Decision," March 31, 1911.
   Hearings, House Committee on Territories. 61st Congress, 3rd Session. "Letter of January 14, 1911, from S. W. Eccles, President, Copper River & Northwestern Railway, to E. L. Hamilton, Chairman of the Committee." 1911, pp. 211-12.
   The Katalla Herald. "Coal Mine a Good One," "Vast Coal Deposits" and "Work on Railroads Will be Pushed During the Winter," all September 21, 1907. "Pile Driving at Camp 7" and "Plenty of Coal Awaits Shipment," October 13, 1907.
   Shiels, Archibald W. Letter, October 1, 1963.

2 BALLINGER-PINCHOT CONTROVERSY BEGINS
   Ickes, Harold L. *Not Guilty: An Official Inquiry into the Charges Made by Glavis Against Richard A. Ballinger, Secretary of the Interior, 1909-1911.* U.S. Government Printing Office, Washington, D.C., 1940.
   Pinchot, Gifford. *Breaking New Ground.* University of Washington Press, Seattle, 1945.

3 CONTROLLER BAY RAILROAD SURVEYS
   Map of Controller Bay Coal Fields, Alaska, compiled by Watkins, Seattle, February 11, 1909.
   Railway maps of the described railroads.

4 "DICK TO DICK," ANOTHER RED HERRING
   Collier's Magazine. "The Latest in Alaska" by Mabel F. Abbott, May 6, 1911.
   Nichols, Jeanette Paddock. *History of Alaska Under Rule of the United States.* The Arthur H. Clark Co., Cleveland, 1924, pp. 374-76.
   The Outlook. August 5, 1911, pp. 750-51.
   The Public. "The Controller Bay Scandal," July 28, 1911.

5 WICKERSHAM RIDES ROUGHSHOD
   Hearings, House Committee on Territories. "Railroads in Alaska," beginning March 28, 1910, pp. 605-63, 669-71, 674, 694, 699, 717.
   Some interesting information is also contained in Hearings of the House Committee on Territories, 61st Congress, 3rd Session, 1911, pp. 202-209, including the following exchange when Delegate James Wickersham was questioning Mr. Steele, the attorney for the Guggenheim interests:

Wickersham: Do you know that the man he [Hasey] shot was walking along with his pick and shovel on his back, going to work?

Mr. Steele: No, I have heard that they had 200 or 250 men there trying to rush this little band of our people, trying to take possession of this property.

Wickersham: Now let me ask you another question. Is it not true that at Valdez you people did everything you could, after you abandoned that town, to prevent the people of the Home Railway Company from going to that town?

Mr. Steele: No, we never did a thing.

Wickersham: Is it not true that you even put men up in the canyon with instructions to shoot the men belonging to the Home Railway Company, and that Hasey, a man in your employ, did shoot them, and that he killed one man?

Mr. Steele: That is true, that Hasey did shoot one man. Hasey was a United States Deputy Marshal, sworn in, and put in charge of that property by the United States Marshal of that district.... Our men were there in possession and working a cut which, compared to this room, was not quite so wide and a good deal longer. As I have been told, there were 25 or 30 of them there. A man by the name of Reynolds had organized what he called the Home Railway, and got a good many subscriptions from the people of Valdez, the subscriptions being payable, first, so much when so many miles were completed, and so much when he got so many more miles completed. They went on with the work and came to where this cut of ours was, and I have been told by Mr. Hawkins, who was working there, that they had a force of 200 to 250 men, and some people got up and spoke to these men and told them: "Your only way of getting any money or anything is to jump this cut and take possession of it," and these 200 or 250 men attacked this small force of ours that were there at work, and the United States Deputy Marshal, Hasey, as I have been told, told them to stop and keep away, and they did not stop, and they came on, and he shot, and I think he killed one man, did he not?

Wickersham: Yes.

Mr. Steele: And wounded one or two more.

Wickersham: Yes; and is it not true that your people are paying him while he is in the penitentiary?

Mr. Steele: No, sir. That is not true.

Wickersham: You defended him?

Mr. Steele: Undoubtedly we did. They came and told us that the United States officials were all against him instead of standing up for him, and we, out of motives of humanity, furnished money to conduct his defense.

Wickersham: How much did you furnish?

Mr. Steele: I can not tell you that.

Wickersham: $70,000?

Mr. Steele: I do not know....

Wickersham: Did you ever see the receipt for $3,000 that went to bribe a deputy district attorney?

Mr. Steele: I never did.

Wickersham: You never heard of it?

Mr. Steele: No, sir.

[A letter and a voucher, both taken from the files of the Katalla Company by an auditor, H.J. Douglas, when he learned that he was to be fired, were introduced in evidence before the committee. These showed disbursements by M. B. Morrisey, an accountant, including expense entertaining witnesses and jurymen and cash advances to a number of individuals.]

Mr. Steele: ... I think you will find that that matter on its face reads very, very badly, but it is all capable of a perfectly fair and honest explanation. What I wish to say, Mr. Chairman, is that so far as the syndicate is concerned, we knew nothing of it at all before we found it out from Judge Wickersham. That account and the letter were stolen from the files of the Commercial Company by the auditor, Douglas, who approved the claim, and on whose approval it was paid. That auditor never made the slightest objection to a single official of the company out there, he never said a word to us in New York about it, but he approved the claim, and the claim was paid. Then he stole that letter, and the account from the files of the company, and the first we in New York ever heard of it was when Judge Wickersham told Mr. Birch about it. . . .

The Chairman: Now, Judge Wickersham has stated that it cost $70,000 to defend Hasey. . . .

Mr. Steele: . . . I would say that Mr. Carson told me that the reason that amount was so high was that the expense of witnesses was tremendous. I think one of the witnesses had to come from the Arctic Circle. . . . They had to come through all kinds of weather and be kept there; and they paid the witnesses, they said, exactly the same fees as were paid the witnesses for the Government. And in regard to the Government's witnesses there, allow me to say this: that Mr. Carson said that the Government summoned a great many witnesses there to testify against Hasey, and when they got there the Government found that their testimony would be favorable to Hasey, and then the Government did not want them, and Carson kept them there, kept them as witnesses for the defense.

Mr. Southwick (of the Committee): Was this man Hasey the man that defended your property against this mob?

Mr. Steele: Yes, he was a deputy marshal of that district.

Mr. Southwick: He defended your property against this mob at Valdez?

Mr. Steele: Yes, he tried to.

Wickersham: What about this expense of entertaining witnesses and jurymen?

Mr. Steele: That is a thing that is done in Alaska. After the first trial was all over, then the counsel for the defense gave the jury and some of the witnesses some kind of entertainment. I suppose it is a little exaggerated form of what we have in the East. When

a man has been acquitted in the East the accused and his counsel go up and shake hands with the jury. . . .

. . . And it has always seemed to me that if anything wrong had been done by any of those gentlemen out there the proper thing would have been to have them indicted, or not to have them indicted, because the grand jury might not have done that, or to have the matter called to the attention of the authorities out in Seattle, where those gentlemen would be present and where proper proceedings might have been had, and if they had done anything wrong they could be punished; but so far as the syndicate is concerned they never heard of it and knew nothing about it until it was brought to their attention here.

6   MARCH OF FORGOTTEN MEN
     The Cordova Alaskan. November 3 and 4, 1910; March 31, April 4, 11 and 29, May 1 and 4, 1911.
     Ickes, Harold L. *Not Guilty: An Official Inquiry into the Charges Made by Glavis Against Richard A. Ballinger, Secretary of the Interior, 1909-1911.* U.S.Government Printing Office, Washington, D.C., 1940.
     Pinchot, Gifford. *Breaking New Ground.* University of Washington Press, Seattle, 1945.

7   CORDOVA'S BOSTON TEA PARTY OVER COAL
     Chase, Dr. Will H. Personal interview.
     The Cordova Alaskan. May 4 and 8, 1911.
     The Seattle Post-Intelligencer. May 6, 7 and 8, 1911.
     Wolf, Walter. Personal interview.

8   PINCHOT VISITS ALASKA
     The Cordova Alaskan. June 9, September 6, 11, 19, 20, 21, 22, 23, 25 and 26, December 4 and 5, 1911.
     Nichols, Jeanette Paddock. *History of Alaska Under Rule of the United States.* The Arthur H. Clark Co., Cleveland, 1924, p. 379.
     The Valdez Miner. January 14, 1912.

9   DELAYED DECISION: AN AMERICAN DREYFUS
     Ickes, Harold L. *Not Guilty: An Official Inquiry into the Charges Made by Glavis Against Richard A. Ballinger, Secretary of the Interior, 1909-1911.* U.S. Government Printing Office, Washington, D.C., 1940.

PART FOUR
THE CR&NW—CAN'T RUN AND NEVER WILL

KENNICOTT ALASKA

GUY F. CAMERON PHOTO

PART FOUR
THE CR&NW—CAN'T RUN
AND NEVER WILL

1 COPPER DAY IN CORDOVA

All the frustrations and bitterness of the Ballinger-Pinchot years could not detract from the brilliant accomplishment of building the Copper River & Northwestern Railway. The driving of the copper spike marked the completion of perhaps the greatest engineering achievement, under the most adverse conditions, in the history of Alaska. And it remains so, although little physical evidence of that former achievement remains.

A week after the simple copper spike ceremony at Kennicott, the first ore train moved down the line. It was loaded with ore so rich that it was not even milled, but simply shoveled into sacks as it came from the mountain. The ore from the mine averaged 70 percent pure copper.

The first copper train was expected to be 60 cars long to bring down the great backlog of ore; however, since insurance could only be obtained on a value of up to $250,000 the train was reduced to 35 ore cars. These cars carried 1,200 tons of copper ore, valued at the maximum insurable amount, $250,000.

The first week after driving the copper spike, while the ore train was being loaded, was a week busy with last minute finish work, snow clearing and other details.

Opposite—**An early view of the mill at Kennicott.**

In Cordova mighty preparations were under way for the arrival of the first ore train from the famous Bonanza Mine. Saturday, April 8, 1911, was officially proclaimed by the Mayor as "Copper Day" in Cordova. On that day the ore train would steam into town. Tourists from Valdez, Seward and other towns were arriving. Excursions were planned by two steamship lines serving Cordova, the Alaska Steamship Company and the Pacific-Alaska Navigation Company. The Copper River & Northwestern had rail excursions set up for the day. Five big steamships were in port: the *Northwestern, Seward, Bertha, Edith* and *Jeanie.* A huge dance was to be held at the Eagles' Hall to allow the crews of these five vessels to attend.

A delegation from the City of Cordova departed town on Friday morning, bound for Mile 27. They had discovered the train was due in on Friday and their mission was to hold the train over until next day because of the celebration plans. The delegation took advantage of the delay to decorate the train with bunting and streamers.

In town schools were not in session so the entire town was out, young and old alike. At 9 a.m. the excursion train left for Mile 27 to join the copper train and escort it to town. Aboard were several hundred citizens and the Eagles' band.

People in town waited all along the tracks for the first sign of the train.

At last they heard it. As the locomotive and its long string of ore cars approached Cordova with the excursion train ahead of it, the Eagles' band was playing, and the entire passenger complement was cheering and waving. All the bells in Cordova were then rung, whistles blew, and dynamite blasts rocked the air. Everyone had a shrieking good time as the train puffed its way slowly through town to the dock.

As it neared the dock, the five ships, gaily decorated with bright bunting, began to toot their whistles and add to the joyous din.

Public exercises followed with prayers and speeches delivered by M. E. Koonce and General Manager E. C. Hawkins. Cheer after cheer was raised to the men who had made the first rail connection with Interior Alaska possible. The Eagles' band played and schoolchildren sang patriotic national and Alaska songs.

Telegrams of congratulation were dispatched by the Mayor to President Taft, J. P. Morgan, the Messers Guggenheim, S.W. Eccles, president of the Copper River & Northwestern, Governor of Alaska Walter E. Clark and Secretary of the Interior Walter L. Fisher. Replies, also of congratulation, poured back over the wires for the next few days:

New York, April 10, 1911
Hon. W. H. Chase, Mayor, Cordova, Alaska
We thank you for your courteous and cordial expressions of good will in regard to the opening up of Alaska. Please accept in turn our hearty congrats and best wishes for your continued prosperity.

—J. P. Morgan & Company

The *Northwestern* began loading the ore for shipment to the Tacoma smelter. Nor did the festivities end there; when the vessel entered Seattle harbor nearly a week later, she was trimmed out in holiday attire with bunting and long streamers reading:

"First trainload of copper from the Bonanza Mine. Worth $250,000. A million tons to follow. We also have coal of our own. Let us mine it."

It had been a most historic day, and Cordova had done it up proud. She was now launched officially as the "Premier Copper Port of the World," although at that time the full potential of the fabulous Kennecott Mines was barely even dreamed of.

At this time the rolling stock consisted of 15 locomotives, 8 coaches, 256 cars, 4 steam shovels, 2 spreaders and 1 dozer. The locomotives were built by the American Locomotive works and included several consolidation engines of the latest type with electric headlights. These fine big engines were used exclusively for hauling passenger and mail trains. The older, smaller and less modern

engines were reserved for the hauling of copper and for maintenance on the line. The rolling stock was of the very latest and best available design. The railroad was standard gauge, a common carrier which had begun passenger service in 1909. Dining car service was inaugurated in January of 1911.

As with any new railroad, the rebuilding began almost as soon as the building was finished. A month after the first copper train moved down the line, the ice went out in the Chitina River, taking with it the bridge under construction there. It was quite a blow, as every effort was being made to build a wooden bridge that would be substantial enough to hold. For two weeks before the breakup, crews had been hard at work trying to reinforce the trestle and add five 60-foot spans, but only four were completed when a huge floe of ice broke from a large ice jam and swept everything out; piers, spans and all. Two of the spans were retrieved and anchored about 300 yards downstream, a third one lodged crosswise on a bar in the middle of the river and the fourth was last seen piled up in a jumbled mass of ice clear down in Woods Canyon. A few days later the canyon was reported completely clear of ice and obstructions—no sign of the span was ever seen again.

Small boats were pressed into service at the crossing until redriving could begin. The driving of a new pile trestle was begun as soon as the ice was out of the river, and from that time forward, the company abandoned plans to build a substantial bridge at the Chitina Crossing. Each year the trestle was allowed to go out with the ice, and a new one driven after the breakup.

There was a great deal of improvement work to do on the line before it was ready to be formally turned over to the Katalla Company as a finished railroad, and the entire summer was consumed in this work.

Late in 1911 it was accomplished, and chief engineer Erastus C. Hawkins made ready to leave for the States, his tour of duty done. He was given a rousing and warm farewell reception in both Chitina and Cordova. There were toasts, resolutions of tribute and speeches. Hawkins' health was drunk in good Irish whiskey, from a bottle brought from Ireland over 20 years before by his long-time friend, Judge Healy.

The toasts were followed by shaggy dog stories and much laughter. Mr. Hawkins' achievements were recounted in detail, both in speeches and in the papers. One of the innovations he was credited with was a system of laying rails so that no two joints were laid opposite each other, resulting in a smoother ride.

Hawkins said that his one disappointment was that he had to leave before his greatest ambition was achieved, that of building the railroad clear to the Yukon River.

2 THE NAVY REPORTS

As interest returned to the coal fields with the proposed military tests, Jack Dalton struck again. This time his target was the nose of a government clerk who had tried to tell him how to do his job. J. W. Swift was a government dispersing agent for some $85,000 allocated to Dalton to move 900 tons of Matanuska coal across the trackless wilderness to tidewater for the Navy coal tests. Swift maintained that Dalton was wasting government money—using more men and materials than were necessary for the job. Swift refused to pay some of Dalton's men, and there was a heated exchange of words that came to an abrupt stop when Dalton put a hard right to Swift's nose.

The man whose nose had been thus violated picked himself out of the nearest snowbank and went storming off to the town of Knik to demand retribution. The $5 fine levied on Jack Dalton did little to soothe ruffled feelings, and the little town of Knik also jumped into the act. The Knik Commercial Club held a protest rally and sent letters to Washington pointing out the difficulties of Dalton's assignment and taking to task both Swift and the commissioner who had levied the fine. Dalton maintained that Swift had done everything he could to obstruct his work, and many of Dalton's men continued to work even though Swift had withheld their wages.

It was not an easy task to move 900 tons of coal from the Matanuska coal field to tidewater. There were no roads or trails. The frozen Matanuska River could be used for most of the journey, but at least 42 miles of road would have to be built, including some small bridges. The test mining had been begun by J. A. Holmes, director of the Bureau of Mines, but it now appeared that the entire 8,000 sacks which had been prepared would have to be resacked. Dalton went to Seattle and brought north an outfit for winter sledging and about 500 tons of supplies, 30 horses and 9 men. He continued hiring as he sailed north. Then he set part of the crew to work building road and another group mushing in to Matanuska to resack the coal.

Meanwhile, another force of men under a mining engineer named R. Y. Williams was doing similar work in the Bering River coal field, where 855 tons were brought down to tidewater from the Tenino claim of the Cunningham group; 674 tons of it from a single opening.

The Navy's steaming tests were conducted aboard the *USS Maryland*. Bering River coal had been burned in boilers of the *USS Nebraska* in 1908 with good results, so there was considerable confidence in Cordova.

With great interest Alaska awaited the results of the 1914 tests. On those tests might depend some of the decisions still pending in regard to government railroads in Alaska.

There were some surprises in store.

"It is with regret, then, that the department reports that the recent tests show conclusively that Bering River coal, mined from selected veins in one of the most promising portions of the field, is entirely unsuitable for naval use. . . ."

That was perhaps the biggest bombshell to be found in the 1914 Naval coal test report. A great many things had been said and done on the seemingly warranted assumption that Bering River coal was almost certainly acceptable for use in the Navy's coal-burning Pacific fleet ships. Perhaps as much of a surprise as the failure itself was the reason for it:

"Formerly the defect that gave the most concern was the generally crushed condition of the coal, from which a large percentage of slack might be expected. An adequate amount of lump was found, however. . . . The coal . . . failed on account of its property of developing large tenacious clinkers—probably the most serious defect that can be developed by a coal for marine use. Whether or not a nonclinkering coal of good chemical and physical properties exists in the field is an unsolved problem. The Bering River sample tried in the *Nebraska* in 1908 did not clinker at the low rate of combustion and consequent low furnace temperatures pertaining during that inconclusive trial. However, neither did the Bering River coal recently tested clinker under natural draft. . . .

"The clinkering of coal is a subject on which but little of value is known from analysis. . . . A coal suitable for naval use . . . can not be spotted by chemical or physical excellence, but must be searched out by the laborious and expensive but conclusive methods of trial under service conditions. . . .

"This must not be regarded as a conclusive test of the quality of coal in the entire Bering River field. . . . There are many beds in the field and much variation in the quality of the coal in different parts of the coal-bearing area. Therefore, while the test recorded above showed that the beds mined do not carry the high-grade coal demanded for naval use, yet this does not condemn the entire field. There can be no doubt that the Bering River field includes a large amount of steaming coal in beds that can be mined."

In direct contrast to this gloomy report were both the port test and the steaming tests aboard the *USS Maryland* on the 900 tons of coal brought to tidewater the winter before by Jack Dalton and his crew.

The coal passed the port tests with flying colors, but the marine tests aboard the *Maryland* were really the clincher:

"20-knot test—The excellent steaming properties of this coal were plainly shown in this test. . . .

"10-knot test—Six boilers were lit for this run, but one was banked almost at the start of the test, and later it was cut out. About two and one-half hours later a second boiler was banked and cut out when the test had been in progress for nine hours. During the remainder of the test four boilers were used, these furnishing plenty of steam . . . Practice has been to use six boilers on Pocahontas coal. So far as is known the *Maryland* has never before made turns for ten knots with only four boilers in use.

"General Remarks—No tendency to heat noticed when damp; friable; from the standpoint of smokelessness the coal is also desirable. . . .

"The board found that this sample of Matanuska coal tested is suitable in every respect for use in the naval service."

Everyone assumed that the government would follow the recommendations of the Alaska Railroad Commission and build two railroad lines in Alaska for the purpose of opening the entire territory to development.

The Navy coal report furthered the assumption when it noted that: "Now that the Alaskan railroads will be built, a line extended into the Bering River fields, and the coal fields probably opened to leasing, the further test of coal from these [Bering River] fields for naval use should be resumed as soon as possible after the completion of the road, and after general development has set in in the coal fields, by the trial of large samples (cargoes) from various seams. In this manner only, in the department's opinion, can the existence of a satisfactory coal for naval use be ascertained." (The report had noted that the coal was all taken from one single part of the field, the Cunningham area. But it was well known that the coal that was burned so successfully in the *Nebraska* in 1908 had come from the MacDonald mine, nearly 20 miles away.)

Alfred H. Brooks of the U.S. Geological Survey also assumed that both railroads would be built, or at least the ones into Bering River and Matanuska. In the 1914 "Report on Progress" of the U.S. Geological Survey, he discussed the stimulating effect of the proposed railroads, and talk of a smelter cropped up again: "The certainty of railroad connection with the Yukon basin and the probability of an early development of the coal fields greatly stimulated the search for mineral deposits in Alaska during 1914. . . .

"A noteworthy feature of the mining industry in 1914 was the great number of investigations that were made on behalf of capitalists looking for properties that would warrant development on a large scale. This was true in nearly all the mining districts, but as was

to be expected, it was more pronounced in the south-central region, which will be directly benefited by the building of the government railroad. With the consequent opening of the coal fields we can now look forward with confidence to the early establishment of copper smelters in the coastal districts, and possibly at no distant day to the utilization of some of the iron ores."

Numerous bills for coal leasing had been introduced in Congress during the Ballinger-Pinchot years. None went very far due to the extreme confusion and high emotion surrounding the entire affair. Finally, on October 20, 1914, a coal leasing law went into effect, clearing the way for final disposition of the Bering River coal cases—in fact, the law made it mandatory, and allowed one year to review and make final determinations on the various claims.

The Cunningham claims had been canceled in 1911, and Secretary Fisher refused to grant an appeal. In 1914 the claimants once again applied to the General Land Office for a new hearing, but the motion was denied.

In January 1915, the charge against the MacDonald group of claimants, that the land located was not the same as that applied for, was dismissed. The land office announced that these claims would now go to patent. However, records of the local Cordova Forest Service office show only one patented claim in the MacDonald group, that of Morris A. Arnold, 157.18 acres, granted May 5, 1915. The article in the *Cordova Times* on the subject said that MacDonald and associates had made a strong fight for the land, and that one claim of the group had already gone to patent. The others had been held up by the land office charges, but they would now go to patent. Apparently, they did not, for unknown reasons.

In June, the *Cordova Times* announced that 40 claims in the rich "Green-Young" group were canceled. The charges were sustained that the claims were not made in the interests of the men whose names were used. The government also charged that mines had not been opened as required by the law. "The claim of L. A. Thurston, known as the Glen, is also included in the decision. The charges that a mine had not been opened were found by the land office to be not sustained, and they recommend that this claim be granted a patent." The claims known as the Tacoma and St. Louis, on which considerable work had been done, were reported relinquished by the claimants and their money returned. It is the only known instance where money was returned to any of the Bering River coal claimants, and this was a voluntary relinquishment.

So it went. In an effort to meet the one-year deadline Special Agent W. H. Lewis from the Department of the Interior was sent to Juneau in March to assist in reviewing the vast backlog of cases.

Rules and guidelines for the leasing of Alaska coal claims were finally laid down by the Department of the Interior in 1916. By then almost all of the capitalists—and capital—had cleared out or been cleared out of the Bering River coal fields. The coal leasing system in Alaska can be called nothing but a socialistic experiment, and it was a resounding flop. The Katalla-Bering River area, until North Slope discoveries, was the richest mineral section of Alaska. Today it boasts not one single resident.

Still, development could have succeeded if the conditions for its success had been brought about at the same time as the leasing was begun. There were those who tried to make a go of it, but it was economically unfeasible.

There is evidence that it was the personal animosity of President Wilson, combined with political expediency and pressure, that completed the disaster.

It was up to President Woodrow Wilson, in the last instance, to decide once and for all, what railroads would be built in Alaska to promote that Territory's development. He announced that his decision would be made public on February 15, 1915.

3 AWAITING THE DECISION

On the last day of December 1914, J. Pierpont Morgan opened negotiations with Secretary of the Interior Franklin K. Lane regarding the sale of the Copper River & Northwestern Railway to the United States government for the appraised physical value. Secretary Lane, when pressed by reporters, admitted that a verbal offer had been made by Mr. Morgan, but declined further comment.

Two weeks later J. P. Morgan submitted operation and maintenance figures to Secretary Lane in connection with the offer to sell to the government.

Great secrecy surrounded most of the decision making regarding the choice of routes, but rumor held that the asking price was $12 million, a tremendous bargain if true.

President Wilson's announcement of the intended purchase of the Alaska Northern Railroad came on schedule, but the news only made vague references to a "possible" purchase of the Copper River & Northwestern. There was much behind-the-scenes activity; Cordova's Chamber of Commerce sent its president, George C. Hazelet, to Washington, D.C., to make a showing of the resources of the Copper River valley and adjoining area because the Alaska Engineering Commission—successor to the Alaska Railroad Commission—had "practically neglected to make any investigation of resources of this section, or its adaptability as a trunk line route, either through lack of instructions from the Administration so to do, or an intentional desire to pass this section by."

There was much political pressure against the President's buying the Cordova railroad. The *Cordova Daily Times* of February 23, 1915, reported that Wilson was "vexed" over railroad rumors: "It is generally reported that President Wilson is much vexed over the attacks made on the administration over its alleged intention to purchase the Copper River & Northwestern Railway in Alaska, in connection with the proposed government railway line in Alaska. This reason is assigned by the President for not asking for a larger appropriation for the Alaska railroad at this session." (Two million dollars for the Alaska railroad in the Sundries Civil bill.)

A letter written to Harry Thisted by Donald A. McKenzie of the Nelson townsite said that many Democratic senators and Congressmen called on the President and protested because they were afraid of the political effect on the party if the Guggenheim road were purchased by the government. "I am satisfied," wrote McKenzie, "that Secretary Lane fully appreciates the great resources of the Copper River country and if the matter had been left entirely to him to decide I believe he would have taken over the Copper River road; and I have a strong opinion that this will yet be done. . . . Should the government not take over the Copper River road, the present owners will be compelled to build into the Bering River coal and extend their main line to save their present investment."

In a move against the possible purchase Richard Ryan of the erstwhile Controller Railway & Navigation Company turned up again in Washington. "Richard S. Ryan, promoter of the proposed railroad from Controller Bay to the Bering River coal field, in his effort to prevent the government from purchasing the Copper River & Northwestern Railway, has submitted a proposal to Secretary Lane to furnish transportation to Copper River copper ores and the Bering coal. Mr. Ryan would build a line himself from Mile 40 on the Copper River road to the coal fields, and thence down to tidewater on Controller Bay.

"He would erect smelters at the coal fields to smelt the ores from the Copper River. He estimates that for $800,000 a breakwater could be built which would make Controller Bay safe. The Brooks [Alaska Railroad Commission] railroad commission two years ago estimated that the breakwater would cost two million dollars.

"Mr. Ryan tells Secretary Lane that all he wants is permission from the government to build on his own account. The proposal is under consideration."

Kennecott Copper Company's Jumbo Mine at the foot of Castle Rock. (Nicolai Jensen photo, Alaska Historical Library)

Falcon Joslin, who had built the Tanana Valley Railroad at Fairbanks, jumped into the act with his own proposal to build. His offer, in conjunction with Clyde Morris, a railroad contractor and builder, was to build from Chitina to Fairbanks and from Mile 38 on the Copper River line to Bering River coal. They submitted specifications and plans for the proposed routes. They would build, they said, under the supervision of the Alaska Engineering Commission, at a sum not to exceed a certain sum per unit mile, and do the work within three years. After construction they proposed to lease from the government and operate for a period of 25 years, and pay three percent interest on the total investment, giving bonds for the faithful performance of the contract. Although it seemed an attractive proposal, it was turned down, why, no one seems to know. It seemed a safe proposition for the government and a good way to open up a large segment of the Territory.

But the Copper River & Northwestern Railway still had a life to live. On April 13th George W. Perkins, a member of the Guggenheim-Morgan Syndicate, praised the government's decision to buy the Alaska Northern and Tanana Valley railroads and the selection of the Susitna River route to the Interior. In an interview he said that the Copper River route was better from an industrial standpoint and that its extension into the Tanana Valley agricultural regions would still be far enough from the route of the government railroad that they would not be competitors. "I am not sorry it was rejected [the Copper River route] because we will now develop it for future business." The interview was taken to mean that the Copper River & Northwestern would now be extended, as the plans had originally called for.

All these separate proposals by private capital may have had some bearing on the government's actions. Actually there were two decisions involved. Now that the Copper River & Northwestern would not be purchased, there was still the decision whether or not to build, at government expense, the line to the Bering River coal field. The feeling was that since the government was prepared to spend $10 million to tap the 19 leasing blocks in the Matanuska field, it surely would be ready to put up a mere $1 million to reach the 60 leasing blocks in Bering River.

In May of 1915 a party of surveyors with its outfit went north and headed for the Bering River. At first it was thought that their mission was to survey the routes from the Copper River line into the field by way of Lake Charlotte, and to Controller Bay to tap Bering River coal.

But it turned out that this survey team, under John P. Walker, assistant supervisor of surveys for Alaska, and Thomas Hargh, U.S. mineral surveyor, had nothing to do with railroad routes. Instead, they were charged with surveying the Bering River coal field into townships and sections preparatory to leasing. They were part of the 1915 effort to clear the old prospectors and claims out of the way so that leasing could be set up. All the coal in Alaska was to be surveyed. Part of it would be set aside for the Navy; the rest would be set up for leasing.

In fact by 1916, there was still no government effort in sight to build to the Bering River field. The Senate Committee on Territories, noting this fact, passed a resolution endorsing its construction. The resolution read:

"Resolved, that the chairman of the committee is directed to advise the Secretary of the Interior that it is impressed by the representations made to it that the public interests require the speedy construction of a railroad into the Bering River coal field in the Territory of Alaska, and will be pleased to receive any communication he may care to make on the subject."

Secretary Lane replied in a letter which stated that ". . . if private capital cannot be induced to enter the field, government capital should be used to build such a road. I have been of the impression that it was wise to leave the development of the east side of Prince William Sound entirely to private capital, inasmuch as it had already been practically opened by the Copper River road. . . . It is my belief that during this summer the President should come to a determination as to whether it is necessary for the government to construct a road opening this coal field. . . ."

This pronouncement had in it the current administration thinking that they really wanted nothing to do with the Bering River area. The insistence that private capital should build can only be attributed to President Wilson and the political phobia against the Guggenheim or the Bering River coal claims associations. It was a hangover from the Ballinger-Pinchot days—a sleeping dog nobody wanted reawakened.

Despite every effort of Cordova and Katalla residents to convince the government it was wise to open the Bering River field, the government clung stubbornly to its insistence that private capital open up the Bering River coal fields. The government would not, although it was spending far more to open the Matanuska field on its government-financed and operated railroad, the Alaska Railroad.

It is difficult to understand the government's reasoning. A full-page editorial on January 17, 1917, in the *Cordova Daily Times* cited the questionable government action saying, "A railroad must have coal for traffic as well as for use. . . . [But in Bering River] a railroad can neither lease nor own nor have any interest in a coal mine.

"Conversely, a coal company cannot own a railroad.

"But if the two companies should enter into an agreement, it would be an unlawful combination or conspiracy. Section 8 of the lease law is specific on this.

"The government evidently expected that when the coal was opened some private corporations would build a railroad to the Bering River field. It has often been said that owners of the Copper River & Northwestern would do so. But this is a false hope. The Copper River people did plan to build a railroad there at one time. They took an option on 5,280 acres of coal land, made surveys for a railroad to it, and would no doubt have built a line and opened a coal mine. But the government interposed, charged the parties with a conspiracy to monopolize the coal field, canceled the title to the coal land and thus stopped the proposed railroad building....

"If the Copper River & Northwestern should venture again to build to the field, they could again be charged with conspiracy to monopolize the coal. The coal lease to which they proposed to build would be subject to cancellation.

"Not under existing laws could they do it."

The editorial charged that Bering River coal fields had been the victim of "malignant politics," and asked, "If it is criminal for a private corporation to strangle and kill one locality while it upbuilds another, should not the government itself refrain from doing the same thing?"

And in Katalla, where protest movements had become almost a way of life, the residents were organizing still another protest. This one would be its last.

A heavily attended meeting of Katalla citizens drew up and unanimously adopted a petition asking the government to build a railroad to the Bering River coal fields, and asking that $3 million of the $35 million appropriated by Congress for Alaskan railroads be earmarked for such a road. The petition listed 11 reasons for the request.

But this petition received no more consideration than all the others adopted by the strangled and dying community of Katalla.

And what of the extension of the Copper River & Northwestern which many said the Syndicate would have to build to protect their large investment? They never built the coal spur to Katalla. They had no reason to do so; their engines were now oil-fired; coal was still effectively bottled up and the Katalla region was dying.

Similarly, there was no visible economic reason for extending to Fairbanks, and there were a lot of political ones for not doing so. Only in the Kennicott copper region were things different. The price of copper was rising, and at the same time, the mines in the area began producing. Prodigious and unexpectedly rich veins of ore were struck.

In May 1915, a train of copper ore 25 cars long arrived in Cordova with a single shipment valued at $345,050. It was a shipment of copper glance from the Bonanza and Mother Lode mines, 1,250 tons of it. That month the Copper River & Northwestern increased train service between Chitina and Kennicott from one to three trains per week. The value of copper ore that month was over $1.5 million. The Copper River & Northwestern, which had been offered to the government a few months earlier at its appraised physical valuation, now was not for sale at any price. The company was suddenly earning a profit.

4 KENNECOTT AND COPPER

The Bonanza and other Kennecott copper mines were situated in some of the most spectacular country in Alaska. The Bonanza copper had been found on the very sawtooth pinnacle of a ledge, 5,000 feet above the valley floor. This ledge ran in a roughly north-south direction, a long razorback of mountains

ALASKA HISTORICAL LIBRARY

The Mother Lode Mine, Kennicott.

towering between two valleys. On one side the mountain plunged nearly straight down to McCarthy Creek; it was on this side that the Mother Lode Mine was located. The other side overlooked the beautiful expanse of Kennicott Glacier.

(The town and glacier were named after Robert Kennicott, early Alaskan explorer; the mining company was supposed to take the same name, but the name was inadvertently misspelled, and it remained so. Hence, the seeming discrepancy in spelling.)

It was on this side that the town, the mill, mine and concentrator were all located. The railroad, when it was finished, ran along the rocky moraine in front of Kennecott Glacier before beginning the sharp ascent to the camp of the Kennecott Mines Company.

The main buildings of the Jumbo-Bonanza and Mother Lode mines were described in a 1920 Bureau of Mines report as follows: "They are closely grouped together almost at the extreme summit of a lofty and rugged mountain top. The main buildings are at an elevation of 6,000 feet and may be said to be perched on the narrow shoulders of the mountain at the base of a cliff fantastically sculptured into hoodoo forms by the action of erosion. The bunkhouses are on rollers held by cables."

In 1907, the Guggenheims decided that, pending a rail connection with the mines, all of their efforts should be concentrated on the development of the Bonanza Mine, the most promising of the area. In order to get supplies to the mine, some temporary means of transportation was necessary. It was for this reason that the steamship *Chittyna* was brought in over the Tasnuna Pass that spring.

Now supplies for the construction of necessary facilities could be brought in by river steamer during the navigation months. In 1908 construction was begun on an aerial tram to carry ore from the mine to the steamer landing. The tram was to be three miles in length, divided about halfway down by an angle station into what was essentially two individual trams. The difference in elevation between the mine and the concentrator and ore bins, where the tram ended, was 4,000 feet. The capacity of the aerial tram was 100 tons per day. It was completed in 1909.

In 1910 construction began on the concentrator. Two hundred thousand board feet of lumber were cut for the concentrator building by sawmill machinery brought in over the trail. The building, when finished, was 44 feet wide, with six stories of benches ranging from 16 to 22 feet. Also built that year were tram terminals, transfer bunkers, ore chutes and 375 feet of snow sheds between the mine and the ore bins, plus offices, cottages, bunkhouses and a warehouse. A dam was built on nearby National Creek to furnish water for the crushers and concentrators, and hydroelectric power for electric and steam plants.

Thus, with the necessary work of building facilities, not much real mining had taken place by Copper Day, 1911. About 1,000 feet of tunneling had been finished with 150 feet of raise. The first train hauled away 1,200 of the first 2,000 tons of ore. There was an estimated $6 million in ore in sight.

While the development of these mines was promising, it was not enough to justify the kind of money being spent on the Copper River &

Northwestern. Tonnage from the many other properties strung all along the Chitina River valley was needed. The four groups of claims owned by the Alaska Syndicate were but a small portion of the 200 groups of some 4,000 copper and gold claims in the area. Of the non-Syndicate properties, the most promising were the holdings of the Great Northern Development Company, which had already expended $800,000 and had 140 men employed at their Copper Mountain mine on the Kotsina. A branch line of the railroad was planned to go 12 miles up Strelna Creek to the properties.

Other properties working on a considerable scale that summer of 1911 included the Dillman group and the Westover on Dan Creek; the California-Alaska Development Company backed by Capt. A. E. Lathrop and others; the Hubbard and Elliott; McCarthy Company; Guillaneau Mining Company; and Deyo and Price properties.

Many of these included large amounts of lower grade ores which would have been more than feasible to bring out if the smelting could be done in Alaska, but that became impossible because of the turbulent coal situation. It was estimated that, if the smelter could have been built as planned, 1,000 more men would have found immediate employment in the Copper River valley. But coal was the key to it all.

In the end, it was only the rich producers who could afford to operate after the first few years of development. Their success made for spectacular production figures that electrified the world, but these figures masked the loss of the low grade ores which were left in the ground.

In 1910 the first development work was begun on the Mother Lode Mine. Work proceeded slowly on this property until 1911 and the arrival of the railroad when all work speeded up. Development was begun on the Jumbo and Erie groups, and these mines reached their full production by about 1914.

It was during these early years of operation of the Copper River & Northwestern that the railroad was offered for sale to the government. At that time it was thought that there was only enough ore for six to ten years of operation at the mines above the company town of Kennecott. But little was known at that time of the peculiar characteristics of the deposits.

In describing the peculiarities of the area the Geological Survey said, "A common experience in mining these ores is to find that an ore body terminates abruptly or that a tiny stringer of copper minerals, apparently of no value whatsoever, if followed a sufficient distance, opens out into a large

Opposite—**The Bonanza Mine, Kennicott.**

mass of ore. It was necessary therefore to explore every indication of mineralization, for otherwise valuable ore might be missed. . . .

"No other ore bodies remotely comparable in size and richness with those at Kennecott have been found in Alaska, and few have been found elsewhere, if both size and richness are considered, although other mines have produced and will produce more copper."

By mid-1915, all the mines except the Mother Lode were in full production, and new and unexpectedly rich finds in the "Glory Hole" of the Bonanza and Jumbo mines were startling the mining world. May 1915 saw $1.5 million in copper ore pass over Cordova docks, and a month later the *Cordova Daily Times* ran banners reading "Copper Ore Shipments from Cordova Alone are Over Two Million Dollars a Month!" In June the *Cordova Daily Times* asked editorially if perhaps President Wilson had not made a mistake in not buying the Copper River & Northwestern Railway when it was offered at a bargain price.

In two days, July 21st and 22nd, ships left Cordova with copper valued at $750,000. By 1916 the Mother Lode reached full production.

At the same time the copper mines were just coming into their full productivity, the war years shot the price of copper out of sight. The Syndicate was being more than amply repaid for its tremendous investment in the railroad.

In 1915, 227 men were employed in the two mines, Kennecott-Bonanza and Kennecott-Jumbo; 109 of these men were employed underground. Both mines had aerial tramways about 16,000 feet long connecting the mines to the mill. About 750 tons of ore were mined daily from both mines in 1915, a 300 percent increase over 1914.

That same year saw the installation of the ammonia process at the Bonanza, the first of its kind and size in the world, with a capacity of 450 tons per day. Ore treated by this process yielded 74.5 percent copper when smelted.

Nineteen hundred and sixteen was the peak year in both production of copper and value of copper produced. In 1915 the production was 86,500,000 pounds, valued at $15,100,000. In 1916 the figures rose dramatically to 120,850,000 pounds worth $32,400,000. This copper production came from 15 mines in 1915 and 18 mines in 1916, only three of which were in the Chitina district. (All the separate mines in the four Kennecott groups were classed as a single mine, the Kennecott.) The output of the Kennecott mines completely overshadowed the production of all the others in Alaska. The principal mines in operation that year were the Jumbo and Bonanza. The Mother Lode was producing some, and

other copper mines in the district were in varying stages of development. Transportation and smelter capacity prevented the mining of any more ore.

The Kennecott Copper Company announced that $7.5 million would be spent to develop and improve the mines. In 1917 a new mill was built and new kitchens and dining rooms were constructed at Bonanza and Jumbo. Various other improvements were made to their properties in Prince William Sound.

New equipment was needed, too. Early in 1917, over $1 million was allocated by the company for new equipment and improvements to the roadbed and other facilities. To be purchased were two new locomotives of the Mikade type, the same as the 70-ton class locomotives. Also on order were 40 flatcars, 5 boxcars, 2 oil cars, 1 steam shovel for the Chitina branch, 6 additional motorcars, 1 locomotive crane for the yards and for other construction work, and 1 gasoline-driven air compressor for tie-tamping, which also would carry its own tools. This latter item was something new in the West, but was reported in use in the East with great success.

Improvements to the line would include a large new store building at the terminal grounds, several other buildings for storage and other uses, the construction of 600 linear feet of snowsheds in Abercrombie Canyon, the replacement of 55 miles of line with new ties of Douglas fir and other conversion of the existing oil-fired locomotives to superheat, an economic device that was said to increase efficiency and power by 20 percent. New fireboxes would be installed in some of the old locomotives, and all would receive a general overhaul.

By 1917 the Mother Lode was sledding large amounts of copper ore over the winter trail to the railway, and the company had another million dollars set aside for further development of this mine and others. Non-Syndicate mines were working hard at this time too, especially the Alaska Copper Company properties near McCarthy, and the gold quartz claims on McKinley Lake.

These were the big years of copper production, when the famous Kennecott mines were riding high on the twin incentives of rich new discoveries and a skyrocketing price for copper.

The towns created by the railroad and the mines were booming. Kennicott was the company town; staid and very proper, where the neat red and white houses were the homes of company officials. McCarthy was the booming, roistering miners' and railroaders' town; wide-open and roaring. Both were small towns, completely dependent upon the area's mines for their existence and their prosperity.

Chitina was only a little less dependent. It was a railroad junction town, even though the railroad was never extended to Fairbanks. The Copper River & Northwestern remained, until the Alaska Railroad was completed in 1923, the only route to the Interior other than the government wagon road out of Valdez, which was now being improved as an honest-to-goodness auto road. The auto was still in its embryo stages. Railroads were both faster and more dependable than the automobile. Chitina was reached by rail in October of 1910, and immediately sprang into life as a small and bustling Alaskan city. In November the Chitina-Tonsina road was completed, and wagon service was soon inaugurated by the Orr Stage Lines. Matched teams of six white horses met the northbound trains from Cordova and carried passengers and freight on into the Interior. Mail contracts were let that same month.

The Hotel Chitina, one of the finest hostelries in early Alaska, was finished in November and was advertised as ready to serve Interior travelers.

5 COPPER RIDES THE RAILS

From the beginning, the Copper River & Northwestern was really more than a mining railroad. It was glamor, adventure and excitement. Its construction had truly been "man against the wilderness." Its people, such as M. J. Heney, E. C. Hawkins, Dr. Whiting, Jack McCord and "Big Mike" Sullivan, seemed bigger than life, their achievements almost beyond the power of description, and therefore a challenge to writers to try, somehow, to describe them.

For this reason, its building had been thoroughly covered by scores of journalists, especially the dramatic events of the construction of the famous Miles Glacier "Million Dollar" Bridge.

Then came the book about it all: *The Iron Trail,* Rex Beach's classic tale, which took many actual events and characters and wove a fictional romance around them. The events were close enough to serve as the only real account of the building of the Copper River & Northwestern (or, as he called it, the Salmon River & Northwestern) that was available in book form. (A comparison of the real events and characters with those of *The Iron Trail* adapted from a letter written by a man who remembered it all, is included in the appendix to this book.)

Rex Beach was a frequent visitor at the bridge site during its construction. Beach had a cabin alongside the railroad track at Mile 19, and often stayed at the old Northern Hotel in town. Old-timers report he was well liked as a man, and the release of his book made

the Copper River & Northwestern and the Miles Glacier Bridge the biggest tourist attractions in Alaska.

Tourists were never disappointed in their visits to the area. The rumble, the thunder of huge icebergs breaking away, the tidal waves and the color of the big glaciers, all assaulted the senses out at Mile 49. The ice advance that had begun in the winter of 1910 continued during 1911. The tremendous wall of ice had already approached to within 1,575 feet of the bridge, and in the early summer of 1911 it was still coming. Bridge engineers gathered at the Miles Glacier Bridge to watch in horrified fascination as the wall of ice inched ever closer. If it should reach the bridge, no power on earth could save it. None. Tourists that summer were treated to the awe-inspiring sight of a 300-foot tower of ice looming over the train and the bridge, less than the length of the bridge away! On it came in a relentless advance until June 16, 1911, when it was measured at 1,474 feet from the bridge. This was its closest advance. From that date on, it began a slow retreat.

The retreat of the ice did not lessen the drama of the visit to the glacier area. Tourist trains stopped for an hour and a half to view the spectacular performance of the glaciers sloughing off icebergs, and it was never too long for the sightseers.

Tourist excursions tended to be exciting along the "Iron Trail." Engineer Sal Reed recalled that "One time I went out on an excursion to Miles Glacier. Oscar Larson was conductor, Roy Badden and Tim Eckstrom were braking, and Alvave Larson was firing for me.

"Coming back from Mile 49 [that is, the glaciers and the bridge] I saw something up ahead of us on the track. I asked Alvave if there were any prospectors or trappers that he knew of who had a white dog.

" 'Not that I know of,' replied Alvave.

"So I said, 'There's something up ahead of us on the track that's white and it's running.' So when we got up closer we could see it was a big goat.

"Well, I slowed down, and Alvave said, 'I'll cut off the bell and see if I can rope him.' So he did, and he tied one end of the rope to the hand rail on the smokebox and made a loop.

"Then he said 'Now, when I throw the rope, you stop.'

"So Alvave was standing on the pilot-beam and I ran in as close as I could, and Alvave threw the rope and lacked about six inches of getting the rope over the goat's head. By this time the train crew and the passengers knew something was going on up ahead, and were all trying to see what was happening, hanging out the windows and platforms of the coaches, and when the rope missed, the goat went

back along the side of the train, and I don't think anyone got a picture of it, as they were all trying to get to the back end of the last coach at once."

The Copper River & Northwestern was a part of a number of touring loops during its heyday; tours that took the sightseer into many interesting parts of Alaska. Many famous visitors rode the rails, along with the famous Kennecott copper.

Certain places along the right-of-way were to cause recurrent maintenance problems. The rails laid on top of the Allen Glacier for five and one-half miles had to be relaid almost completely every year, although the tons of gravel and overlayment dumped on top of the ice acted as a surprisingly stable insulation.

The tunnel beyond the Chitina Crossing had a nasty habit of sloughing down tons of mud each spring, and the Chitina Crossing itself had to be redriven each spring. Just before breakup, crews were sent out to lift the rails and the entire wooden trestle was allowed to go out, then was replaced after the ice was gone.

One of the more spectacular rebuilding jobs was the replacement of one of the icebreakers in front of the Miles Glacier Bridge. The breakup of 1915 completely turned the icebreaker in front of pier #2 on its foundation. It may be remembered that one of the caissons for these protective pyramids had refused to sink to its desired depth, despite every effort of the builders. Now A. C. O'Neel returned with a crew to rebuild the faulty structure.

The weather led to one of the few accidents recorded on the rail line. During a howling snowstorm in mid-February a local carrying passengers for Chitina and a great deal of freight for the rebuilding of the icebreaker stopped just short of the bridge to unload its cargo. Meanwhile the rotary went on across the bridge to plow the way clear. The local followed too closely and because of the thickness of the swirling snow it collided with the rear end of the rotary. The two trains telescoped and wrecked the caboose of the rotary and a number of freight cars on the local. No one was injured. The shaken passengers and the damaged cars were taken back to Cordova by the southbound train from Chitina.

The icebreaker was completed without further mishap, at a cost of $80,000. Both icebreakers still stand firm, 60 years later.

During this phenomenal growth period the fisheries of the Prince William Sound and Copper River were coming into their own. Nine canneries were operating in or near Cordova, and one cannery, the Copper River Packing Company, had a cannery at Mile 55 in the Copper River, just above the Miles Glacier Bridge and Abercrombie Canyon. Commercial fishermen dip-netted salmon from platforms along the edges of the Abercrombie Rapids, and gill-netters fished among the icebergs in Miles Lake. They delivered their catch to the train, and the train took them to the various canneries.

One of the dip-net fishermen was Dick Janson Sr., who was also there at the time of the filming of the movie *Days of '98*. This was one of the two movies filmed on location along the Copper River & Northwestern, the other being Rex Beach's story *The Iron Trail*.

For the movie *Days of '98*, Eyak Lake was used as Lake Bennett, and the Abercrombie Rapids as the Five Finger Rapids of the Yukon River. "The trouble was," said Mr. Janson, "that the Abercrombie was so much worse than Five Finger. Three stunt men were drowned trying to run the rapids for that picture.

"I was offered a job running the rapids for them once, while I was dipnetting in the rapids. I guess they thought that because I fished in the eddies of the river that I was a white-water man. I told them I'd have to get $1,500 for it. They looked shocked at that and said, 'We can get all the stunt men we want for ten dollars a day.' But I guess they couldn't get all they wanted after those other men drowned, because they wound up filming the sequence with dummies in the boats."

The other picture was of Rex Beach's novel. For scenes in *The Iron Trail* showing the falsework going out from under the Miles Glacier Bridge, they ran in shots of the Chitina trestle going out.

In 1916, as the copper mining hit its all-time high, old-timer Jack Dalton bowed out of the Cordova scene. The Copper River & Northwestern purchased the properties of Jack Dalton. Included in the deal were Dalton's three mining claims over which a battle in court had been waged for five years, the Dalton mill, buildings, machinery, water system, (including a dam he had built), his newly built hotel, residence, furniture—all his property, real and personal. This gave the railroad company title to all the shore lands near the dock and settled, presumably to the satisfaction of all concerned, the dispute between Jack Dalton and the railroad company over those lands.

"While the people of the town will regret losing in Mr. Dalton one of its old-time and popular residents," commented the *Cordova Times*, "The closing of the deal meets with general approval among the citizens of Cordova, for in the acquisition of the Dalton properties the railway company will be in a position to encourage industries desiring factory and business sites adjacent to deep water, and the company itself is

Opposite—The famed Million Dollar Bridge, which actually cost more than a million and a half. One span was dropped by the 1964 earthquake. Childs Glacier is in the background.

also in possession of ample ground to enable it to develop its own operations, and the business of its allied companies." And so passed from the scope of this story a true pioneer, a vigorous and energetic man who would take on any difficult job at hand and carry it to a successful conclusion. He was a man whose story to this point had been intertwined at scattered points all along the way with the building of the Copper River & Northwestern, though he personally did not participate except in that early survey up the Copper River for M.J. Heney.

Another familiar name cropped up that year of 1916:

> To independent mine owners and operators in Prince William Sound: Gentlemen, you are invited to attend a conference at Valdez Saturday, August 5, to consider and act upon a plan in our mutual interests, to market our copper output to the best advantage in the present high market.
>
> —H.D. Reynolds

Reynolds, whose name had roused such passion back in 1907 in Valdez, was back and ready to get into the game again. He had just passed through Cordova on board the *Admiral Watson* on his way to Valdez. The *Cordova Times* pointed out that it was scarcely necessary to introduce Mr. Reynolds to anyone who had lived in Alaska prior to 1906, but that Mr. Reynolds still owned many of his mining properties and would attempt to improve the marketing conditions as they applied to copper in the Prince William Sound area.

There was indeed a problem; that of the lower grade properties which needed some access to local smelters, operated by the use of Alaska coal or coke, for them to prove feasible. It was to this difficulty that Reynolds and his retinue of copper mining engineers were to address themselves.

Reynolds received a distinctly frosty welcome in the glacier city. The *Valdez Miner* cautioned its readers about this "Moses arriving to lead them out of the wilderness into a promised land—with a diversity of schemes to separate the people from their Mazuma."

Little is known of the subsequent success or failure of the former "High Panjandum of Valdez," but it is certain that his name carried the powder burns from the guns of Keystone Canyon.

There was one other name-that-makes-news that should be mentioned in connection with the years of the Copper River & Northwestern: that of President Warren Harding, the first President of the United States to visit Alaska. The occasion of his visit was the driving of the golden spike marking completion, at

long last, of the Alaska Railroad. Alaska finally had her "All-American route," 25 years after it first was proposed.

After the ceremonies at Nenana that summer day in 1923, President Harding entrained back to the coast via the brand-new railroad-created town of Anchorage and south to Seward. From there he traveled to Cordova, where he took the excursion train to the glacier area. Indeed, in those days, no tour of Alaska was considered complete without a visit to this famous spot. It was a warm summer day, and the glaciers were performing spectacularly. After about three-quarters of an hour, there was a pause in the glacial activity, and the President asked a Secret Service man to fire his pistol at the face of Childs Glacier to see what would happen. The Secret Service man did so, and a huge chunk split away with a thunderous report. The President, it was reported, "looked pleased." On the way back to Cordova the President handled the throttle of the locomotive for 20 minutes, and "there were no complaints from the dining car," where passengers were eating lunch.

In Cordova, he was taken on a tour of the town and given all the VIP treatments that were common. Secretary of Commerce Herbert Hoover, with the party, commented that there must be some special greatness about Alaska, because the problems of its 55,000 people caused so much trouble for the other 105 million people in the United States.

6 ALASKA ANTHRACITE RAILROAD

Back in 1906 when Clark Davis was building the Catalla & Carbon Mountain Railroad from the Bering River coal field to tidewater, he made the boast that his railroad would beat both the Bruners and the Guggenheims to the field, and would be the first to haul coal. By a strange quirk of fate, he was right. His prediction was to come true in 1918, 12 years later! Clark Davis' original survey—he was no longer connected with it—was revived and finished in that year under the name Alaska Anthracite Railroad. By now both of the big rivals, as well as the other Controller Bay railroads, were out of the picture.

In 1916 the property of the Alaska Petroleum and Coal Company was granted a patent to 160 acres in the Bering River coal field. It began plans to develop the mine there and undertook the building of 17 miles of railroad. Engineers for the company had estimated not less than five million tons of merchantable coal was to be found in the claim.

At the same time it was announced that Washington's U.S. Senator George Turner was planning on suing the United States government for patents to the other coal claims in the Bering River region claimed by the company, and to which patent had been denied.

Officers of the Alaska Anthracite Railroad were John H. Campbell, president; James Campbell, vice-president; Charles Kinnear, vice-president; and Charles D. Davis, general manager. Chief engineer for the enterprise was Manche O. Bennett, and the contractor for the job of building the line was George Nelson.

Nelson began clearing the right-of-way in 1916. In March of 1917 it was reported that the company had purchased 2 locomotives and 16 cars in San Francisco and the contractor was ready to begin work in earnest. About 17 miles was completed before war shortages brought progress to a halt. One 0-4-0 saddletank engine affectionately known as "Ole" was in service at that time. The mine in the eastern part of the field near Carbon Mountain was now connected to a landing on Bering River at the mouth of Canyon Creek. This terminal was commonly called Goose City.

remained the only rail connection with the Bering River coal field.

One other patent was granted to lands in the Bering River coal field: the property of the MacDonald mine on Bering Lake. Little or no mining was ever done under the leasing system in Bering River. The largest amount of work was done on the property served by the Alaska Anthracite Railroad. The mine closed in May 1921.

The report of the Territorial Mine Inspector of that same year described the mine in saying that "... On the property there is a very comfortable camp, also a power house, stables, warehouse, in fact everything necessary to develop a mine.

"Prospecting has been carried on for some time. All work has been done on the water level. The Carbon tunnel crosscuts the strata for a distance of over 1,300 feet. Several beds have been cut and three gangways have been extended a distance of from 200 to 400 feet.

"The south tunnel, the portal of which is directly opposite the portal of the Carbon tunnel, is 800 feet in

ALASKA ROAD COMMISSION COLLECTION. ALASKA HISTORICAL LIBRARY

Goose City, on the Bering River 3 miles from Chilkat, was the terminus of the Alaska Anthracite or Bering River Railroad.

Construction costs were given as $457,684 for 17-plus miles and some additional right-of-way clearing, a cost per mile figure of $21,796.

Details about this railroad are very sparse, although it is known that it was completed on October 7, 1918. The first two loads of coal, of "a good quality," passed over the rails soon after, and were shipped to Cordova.

Other roads were contemplated for the Bering River field. About this same time, 1918, a lease was granted to the St. Elias Oil Company on a vein of coal which had been part of the holdings of the old "English company." Backing this project were Falcon Joslin and George C. Hazelet. It was reported that the work of prospecting would begin at once and if the vein proved as good as hoped, these gentlemen would go ahead with an independently owned spur line to Mile 39 on the Copper River & Northwestern. Although some work was done on this mine, nothing ever came of the planned spur. The Alaska Anthracite Railroad

length. From this tunnel a gangway was driven a distance of 300 feet. About 800 feet north of the Carbon and South tunnels, the Shields Tunnel was started and from its intersection with No. 16 bed a gangway was driven for about 1,000 feet along the bed.

"The coal at this mine is semi-bituminous, suitable for blacksmithing and coking and though no test has been made it is most probable that it would be suitable for navy purposes. Analysis of the coal indicate it to be of navy grade.

"The Bering River Coal Company is the only company that operated in the field during the past year."

In 1921 the company was granted permission to issue bonds in the amount of $1,500,000 to finance further construction, especially a three-mile extension to tidewater on Controller Bay and a five-mile spur, cutting off at Mile 20 to tap the Alaska Coke & Coal

Company property at Cunningham Mountain. However, this work was never completed, for reasons unknown. Although the line was 22 miles in length, and hauled from 18,000 to 20,000 tons of coal to the Goose City terminal, it was never profitable.

Plagued by inadequate finances, improper construction and economic unfeasibility—too little tonnage, brought about by the stagnation in the field under the leasing system—the Alaska Anthracite Railroad was the Toonerville Trolley of the North, to judge by the off-the-cuff stories told of it.

One adventure was related by Dick Janson Sr., who was working as a station man on a section of reconstruction of the line.

"We were building a new grade near Shepherd Creek over the top of a hill. It was to replace the old grade around the bottom of the hill, which was in danger of washing out.

"One time engineer Harding stopped at our camp with supplies on old 'Ole.' He was going on up the line, but we told him he was crazy to take his engine around the hill on that old grade; it was unsafe. We tried to warn him of the danger, but he waved it all aside as of no importance. 'Don't worry about me,' he said, 'I'll get back all right.' So, while we were watching, he climbed up into the cab on Ole and commenced to setting all the controls just so—set the Johnson Bar or whatever it is they do—and as the engine puffed slowly away, he climbed down out of the cab.

"'So long, Ole,' he said, patting the engine fondly, 'I'll see you later.' Then, while we stood there watching, Harding, who must have been 70 years old if he was a day, took off at a dead run over the new grade across the top of the hill. We ran after him to see what he'd do, and sure enough, when he got to the bottom of the hill, around the corner came Ole and he caught her on the fly as she went by."

There were only a couple of lessees who tried to make a go of it, and after a very few years they gave up. The Alaska Anthracite Railroad went out of business. Bering River reverted to wilderness after 15 years of costly and heartbreaking effort.

7 THE LIFE AND DEATH OF KATALLA

While Cordova was riding high on the prosperity of Kennecott copper, Katalla with all her coal and oil was staggering under a government-induced depression. No coal could be mined until the leasing system was established, and even then the conditions were such that coal mining completely failed. No oil could be produced due to the oil land withdrawals of 1910, except for the single 160-acre patented property of the Chilcat Oil Company. A certain amount of winter trapping and summer fishing augmented this small industry for the town.

Katalla had a brief rebirth in 1920 when the oil-land leasing law passed. Bill provisions allowed the first persons on the ground after the bill was signed, preference for land lease. This precipitated an old-fashioned "oil rush." In Cordova, as well as all along the west coast, preparations were being made to rush to the fields and stake out oil claims. The bill was signed by President Wilson on February 25, 1920, and was effective immediately. The oil rush was on.

The big oil rush gave Katalla a nice short-term economic boost in the early twenties. By 1928 The All-Alaska Review reported that 22 wells had been drilled, and although only 13 produced paying quantities, none had ever produced a dry well. More drilling equipment was on the way, and 1,000 barrels a month were produced, all of it used in Cordova and vicinity. Several other properties were being developed and by 1929, 16 producing wells were reported.

The oil was a very high-grade paraffin base; most of that refined was for kerosene. The gasoline produced by the small refinery was pure enough to be used by the Copper and Bering River fishermen in their boats, and for planes.

The early thirties hit hard at copper, coal and oil production, although the Chilcat Oil Company continued to pump and refine for local consumption through 1933.

It was the last year of oil production at Katalla, for on Christmas Day, 1933, the refinery caught fire and burned.

Stella Janson, an old-time Katalla resident and daughter of Bill Hansen, recalled that "It was very early Christmas morning that we heard the steam whistle blowing the alarm. There was a lot of snow that year. All the men ran over to help fight the fire.

"The refinery building was a tin building, with just tin over 2 x 4's. It was a very cold place, with no siding or inner lining. The watchman had one corner that he stayed in, with a padded cot and a natural gas-fired stove (all our stoves burned natural gas). His corner had blankets put up around it to hold the heat. We figure the dog knocked the blankets down; they fell on the stove and started the fire. The watchman was out on his rounds and by the time he got back, the fire was too far gone.

"It was a hot fire. Everyone was down throwing snow on the oil tank. [That is, the oil storage tank.] We were afraid if it broke, the oil would flow burning down onto the gasoline tanks below. Then everything would blow.

"My younger sister was out in the snow clutching her doll and wailing; she was worried about Dad. It was an eerie scene that Christmas morning: fire, blazing fiercely and crackling; men furiously throwing snow onto the oil and gasoline tanks to prevent an explosion; and a little girl standing out in the snow clutching her doll and crying hysterically while Katalla's last vestige of industry went up in smoke."

The refinery was never rebuilt as, "It was considered undesirable to replace the building and equipment, because the outlook was not encouraging for the profitable operation of the property," according to the Geological Survey Bulletin of 1937.

Copper mining was resumed in 1934 and continued on a small scale for a few years thereafter, but it was clear that the Copper River & Northwestern Railway's days were numbered. New copper mines in Chile were now in operation, and their cost of production was far cheaper than in the distant mountains of Alaska.

8 CONVENIENCE AND NECESSITY: A DEATH KNELL

The years of World War I had been the big years for copper. In those days, while $2 million worth of copper a month was shipped through Cordova to Tacoma smelters, that Alaskan town loudly proclaimed her superior military advantages: fine harbor with ample anchorage; railroad; and the three most strategic minerals, coal, copper and oil, close at hand. And someday, a smelter!

By the 1920's the golden dream had faded. Still riding high on Kennecott copper, Cordova remained the "Premier Copper Port of the World," with still a million dollars a month of the red metal coming from the Wrangell range. But the handwriting was on the wall. A railroad without coal was doomed from the start, at least in far-off Alaska. So while copper poured from the mountains, time was running out.

Nineteen hundred and thirty-two was the last year the railroad ran in the wintertime. In 1933 and 1934, very little copper was mined at all. These were the depression years, years that touched Alaska as a whole very little, but which were felt in her meager industries. The Copper River & Northwestern and the Kennecott copper mines were among the stricken. Copper production was resumed on some scale in 1935, but the line continued to lose money and was closed in the winter.

The Geological Survey Bulletin for 1933 on the Mining Industry of Alaska summed up the situation saying that, "The production of copper from Alaska mines in 1933 was insignificant . . . brought about by the extremely low price paid for copper, which led the two principal copper mines in the Territory to choose the alternative of closing rather than a heavy operating loss. . . . The necessity of suspension of the large Alaska copper mines is not only to be regretted as a serious direct loss to the mining industry of the Territory but has even greater indirect effect through curtailment of the transportation facilities. . . .

"By no means have even the known deposits of copper been exhausted, so that had the price of copper stayed up, the mines would doubtless have continued to operate, but it would be folly to do so, in the face of heavy financial loss.

"It must be remembered, though, that the mines near Kennecott, which have contributed perhaps 90 percent of the Alaska copper, have been mining a unique deposit, not comparable with any other known deposit in the world, so that inevitably their mineral wealth is being depleted, and there is no justification for expecting that their loss will be offset by new discoveries of equally marvelous lodes."

The Bering River coal situation and the reasons why it had no chance of success were stated neatly: "In the Bering River field, where extensive deposits ranging in composition from bituminous coal to anthracite have long been known, prospecting and other development work . . . was apparently at a standstill in 1933. Rumors of renewed activity in this field were heard from time to time, and requests for extensions of some of the government permits . . . were received. [However,] work already done in this field indicate some complex geological conditions will be encountered, so that desultory prospecting by poorly financed, small, or technically unskilled operators holds little promise of success, and full development must await a company that is able to go into the matter in a large way and to bear the necessary expense of exploring a new field."

The companies meeting that criterion had long since been driven out of the Bering River coal field.

The oil picture was only a little less gloomy: "The only oil produced in Alaska [in 1933] comes from the wells of the Chilcat Oil Company in the Katalla field . . . no new drilling in 1933 . . . a small refinery is operated at Katalla by the company, and the products—gasoline and distillate, which are of especially high quality—find a ready market near at hand, especially for use by the fishing fleet near Cordova. . . ."

The burning of the boiler house and refinery put an end to Katalla oil production.

On September 13, 1938, the railroad company applied to the Interstate Commerce Commission for a "certificate of convenience and necessity" to abandon the Copper River & Northwestern Railway, and notices to that effect appeared in the newspapers. At a meeting of the Cordova Chamber of Commerce, the company's attorney, Thomas M. Donohoe, stated that in order to give the communities of Cordova and Chitina and the Transportation Workers Union, who wished to protest the abandonment, a chance to appear at the hearing and testify, the railroad company was offering to pay transportation charges of representatives of these groups, to and from Seattle.

The hearing took place on January 16, 1939, in Seattle. After a long day of testimony and consideration, the railroad company was granted a certificate of convenience and necessity to abandon, and thus the "Iron Trail" died.

The report of the Interstate Commerce Commission hearing constitutes the death certificate, will and funeral eulogy of the Copper River & Northwestern Railway. It told what the line was, had hoped to be and the causes of its demise.

The line was described as a single-track railroad, laid with 60- to 70-pound rails, with gradient ranging from 0.8 to 4 percent, and a maximum curvature of 12 degrees.

"In support of the proposed abandonment, the applicant avers that the mineral resources of the Copper Company have become entirely exhausted; that its mines have been closed; that all mining equipment and machinery have been shipped away; that the remaining traffic in the tributary territory is negligible; and that the railroad can no longer be usefully or economically operated.

"The line in question, the construction of which was completed in 1911 . . . was built primarily for the purpose of transporting copper ores from the copper company's mines at the northern terminus, to Cordova, its southern terminus. Cordova . . . has a population varying from 1,500 in the winter to 2,000 in the summer. . . . Kennecott was formerly a mining camp having about 200 inhabitants, all of whom were employees of the copper company. At the present time there are only two inhabitants in that community.

"When the line was constructed it was hoped that it would prove to be an inducement for other mining interests to aid in the development of the natural resources of the tributary territory and that there would be much additional traffic from that source. However, such traffic failed to materialize and the applicant has been almost wholly dependent on revenues from the traffic handled for the copper company."

So much for the golden, defeated dreams!

"Service on the line is performed by a mixed train making two round trips weekly. In recent years, during the summer months, special tourist trains have been operated between Cordova and Childs Glacier. . . . The line has not been operated during the winter months for the last five years, owing to heavy snows. . . ."

"The investment cost of the line, including equipment and general expenditures, is shown as $28,647,034. The net salvage value of the applicant's rolling stock, locomotives, snow plows, and miscellaneous equipment, is estimated at $100,000. No value is placed on the rail and bridges for the reason that the cost of removal and transportation would exceed the scrap value. There appears to be little or no deferred maintenance on the line at the present time."

The railroad company gave a statement of passengers handled and freight hauled, with the percentage of freight which was Kennecott Copper Company's (owned by the same syndicate), and a financial statement.

SUMMARY OF FINANCIAL STATEMENT			
Year	Passengers	Freight	Net Loss
1933	1,265	2,849 tons 26.1% Copper Co.	$1,444,409
1934	1,573	3,618 tons 11.0% Copper Co.	1,384,077
1935	2,047	27,179 tons 88.9% Copper Co.	1,085,745
1936	1,323	34,278 tons 95.5% Copper Co.	1,148,018
1937	1,880	46,318 tons 95.7% Copper Co.	891,624
1938 (7 mo.)	-	- 94.4% Copper Co.	701,232

Figures for 1933 and 1934 reflect the relative inactivity of the mines in those years, and suggest the low level of business to be expected independent of the mines.

The application did not go through without protest. Among those appearing to protest were Bryce Little, Walter H. Hodge, Martin Hegeberg, George A. Robison, C. Chester Carlson and John Rosswog. Most of these persons were Cordova residents and businessmen, though some represented the towns of McCarthy and Chitina. The cost of air service for the remaining small gold miners, the possibility of opening up new mineral sources, and the loss of income both to towns and to long-time railroad men were cited if the railroad ceased operation.

"Some of the witnesses for the protestant believe that there are vast quantities of mineral deposits but admit that they may not be discovered for many years.

"Cordova, according to the testimony of a representative of its Chamber of Commerce, is an

ALASKA HISTORICAL LIBRARY   AUTHOR'S COLLECTION

ALASKA ROAD COMMISSION COLLECTION. ALASKA HISTORICAL LIBRARY

K. KENNEDY PHOTO. ALASKA HISTORICAL LIBRARY

Top—Katalla in early years. The post office was later built on the foundation to the right of the saloon. The Hotel Northern behind it had a famous back bar, part of which was later moved to the Alaskan Bar in Cordova.
Middle left—Warehouses and the tramroad of the Chilcat Oil Company near Katalla.
Left—Flag Day in Cordova, *circa* 1915.
Above—Scene on the Ocean Dock at Cordova in the late 1920's.

important port containing numerous industries, chiefly the applicant's railroad and fishing. The witness has found that the total payroll of the applicant is over $500,000 a year, of which Cordova would lose about 40 percent if the railroad were abandoned. . . . Practically all the territory tributary to the railroad is within the trade area of Cordova and the proposed abandonment would cause a further loss of volume of business handled by various inhabitants of that territory, the losses anticipated by the witness would seem to be somewhat overestimated.

"A member of the town council of Cordova testified that the proposed abandonment would cause considerable depreciation in the value of private property and that the taxes accruing to Cordova would be materially reduced as a result of such depreciation. Matters of that nature, however, are not controlling in the determination of abandonment cases.

"It is undoubtedly true," admits the report, "that the loss of rail transportation facilities would work a hardship upon the people of the territory served, especially those in the town of McCarthy. . . ."

McCarthy was to be provided for in rather unusual fashion: "The superintendent of highways in the Chitina district, whose work is under the supervision of the Alaska Road Commission, hereinafter called the Road Commission, testified that he had made a study . . . and recommended that the Road Commission take immediate steps to maintain the railroad between McCarthy and Chitina, and operate it by means of light equipment. The Road Commission has purchased a so-called speeder and some push cars for the purpose of experimenting with that method of transportation." The aerial tram was to provide the missing link, the Chitina Bridge.

This stopgap type of solution was not greeted with very much enthusiasm by McCarthyites at the hearing. "Evidence tending to establish the necessity for continued operation of the line was adduced by the testimony of several witnesses. The owners of certain small gold mines in the general territory . . . place little dependence upon air service [of which McCarthy had year-round service] because the airplanes serving that territory carry only 700 or 800 pounds of freight and the carrying charges between the gold mines and the port of Cordova are at the rate of $200 to $240 a ton. For various reasons they believe that the use of the railroad for the movement of light freight between McCarthy and Chitina, as contemplated by the Road Commission, would not be practical, and that the latter should construct a highway in lieu of the railroad between these points. The witnesses estimate that such a highway would cost about $300,000, which would include the cost of constructing a light

suspension bridge across the Copper River for use instead of the tram line previously mentioned. They ask that provisions be made by this Commission for such construction. The Commission is without jurisdiction in the premises."

And so, all the decencies and formalities attended to, the corpse was consigned to its allotted graveyard in history. "It is recommended that division 4 find that the present and future public convenience and necessity permit abandonment, as to interstate and foreign commerce, by the Copper River & Northwestern Railway company, of its entire line of railroad in the Third Judicial District in the Territory of Alaska, described in the application. An appropriate certificate should be issued."

There is a wry irony in the nickname of the Copper River & Northwestern. Using its initials, it was called "Can't Run and Never Will."

One more item of irony in a story loaded with them: If the railroad could have maintained operation for only two or three more years, the need for copper in World War II might have assured its continuance.

On November 11, 1938, the last train moved down the line from Chitina to Cordova with locomotive engineer Sal Reed at the helm.

Up in the small town of Chitina, a World War I veteran named Billy Williams watched the last train chuff through town headed south forever, then went home and took up his pen to write in the poetic style of the times the following verses:

> *For thirty years the Iron Horse*
> *Crept over the winding rail,*
> *To carry the copper from Kennecott*
> *And haul the sourdough mail.*
>
> *The hand of time and the work of men,*
> *Who came in numerous bands,*
> *With sweat and toil, from earth have wrought*
> *The wealth of these great lands.*
>
> *It matters not the end has come*
> *To Rex Beach's Iron Trail,*
> *For men, with grim tenacity,*
> *Will live on and still prevail;*
>
> *To dig from Mother Earth the wealth*
> *That still lies hidden there;*
> *And on their back—as years before—*
> *The burden they will bear.*

Not great poetry, perhaps; but there were plenty of men who remembered only too well what it meant to carry everything over the vast mountains on their backs. To them, the words carried special meaning.

9 OLD RAILROADS NEVER DIE

▌ron Trail Ends 27-Year Career; Last Train In," wrote a columnist in the November 11, 1938, *Cordova Daily Times*. "Railroad Serving Kennecott Mines Ceases Operations After Colorful Period—The last train ever to run over the Copper River & Northwestern Railway arrived in Cordova this afternoon. . . . Few are the persons who could review the remarkable history of these famous institutions without a tinge of sadness at their closing. . . ."

The exciting days of intense rivalry between contending railroad companies, the efforts to build from Katalla, the final granting of the contract to M. J. Heney; all these had passed into "that inert state known as past history. . . .

"From [these beginnings] was started the building of what has been said by many great engineers to be one of the most unique and difficult jobs of railroad building in the annals of railroad construction on the North American continent. For nearly three and one-half years men numbering in the thousands, from the highest official to the laborers who shoveled mud or snow, gave the best that was in them. At times more than 6,000 men were employed.

"At 3:30 p.m. on Wednesday, March 29, 1911, the 'copper spike' was driven at the Kennecott mine, 196 miles from Cordova, announcing to the world the completion of the great project. Early in April the first trainload of copper ore steamed into Cordova and to the terminus at the Ocean wharf. Since that time more than half a billion dollars' worth of copper has been extracted from the mines.

"It has been estimated that more than 40 million dollars was spent by the Syndicate in surveys, purchases and construction of the railroad.

"The Copper River & Northwestern numbers many workers who have been in its employ for a long period of years. Among those who are still in service (according to the most reliable information available) who were working when the railroad was completed in March 1911, and the positions they occupy at present, are: R. J. DeLeo, assistant superintendent; John Day, locomotive engineer; Archie Shiels, electrician; Wm. Hayes, wharf watchman; Arthur Holt, locomotive engineer; Henry Hoffman, track-walker; Oscar L. Larson, conductor; Fred Luppy, roadmaster; George Scott, conductor; and John Vinquist, bridge foreman." Ten men had served from the very beginning to the closing of the railroad. Of these, four men were present at the driving of the copper spike, back in 1911: DeLeo, Hoffman, Luppy and Scott, and were still around to watch the last train come in.

Thomas M. Donohoe, appearing at the Chamber of Commerce, with F. A. Hansen, superintendent of the railroad, explained that arrangements were being made for long-time employees of the railroad. A bonus of two and one-half months pay was to be given to those with 20 years or more of service with the company, with other bonuses scaled down according to length of time employed. Half a month's pay was to be given those most recently employed.

Two large motorcars and a quantity of pushcars had been turned over to the Alaska Road Commission for their proposed service between Chitina and McCarthy. Three other motorcars and several pushcars had been disposed of to private parties. It was felt that these arrangements should take care of needs for persons remaining at the far end of the line.

A few days before the last train came in, a work train was sent up the line to take care of last-minute details. The train crew had instructions to leave stoves, cooking utensils and a quantity of food in each of the section houses along the line for the use of trappers, prospectors and campers—an old-time Alaskan custom. A number of pushcars and hand speeders were left at intervals along the line for the same purpose. Cordova Airlines and a number of private individuals offered to maintain the telephone line of the company, for their own use.

The last train was hardly at rest in the roundhouse before the disposition of the rolling stock began. On that same day, the freighter *Tanana* took aboard a rotary, a locomotive and two tenders, and was expected to depart for Seattle as soon as the blocking of the large deck-freight items was completed.

At the time of the driving of the copper spike, there were 15 engines in use on the Copper River & Northwestern. Besides the six "dinkie" or saddletank engines (numbered 1 to 6), there was "Old No. 50," the original engine bought by M. J. Heney for the Copper River Railway; and No. 51, the slightly larger locomotive purchased from the Alaska Central. There were also three engines in the "100" series, numbered 100 to 102, and four in the "20" series. Of these engines, it is known that No. 51 was scrapped; at least one, and maybe all three, of the "100's" were sent to the Alaska Railroad; and No. 23 also went to the Alaska Railroad.

Another series of five engines, numbered 70 to 74, were bought in 1917 or years thereafter. Of these, the boiler on No. 73 blew up and the engine was scrapped. No. 74 was sold to the McCloud River Logging Company of California, and also one other engine, which one it is not known for sure.

In 1941 some steel salvage work was done on the abandoned railroad line. The *Cordova Times* in describing it said:

"Stirring memories of Cordova's oldest old-timers in the latter part of last week were the activities of the

Copper River & Northwestern's '7-Spot' locomotive, also known as the 'percolator' or the 'goat.' Operated by veteran railroaders Ed Oss and Charles Johnson, the engine is being used to move salvage steel from the road, a fact which gives the venerable little 'percolator' the distinction of being the first and the last on the road. It was the same engine used to push the first steel up the line over thirty years ago when the 'Iron Trail' was in the making."

The engine referred to in the article, of course, was the "Old No. 50," Heney's original engine. "Old No. 50" was sometimes called the "7-Spot" because, on the Copper River & Northwestern's roster of engines, there were six small dinkie, or donkey, engines used on the line. "Old No. 50" was not much larger, and was therefore occasionally dubbed "7-Spot."

Through an unfortunate oversight, all of the railroad's locomotives were shipped out, so that today Cordova does not have even one of the old steam locomotives as a civic memento.

Cordova was affected very little by the closing of the railroad, mainly because she was now riding high on fisheries. The salmon production of Alaska was at its all-time record high, and razor clam production was booming. The town had many canneries, and prosperity was the rule.

Four ghost towns were produced by the closing of the railroad: Katalla, Kennicott, Chitina and McCarthy. The closure of the mines was thought to be temporary, another winter lay-up. In Kennicott houses were simply closed up and locked as if for the winter. Fifty years later, some houses of Kennecott company men still had their owners' fine Bavarian china sitting on the shelves.

Katalla eventually died. Here was a town in the heart of the richest and largest coal district in Alaska, the home of the first commercial oil operations in Alaska, and she became a ghost town, legislated out of existence.

Ghost towns, of course, have their own mystique. In two of these towns, part of their special atmosphere was in having a "ghost auto." In both McCarthy and Katalla, an ancient Model "T" Ford continued to be driven by anyone in the neighborhood. No one seemed to own them, and the addition of a little gas, spark plugs, a fresh battery and oil made them quickly operable again; at least, until the high tides and storms of Katalla reached the ownerless vehicle at that town and took her out to join the bones of the *Portland*.

Despite the fact that the trains no longer ran to the Kennecott mines over the old rails, the tracks remained, as well as the bridges and other physical evidences of the old Copper River & Northwestern, and they had value.

In 1941, the following editorial appeared in the *Cordova Times*:

Poser for Congressman

It was difficult for Hon. Hugh Peterson, presiding at a hearing of the House Committee on Territories to understand that any big corporation would hand the government anything free-of-charge, during the recent transfer of the Copper River & Northwestern Railway's right-of-way to the Federal government.

Delegate Dimond gave reasons why his bill authorizing the Copper River & Northwestern Railway to execute the conveyance should be approved. The transfer carried the stipulation: "For use as a public highway."

Then the following debate took place:

Mr. Peterson: *The passage of this bill does not cost the government a cent?*

Mr. Dimond: *No. There is no obligation of any kind.*

Mr. Peterson: *Is there any opposition to the bill in Alaska?*

Mr. Dimond: *No. In fact the people of Alaska are anxious to follow it up with another bill to authorize the Secretary of Interior to convey to the Town of Cordova some of the property for municipal purposes. That is, property which lies within the city limits, and it would be used by the Town of Cordova for municipal purposes.*

Mr. Peterson: *Is it not a little unusual to have a railroad to voluntarily give away its property?*

Mr. Dimond: *Yes. This is one of those rare things that is almost unbelievable. However, the copper mines are no longer profitable. They took some $210,000,000 worth of copper from the mines. So the railroad did get a return of its money many times over. The grade of the ore finally went down to a point where they could not compete with copper from Chile and South America. Therefore, the company will not operate the Railroad and is quite willing to turn it over for public use.*

Mr. Peterson: *This seems to be one proposition that is almost too good to be true.*

Thus the Copper River & Northwestern right-of-way passed to the federal government for the purpose of building the Copper River Highway, a gift to the people of Alaska from the Guggenheim-Morgan Syndicate.

The last train of the Copper River & Northwestern Railway had passed down the rails to Cordova on November 11, 1938, but it was not the last train to operate on the "Iron Trail." There was still to be one more before the rails were lifted and the railroad story closed. It came with World War II.

Left—A rotary snowplow on the Copper River & Northwestern Railway. The road had four of these plows, the smallest with a cut of 10 feet, 7 inches, the largest with a cut of 12 feet, 6 inches. *Below*—Locomotive No. 20 with a string of boxcars and ore cars.

10 THE CIVAIR RAILROAD

It was in World War II that the airplane came into its own. Airports were being built everywhere in a hurry, part of the all-out total war effort. Cordova was to have one also, on the Copper River flats not far from town. To build this strip the old Copper River & Northwestern was pressed back into service by the U.S. Army.

In the now-or-never fashion peculiar to World War II, the Cordova airport and many others like it were slashed out to accommodate the machines of war. And the ancient engine still left in the roundhouse, Old No. 50, was used for the job. The Iron Trail was back in business, more or less.

The new airport was located on the Copper River flats 13 miles from town, and veteran railroad men in the Army ran the trains for the building and operation of the strip.

But in 1944, with the war's end in sight, the Army pulled out, leaving the Civil Aeronautics Administration to run the airport. It also left that aviation agency (as the *Mukluk Telegraph* put it in a January 1959 article) "13 miles up the track without a train."

It was at this point that the last steam-and-diesel chapter of the Copper River & Northwestern's story began. The men who worked it called this bizarre operation the "Civair Railroad."

For the first winter after the Army moved on, they left behind experienced men to run the locomotives, but in the spring these men departed.

In the meantime CAA personnel were learning something of the operation of the smaller rolling stock of the old railroad. They dragged two or three of the gasoline-powered speeders out of the old roundhouse and put them in operating condition. For the accommodation of passengers the "Civair Railroad" had seats mounted back-to-back on small flatcars. Riding these open-air taxis, fair weather and foul, the children commuted to school and women bought groceries in Cordova. A general passenger service was carried on also. The condition of the line left a lot to be desired; on almost every trip the small speeders would jump the weed-choked track and it was everybody out to help put the Civair "train" back on the track.

But for servicing the CAA station with such large-lot items as gas, these Toonerville Trolleys were totally inadequate. Consequently, the Army had a 25-ton diesel locomotive sent to Cordova from Seward. This was considerably heavier stock than had been handled through Cordova's port for some time, and it developed that, although Seward had the big cranes for handling this behemoth, Cordova had only ten-ton cranes.

The unloading of the diesel was accomplished by sawing out the guardrail of the ship and running rails out to it. At the proper stage of the tide the tracks were connected to those on deck and the engine wheeled gingerly across the creaking, groaning bridge to the dock. After the big boy was ashore there was still no time to sigh with relief, for the entire 13 miles to the airport was on track which had settled and shifted and overgrown with grass and alder. What if this giant should jump the track as the speeders so often did? It would take considerably more than the crew and passengers to put her back on the rails. The train was taken with the greatest of care at low speed to the station at the airport.

In due time maintenance and reconditioning caught up with needs and the Civair Railroad served its purpose admirably.

In 1945 the *Cordova Times* jubilantly announced: "Cordova is to Have a Road!" The Forest Service began work that year on the road to the airport, completing the first 13 miles that summer. Thus ended at last the story of the Copper River & Northwestern Railway and its progeny, the Civair Railroad.

But, of the Copper River Highway, it was just the beginning. . . .

11 EPILOGUE—TALES OF THE COPPER RIVER HIGHWAY

The story of Cordova's 30-year battle for a road over the old Copper River & Northwestern is a story unto itself, a story in direct contrast to the whirlwind night-and-day pace when the "Iron Trail" was slashed out of a virgin wilderness in four years flat. The bland unconcern of the 1950's seemed a complete turnabout from the violent emotions attendant upon its building back in the 1900's.

Such a story would seem strange indeed in the lower 48 states which are blessed (or cursed, as the case may be) with a vast complex of roads and highways, superhighways and freeways. There are many reasons for this disparity between Alaska and the older states, chief among them being that Alaskans shared fully in highway taxes but never shared fully in the funds derived. Caught in an ever-widening "road gap," Alaska failed to get her share of roads, and Cordova was only one of many towns which did not, and do not to this day, have even a single-lane dirt access road.

Still, Cordova had been cast in a bigger city mold, and she fought hard for a road over the old right-of-way, using the railroad bridges and roadbed.

In the forefront of the battle for the "missing link" was John LeFevre of Cordova, who spent great amounts of time, money and effort in promoting Cordova's road. Mr. LeFevre spared no effort to buttonhole anybody who would listen and who might conceivably help to get the road built.

Another who fought hard and colorfully was O. A. Nelson of Chitina, who, it is said, mounted his own bulldozer and dozed out the first mile southward from his town, declaring that the rest was up to the State of Alaska. He had done his part.

Gradually, a few miles at a time, they began to build it. First to Mile 13, then Mile 27, then a few more miles, and so on until in 1958 they reached the Miles Glacier "Million Dollar" Bridge.

Out in the wilderness she stood, abandoned, the bridge on which the fate of the Iron Trail had hung; the bridge the skeptics said would never stand through a spring breakup. Like Rip Van Winkle of old, she slumbered for 20 years after the closing of the railroad, and then in 1958 the old iron bridge awoke to a new promise.

The road builders found her still hearty and strong after 20 years without the slightest maintenance; even the paint was intact. In fact, engineers for the contractor sent samples of the paint out for analysis because of its obvious extraordinary wearing qualities.

There were problems in decking the big bridge for autos. The bridge, built by no-nonsense railroad men of the Katalla Company back in 1910, was of such heavy construction that there were no bridge jacks west of the Mississippi River big enough to lift her brawny spans. They had to send back east for the jacks to handle her so they could replace the rollers.

With concrete decking and new rollers and paint, the bridge, looking once more like a "Million Dollars," was again a tourist attraction, for Cordova motorists at least.

Things are much quieter up at the Glacier Bridge site these days. Childs Glacier has now melted back to a point where it no longer overhangs the river. No longer does she send her awe-inspiring tidal waves rampaging across the muddy waters as a matter of course; now they only come in seasons of high water.

Miles Glacier has melted back also. Today Miles Lake is almost twice the size it was back in those "Iron Trail" days. And in melting back, she has done away with another of the Copper River's almost legendary terrors: the Abercrombie Rapids. It may be remembered that one side of the rapids was a sheer rock cliff; the other was the moraine-covered snout of Miles Glacier. As this glacier melted back, the pressure on the rapids was released, and in 1951 the Copper River changed course, leaving the boulder-strewn rapids high and dry.

And thereby hangs another tale: the story of Alaska's last gold rush!

Bush pilots were the first to discover the riverbed had changed. They carried the news to nearby towns. And somehow the rumor "accidentally" got around that there might be gold among the ten-ton boulders of the dead Abercrombie, but the only ones to strike any gold were the bush airlines, who struck all those golden charters!

In January of 1959, Alaska became a state. Cordovans, motivated by problems of fisheries and roads, voted a thundering 30 to 1 in favor of statehood, and celebrated by burning a fish trap in effigy in the ball park. With statehood, road building was accelerated, and a completion date set upon the Copper River Highway. In 1962, Cordova achieved an auto link of a different sort: tri-weekly service via the ferry *Chilkat* from Valdez. The need for a highway was reaffirmed as the small vessel carried capacity loads and became the only ferry in the state to make money consistently. Work on the Copper River Highway went ahead with renewed vigor until it reached a point several miles beyond the Miles Glacier Bridge.

Things looked promising. But then, on Good Friday, March 27, 1964, central Alaska was ripped by a savage earthquake. Observers at Mile 13 watched awestruck as six-foot earth waves rippled through the mud and sand of the Copper River flats; people in Anchorage dodged falling buildings; in Valdez they watched helplessly as the sea swallowed the city dock with 30 longshoremen on it. For five and one-half minutes—terrifying minutes—the earth shook.

Then the quake was over, but the terror had just begun. Seismic sea waves of devastating force and destruction tore through the coastal cities, many of which were actually raised or lowered in elevation by the quake. Fire lashed out from the huge oil storage tanks near Valdez and Seward, and people were forced to flee without knowing the fate of loved ones. It would be many days before news would come in from outlying areas, and before communications would be restored with such places as Seward and Kodiak.

The cost was high; first in lives, then in shattered homes and disrupted facilities. The rails at Seward ran off crazily into the sea, and the Alaska Railroad was cut off by landslides, fallen bridges and other damage. Later the line had to be relocated in places where the lowering of the land threatened to flood out tracks.

In Cordova the headway gained from 20 years of campaigning, politicking, cajoling, fighting and building on the Copper River Highway was lost. Cracks as deep as a man split the road asunder, and bridges (the new concrete bridges with steel rail pilings) lay twisted and sagging in grotesque shapes.

Underneath, the pilings had been snapped off like so many wishbones.

At first there was time only for rescuing the isolated, searching for the missing and reestablishing essential traffic and communication lines.

Then, a few days later, the rest of the bad news came. Small planes, finally freed from their mercy flights to isolated cabins and villages in Prince William Sound, had flown the Copper River.

The Miles Glacier Bridge was down.

Three of the spans rested on the piers, but the fourth one lay in the river, shaken off its resting place by the violence of the quake.

Despair seized Cordovans who had spearheaded the fight for the highway. Up to 1964, it had taken 25 years to gain 50 miles of highway, an average of two miles per year! At that rate, it would be the year 2004 before Cordovans could drive to Chitina, and vice versa. Now even that progress was gone. "Now we'll never get our road!" they said. Not so, said the State of Alaska. Investigating engineers were sent out to take a look.

The resulting report seemed to seal the doom of the famous old railroad bridge. It said in part: "The north span of the bridge fell into the Copper River. The northern truss span which collapsed into the river is badly damaged. These great truss spans weigh more than 2,000 tons each. . . .

"The northern pier is completely shattered, and will collapse in the near future. The remaining spans are seriously displaced and distorted . . . and remaining piers have been displaced on their foundations.

"Since movements of all piers appear . . . the result of movements of the underlying foundation material, there is question of the continuing stability of all substructure elements." A new bridge was recommended in its stead.

That was the preliminary report. Later investigations were, of course, far more thorough and revealing, and were made with the historical significance of the bridge in mind. By this time it was realized that the question was not merely an engineering one, but must be considered from other viewpoints also.

It was found that abutment #1, pier #2 and span #1 were relatively undamaged. Spans #1 and #2 were displaced in various directions, causing some repairable damage. "Piers #2 and #3 seem to have suffered no structural damage."

Span #4 had dropped off pier #4 and was lying with one end in the river, but because it was lying in relatively shallow water, it seemed in little danger of being carried away.

The major damage was to pier #4, the northernmost pier. "Pier #4 is virtually destroyed. The upper portion has split into three parts, with each of the end pieces separated from the middle by a crack up to 2' wide. The middle portion has a vertical crack running completely through it. The upper half of the pier has also sheared horizontally and has moved about 2' south in respect to the lower half. The entire pier has a list toward the south. . . .

"Span #4 and pier #4 would appear to be total losses. In the event that pier #4 collapses before it is possible to shore up span #3, that is, until the site becomes accessible to heavy equipment, span #3 will also be lost. . . . In any event, the raising, relocation, and rehabilitation of these massive spans will be a difficult and expensive operation." "Massive" is the word for span #3, the critical span, which weighed, with its erection device, three and one-half million pounds. That's just the one span; in the whole bridge there are more than nine million pounds of steel ore.

The bridge damage report had this to say of the famous old bridge: "Because of its rich historical background, the "Million Dollar" Bridge should be given most careful consideration before a decision is made concerning its replacement."

That decision, said the Alaska State Highway bridge engineer, was not really an engineering decision alone, but must be made in the halls of the Alaska State Legislature. If the Miles Glacier Bridge were replaced by a brand-new bridge, a tremendous slice of Alaska history would indeed be lost.

BIBLIOGRAPHY AND NOTES
PART FOUR

1 COPPER DAY IN CORDOVA
Alaska Sportsman. "April in Alaska's History," April 1965, p. 37.
The Cordova Alaskan. March 28, April 1, 4, 8 and 10, May 9, October 16 and 17, 1911.
The Seattle Post-Intelligencer. "Alaska Coal Station Urged," May 8, 1911, p. 1.

2 THE NAVY REPORTS
Alaska Sportsman. "Another Dalton Trail," July 1963, p. 16.
Brooks, Alfred H., and others. *Mineral Resources of Alaska and Report of Progress of Investigations in 1914.* U.S. Geological Survey Bulletin 622, U.S. Government Printing Office, Washington, D.C., 1915.
The Cordova Alaskan. January 5, 1911.
The Cordova Daily Times. January 4, March 9, June 5, 1915; January 7, June 7, 1916; January 31, September 14, November 24, December 19, 1917; January 8, 1918.
Underwood, John J. *Alaska, An Empire in the Making.* Dodd, Mead & Co., New York, 1913.

3 AWAITING THE DECISION
The Cordova Daily Times. December 31, 1914; January 19, February 15, April 13 and 14, May 21, 1915; June 13, 1916; January 25, 1917.

4 KENNECOTT AND COPPER
The Alaska Monthly, Juneau. May 1907, p. 52.
Alaska Sportsman. "Kennecott" by R. L. Button, April 1965, p. 38.
The Alaska-Yukon Magazine. February 1908, p. 454.
The Alaska Weekly. "The All-Alaska Review for 1930." Seattle, 1930, p. 1.
Colby, Merle. *A Guide to Alaska.* The Macmillan Co., New York, 1939, pp. 343-45.
The Cordova Alaskan. "The Bonanza Mines," April 1, 1911.
The Cordova Daily Times. January 16 and 29, February 9, 1917.
U.S. Geological Survey. *Mineral Industry of Alaska in 1937.* Bulletin 810, U.S. Government Printing Office, Washington, D.C., 1938, pp. 45, 67, 77.
Moffit, Fred H. *Geology of the Chitina Valley and Adjacent Area, Alaska.* U.S. Geological Survey Bulletin 894, U.S. Government Printing Office, Washington, D.C., 1938, pp. 120-25.
The Valdez Prospector. "Alaska Copper" by E. S. Harrison, January 24, 1907.

5 COPPER RIDES THE RAILS
Alaska Sportsman. "July in Alaska's History," July 1965, p. 30.
The Cordova Alaskan. "Fishing Industry to be Established Along Railroad," March 29, 1911.
The Cordova Daily Times. January 21, February 6 and 18, July 27, August 9, September 22, 1916; January 10, 1917.

6 ALASKA ANTHRACITE RAILROAD
Brooks, Alfred H., and others. *Mineral Resources of Alaska, 1920.* U.S. Geological Survey Bulletin 722, U.S. Government Printing Office, Washington, D.C., 1921, p. 26.
The Cordova Daily Times. January 18, 1916; January 16, March 29, 1917; June 17, November 11, 1918.
The Pathfinder. "Plan to Complete Katalla Road," August 1921, p. 17.
U.S. Forest Service, Records at Cordova. Survey No. 188 was patented to Morris A. Arnold on May 10, 1915.

7 THE LIFE AND DEATH OF KATALLA
Alaska Sportsman. "January in Alaska's History," January 1966, p. 27.
The Alaska Weekly. The All-Alaska Review for 1928: "Cordova, A City of Conservative Optimism" by E. P. Harwood; and "Alaska, A Great Oil Reservoir to Be" by Alain Craig Faith. Seattle, 1930.
The Cordova Daily Times. February 12, September 30, 1920.
Janson, Stella, former Katalla resident. Personal interview.
MacDonald, Myra, of Cordova. Personal interview.
The Pathfinder. July 1920.

8 CONVENIENCE AND NECESSITY: A DEATH KNELL
The Cordova Daily Times. "Interstate Commerce Commission Gives Report on Closing of Copper River & Northwestern Railroad" by J. S. Pritchard, Interstate Commerce Commission Examiner, March 20, 1939.

9 OLD RAILROADS NEVER DIE
Burns, Frank, of Cordova. Personal interview.
The Cordova Alaskan. Various dates from 1906 to 1911.
The Cordova Daily Times. November 11, 1938; August 18, 1941; May 11, 1961.
Janson, Lone. Personal recollections.

10 THE CIVAIR RAILROAD
The Mukluk Telegraph. January 1959.

Appendix A
REX BEACH'S "THE IRON TRAIL" VERSUS ACTUAL EVENTS AND CHARACTERS

Comparison of Rex Beach's *The Iron Trail* with actual events and characters in the building of the Copper River & Northwestern Railway, from a letter written in November 1962 by Thomas F. Kelly, retired, who worked on the line as an engineer—

"I am giving you an imperfect but fairly accurate identification of people and places mentioned in the book:

Murray O'Neil	Michael J. Heney
Captain Johnny Brennan	Captain Johnny O'Brien
Kayak Bay	Katalla Bay
Halibut Bay	Carter Bay
King Phillip Sound	Prince William Sound
Cortez	Valdez
Salmon River	Copper River
Coast Range	Chugach Range
North Pass & Yukon	White Pass & Yukon
Curtis Gordon	Henry Derr Reynolds
Hope	Ellamar or Reynolds
Tom Slater	Little Willie Robinson
Eldorado	Kennecott
Dan Appleton	Jack McCord and others
Omar	Cordova
Omar Lake	Eyak Lake
Dr. Stanley Gray	Dr. F. B. Whiting
Mellen	A. C. O'Neel
McKay	Murchison
Sheldon	Archie Shiels
Elkins	Frank Williams
Parker	E. C. Hawkins
Eliza Appleton	The red-haired lady on the footbridge
Heidlemanns	Guggenheims
New Omar Hotel	The Burke Hotel, which later became The Windsor Hotel
Mr. Trevor	M. K. Rogers
Smallpox incident	Factual
Salmon River & Northwestern	Copper River & Northwestern
McDermott	McPherson-Joslyn
Garfield Glacier	Miles Glacier
Jackson Glacier	Childs Glacier

"Dan Appleton is a composite person. I think the physical model was Dr. Council, Dr. Whiting's assistant, a 6'4" blond giant from Virginia, a handsome football player who married a daughter of one of the 'Copper Trust.' Dan Appleton is made up of H. L. [E. C.?] Hawkins, who located and surveyed the right-of-way; Jack McCord, who cut a steel cable with an axe, and possibly some of McPherson and Deyo. The so-called 'McDermott Rights' are very likely McPherson's surveys for Joslyn. [Or the Bruner right-of-way.—Author] The subject is hazy.

"Jack O'Niell's father was an engineer on the Guggenheim survey of Keystone Canyon, when the fight occurred. Mr. Hazelet, who was General Manager of 'The Copper Trust' at Valdez is very probably the 'Mr. Blaine' of the book. Mr. Rogers—the Mr. Trevor of the book—was a very highly rated engineer and suffered greatly by the loss of the breakwater.

"In 1909, while I was working on the bridge at Miles Glacier, Rex Beach was our guest. He rambled around quite freely, but I recall that he had one special companion, a wizened old chap who might have been assigned to him as a 'dog robber.' Of course, he got to know Jack McCord quite well, as the commissary was the gossip shop.' The exploit in which Jack McCord figured, the cutting of the steel cable, happened at Katalla (Kayak in the book) and was *not* for 'The Irish Prince,' as Heney was known, but for other interests. Rex Beach makes it occur at about where the two surveys intersected, about Mile 40 of the C. R. & N. W. Ry. There actually was a tentative right-of-way, surveyed from Katalla. Both Caleb Corser and Jack O'Niell think that it was run for a man named Joslyn from Fairbanks who had a small railroad up there and saw a chance to get in the game.

"The man Gordon in the book, so far as I ever learned, was a man named Reynolds who actually did 'sell' the citizens of Valdez the dream of an electric railway up the canyon to the interior. So that chapter is historically factual. Also, the town of 'Hope' seems to have been created around the vicinity of Ellamar and Copper Mountain.

"For other items, Archie Shiels asserts that there was a tussle between two gangs of surveyors in Abercrombie Canyon, above the bridge, but I do not get support of this from others.

"The Katalla Co. was primarily established to get the coal from Carbon Ridge. They did build a million dollar breakwater, and it did wash out. The Guggenheim-Eccles group did consider sharing the harbor with the Katalla Co. and probably as a reserve idea, using the Joslyn route if their own survey up from Valdez proved not feasible, as happened.

"While all the groups were maneuvering, two engineers, McPherson and Hawkins, had scouted the present C. R. & N. W. right-of-way. Apparently McPherson didn't look on it with favor, and a prominent railway engineer named Deyo also ruled against it because of the (Miles Glacier) bridge problem. Hawkins, however, persisted and proved its feasibility to M. J. Heney, who proceeded to plan construction. The 'Copper Trust'—the Guggenheim-Morgan-Eccles group—gave up the Valdez-Thompson Pass route as unfeasible. However, there was a fight in the Keystone Canyon, which was Beaver Canyon in the book. So that's authentic.

"The financial problems, the tight situations, are probably factual because it was British capital that financed the White Pass & Yukon (North Pass & Yukon in the book). Evidence of that is the fact that the New York people had the *S.S. Northwestern*, Captain Johnny O'Brien commanding, commissioned as a private yacht, and an imposing group of financial people came to Alaska in July, as I remember. They visited the bridge camp and were royally entertained; we even had an excursion boat on Miles Lake.

"With the group was a very attractive magazine writer, a lady with red hair and wearing a gorgeous green 'princess' dress. It was because of her that a near catastrophe happened that day. A. C. O'Neel, Dr. Whiting, Douglas (the auditor), the lady and another man were walking south to the main camp over a slender cable footbridge composed of two 3/4-inch cables stretched from pier to pier to shore. On those two cables were placed 2 x 4 crosspieces, with side risers to carry hand hold cables of 1/2-inch steel. On the crosspieces rested 2 x 12 planks for a steel pipe which carried compressed air from the power house to the men down in the caissons.

"There was a stringent rule that people on the walkway should never be closer together than 10 feet. On that day the gentlemen were escorting the lady over the works and were returning to camp with the lady in the middle. Making conversation, they gradually bunched up. I happened to be visiting the north caisson and was talking to a fellow named Hanson. We were talking about how our 'top brass' were 'fussed' by the red-haired girl when it happened. A cocky young peavy man named Harris, from Tacoma, was coming north toward us. Instead of waiting for the bridge to clear, he came on and met the group about halfway. They leaned sideways to let him pass and over went the footbridge. I scampered down, yelling to hang on, with Hanson at my heels. 'What do you want me to do, Mr. Kelly?' he yelled. I replied, 'Throw Harris overboard and then help me.' He booted Harris out of the way and then, straddling the air pipe and using our arms as uprights, we took hold of the hand ropes and with scared people helping to climb up on the pipe we slowly righted the footbridge. We made the lady and the men travel on their hands and knees to the south pier. That incident was never publicized in any report. If Mr. O'Neel and Dr. Whiting were lost that day, the story would be tragically different. I am not sure whether Rex Beach was there that day or not.

"Rex Beach used the wreck of the *Ohio*, which he called the *Nebraska* in the book. She left Seattle on August 26, 1909, and struck in Finlayson Channel, in Canadian waters, two days later. Her captain was not Johnny O'Brien. She carried 234 persons, passengers and crew, and five were lost. M. J. Heney was aboard and helped save some of the passengers. Jack O'Niell tells me that Heney helped his sister ashore and carried her baby in his arms, and Heney did pay for food and clothing needed for the shipwrecked people and did everything possible to alleviate their distress. But the Girard girl is window dressing.

"On or about that date, August 26, 1909, Pier One, the south pier, of the Miles Glacier Bridge was completed. Pier Two, the caisson with Hanson in charge, was down about 15 feet and work was beginning on the two abutments. The

railroad was operating to the bridge site. The machine shops were at Alaganik. For long distances the track was carried on exposed pile bents, and the whole expanse of the delta was a wide waste. Very little of the present tree growth existed then. The book notes that, too.

"The near bridge camp was quite a small town. The power house had 1,600-horsepower in boiler capacity. There were two 45-pound air compressors and one 125-pound air compressor. We had a 200 k.w. dynamo for lights and tools, but most of our tools were compressed air. Our tents were wall tents with board sides and floors, with canvas roofs and flys. The mess hall and offices were frame, and the power house, also. At the north end there was a good sized camp for the grading crews. We took a steam shovel and a locomotive across the ice in April. You will notice in the book that it was one year later—in April, 1910—that the steel crisis took place. The falsework on which the 'traveller' track rails were laid was on 'bents' on the ice, not on piles.

"The narrative is factually accurate and true. The ice did move, and throw the north span out of line, and only by superhuman efforts was it pulled into place. The dramatization is fully justified, especially when you realize that in every pinch, we had to improvise. The source of supply was far away and ship delivery was uncertain at best. The book immortalized that special bridge as a marvel of its day, which it was. I might add that the drama is almost technically factual in its description of details and incidents at the Million Dollar Bridge.

"There is a slightly different version of Heney's financial troubles in the 'Alaska Guide,' by the federal writers project, but it is quite likely that Mr. Heney himself supplied most of the financial information used in 'The Iron Trail.'

"Other men whom I remember of the C. R. & N. W. Ry. group were engineers Browne, Sellem and Wernecke; Van Cleve, the R. R. master mechanic; McDonald, the bridge steel foreman; Jack McCord, the commissary manager; and all of the Boer War veterans, the 'sand hogs' who worked down in the caissons in compressed air and who were all very British and eager to 'get done with the job and get the hell out of Alaska.'

"As I write this, in 1962, the years 1906-13 are long, long ago, so please excuse any errors."

Appendix B
OPENING STATEMENTS IN THE TRIAL
OF EDWARD C. HASEY

The opening statements in the trial of Edward C. Hasey at Juneau in connection with events in Keystone Canyon on September 25, 1907:

FOR THE DEFENSE:

"Immediately after the shooting in Keystone Canyon on September 25, 1907, untruthful and garbled accounts thereof were published in the press, and no accurate statement of the defense has ever been published. Reynolds owned the only Valdez newspaper and also had the Associated Press correspondents with him.

"Keystone Canyon is a box canyon two to three miles in length and varying in width from several hundred feet to less than a hundred feet. Through it flows the Lowe River,

making it impossible to go through the canyon except in the winter months when the river is frozen and teams with freight for the interior pass through. During the spring, summer and fall months, it is necessary in order to get through the canyon, to go over what is known as the 'Summer Trail,' which is a trail constructed by the Government, running over or along the mountainside above the canyon.

"In 1905 the Copper River & Northwestern Ry Co. began work in the canyon, constructing a rock road bed, and expended about $85,000 thereon. The canyon is wide enough to permit several railroad grades to be built therein, and the C. R. & N. W. Co. selected and constructed their grade on the left side of the canyon, blasting out a rock cut along the mountainside. This rock grade is completed for about 2,000 ft. from the entrance to the canyon, and this piece of grading ends against a sheer, straight wall of rock, beyond which it is impossible to pass. In this high wall of rock, the C. R. & N. W. Co. ran two working tunnels, called 'coyote holes'—one being about 40 and the other 45 feet in length. These holes were to be filled with powder and exploded to blow off this wall of rock. The C. R. & N. W. Co. had never abandoned this rock grade, but kept men at work thereon at all times up to September 25, 1907.

"In July, 1907, the C. R. & N. W. managers began to doubt the feasibility of building a railroad from Katalla, and Mr. Hazelet, who was their manager at Valdez, received instructions to return to Valdez from the interior, where he had gone on a short trip, and await orders regarding the work to be done in Keystone Canyon. In August 1907, one H. D. Reynolds appeared in Valdez and announced his intention of building a railroad from Valdez, and formed the Alaska Home Railway. Reynolds at that time conceded the right of the C. R. & N. W. to the rock work they had built in Keystone Canyon, and opened negotiations with Mr. Hazelet with a view to purchasing the property and rights of the C. R. & N. W. Co.

"These negotiations resulted in nothing, and along in September, Reynolds, who had several hundred men employed, indicated plainly that he intended to go upon and take by force the rock work and grade of the C. R. & N. W. instead of building their own grade for which there was ample room. The latter named company had thirty or forty men working on this grade, and in order to avoid trouble, two deputy U.S. Marshals, Edward C. Hasey and Duncan Dickson, were sent up to the canyon, and instructed to allow no one to go upon said rock work and grade. Several officers of the Reynolds company tried at different times prior to September 25th to go upon this rock grade, and were warned off by Hasey and Dickson; repeated warnings were given to the Reynolds engineers and officers to keep off this grade, and written notices were posted thereon. No attempt was ever made to keep the Reynolds company from entering Keystone Canyon or building a grade of their own. The Reynolds people would have had no possible object in wanting to go upon the rock grade of the C. R. & N. W. Co. except to take possession thereof, for the reason that no one could get through the canyon by that route, or by any other route at that season of the year, other than over the canyon by the summer trail.

"Finally, on the morning of Sept. 25th, the Reynolds people mustered a force of about 200 men near the entrance to Keystone Canyon, and armed with pick handles, mattock handles, picks, shovels, and some few having revolvers. After a speech had been made to them by Chas. Ingersoll, the Reynolds Company attorney, they advanced with shouts, and brandishing various implements, to go upon this rock grade and take it. In the first rock cut this mob of men encountered some 30 or 40 of the C. R. & N. W. men, and thrust them out of the way. Several assaults were made. Just at this time, O'Niell, the foreman of the C. R. & N. W. Co., came running toward them down the grade, shouting for them to go back and if they advanced they did so at their own peril. At this, several of the leaders of the Reynolds Company seized O'Niell, threw him down and forced him ahead with them. Biggs, another C. R. & N. W. man, also came running down to warn them, and they also grabbed and assaulted him. Hasey, who was about 250 or 300 feet farther up the grade, standing beside a small rock barricade, seeing O'Niell and Biggs assaulted by the mob, and fearing for

further injuries to them, as well as to himself, holding a gun in his hand, raised one hand above his head and waved the mob back three times, at the same time crying, 'Go back. Go back.'

"The mob continuing to advance, Hasey then fired one shot in the air, over the heads of the mob. They continued to advance, and Hasey then fired one shot low on the ground. The leaders of the mob continued to advance until Hasey had fired four shots. As soon as they ceased to advance he ceased firing. The man Rhinehart, who died, was shot near the knee, not at all a fatal wound, and with proper treatment he would have recovered.

"Just prior to this mob starting to make their attack on the morning of September 25th, one Kenyon, a Reynolds foremen, after a conference with several of the Reynolds leaders, took several sticks of dynamite, with caps and a very short fuse, and went with it up over the hill, so as to reach a point near the summer trail, immediately over Hasey's head, with the avowed purpose of blowing him up if necessary. Fortunately he reached there too late to accomplish such a design, but he left the powder up there where later it was found.

"Hasey's defense is four-fold: First, self defense; Second, defense of others, to wit: O'Niell and Biggs, both of whom were being assaulted before his eyes, and from the appearance of the mob, Hasey had good reason to fear great bodily harm to himself and to O'Niell and Biggs; Third, defense of property, of which he was rightfully in possession; and Fourth, as a peace officer, he was quelling a riot by the only means within his power. The mob constituted a riot, engaged in an unlawful purpose, viz, the forceable taking of property rightfully in possession of others. Hasey sent O'Niell and Biggs down to warn them to desist; he warned them himself, and only after all other means failed did he fire, and fire low, without intent to kill or to use more force than was necessary to stop this riotous mob."

SUMMARY OF THE PROSECUTION'S STATEMENT:

John J. Boyce, United States Attorney, outlined the case for the prosecution. Starting with a geographical and topographical description of the country intersected by the Keystone Canyon, he explained to the jury the peculiar conditions existing there. He then took up the organization of the Copper River and Northwestern Railway Co., told of their application for a right-of-way through Keystone Canyon during the latter part of 1906; how that company secured such right-of-way and constructed a railroad grade partially through the canyon until early in 1907, when they ceased work on the grade and withdrew all their workmen except one man left in charge of their personal property. Later the Alaska Home Railway Company was organized, which company had for its purpose the construction of a railroad into the interior from the coast and, like that of the then quiescent C. R. & N. W., using a grade passing along Lowe River and through Keystone Canyon. The right to do the latter was granted by an Act of Congress passed May 14, 1898, which prevents any one road from having a monopoly on any pass or canyon in Alaska. By September 25, 1907, the latter road had built its right-of-way to or near the mouth of Keystone Canyon and was moving camp into canyon when they were confronted by a rock barricade and saw the man Hasey go behind it with a rifle in his hands. Upon approaching the barricade, Hasey opened fire on the crew, inflicting wounds on several of the men; one man, Fred Rhinehart, being hit in the thigh and injured so badly that he died from the wound five days later.

INDEX

Page numbers in boldface indicate photographs.